MUSLIM MODERNITIES

TABISH KHAIR'S
Essays on Moderation and Mayhem
2001–2007

MUSLIM MODERNITIES

TABISH KHAIR'S

Essays on Moderation and Mayhem 2001–2007

Compiled & Edited by
Renu Kaul Verma

Vitasta

Vitasta Publishing Pvt. Ltd.
New Delhi

Published By Renu Kaul Verma for
Vitasta Publishing Pvt. Ltd.
2/15, Ansari Road, Daryaganj,
New Delhi-110 002

ISBN 81-89766-08-2

First Edition 2008
3rd Reprint 2022
MRP ₹495

Typeset by Vitasta Publishing Pvt. Ltd.
Printed at Saurabh Printers Pvt. Ltd., New Delhi
Cover design by Prabha Singh

Dedicated to

Sanjay, Rajesh, Gyanendra (who died young),
Renu, Vinita, Lata (who also died young),
Deepak, Hemant, Sohail and
all my other schoolmates

Contents

Part II

Part III

Introduction

I was educated in a Roman Catholic school in a small town of Bihar. The girls and boys in my class came from different parts of India, though the vast majority were Biharis. They also belonged to different religions, though most were Hindus. However, there was a high percentage of Muslim students, as the school was located in a Muslim colony.

Years passed. I drifted away. I lost touch with almost all my schoolmates. Then suddenly out of the blue an old schoolmate, Sanjay, sent me a mail. He had been reading my articles and books and he wondered whether I would like to offer a manuscript to a publishing house he was associated with.

I have fond memories of my school days. I also have fond memories of Sanjay, who had been—like me—a studious and quiet boy, not picked too quickly for the class soccer team. As I corresponded with him, I realized that one of the things I missed about my school days was how religious and other identities, though visible, had not been divisive. My Hindu school friends would come and eat at my house for Eid and other Muslim festivals. I would go to their houses for Diwali and Holi. We would all go to the sisters of the Roman Catholic school for Christmas, and not just because cakes and cookies might be on offer. All Muslim boys made *raakhi* sisters, who were often Hindu; all Muslim girls tied *raakhi* too as far as I can recall. These were gestures we grew up with. We took them for granted. They came naturally to us in those days.

They are gestures that, I later realized, remain largely unknown in the supposedly 'liberal' North Europe, and might be dying out in places like India. Perhaps, in our craving for a borrowed 'modernity', Indians are simply mimicking the historical 'progress' of North Europe, where there is space only for the commercialized visibility of Christian festivals today.

So when I decided to compile the essays and papers that I have published largely between 2000 and 2006 in different Indian, British, Danish and other publications, I focused on those I felt I had to write partly as a Muslim. Because, as the reader will discover, 'Muslim' is *not* the only thing I can call myself. And yet, over the years I have had my nose rubbed into this one 'identity' more often than I wish to recall. So much so that I have even started answering to it at times. Let me explain with an example.

When I first came to Denmark, I would sometimes be asked what religion I belonged to. I would reply that actually my parents are practising Muslims, or that I come from a Muslim background. That was the only honest answer I could give, as I did not feel very religious. But over the past two or three years, I have started giving a different answer. When asked, I now reply, 'I am Muslim'.

No, I do not feel any more religious than I did earlier. But after 2001, the answer 'I am Muslim' evokes strange reactions. Some people don't care and some people are taken aback but recover. But some cut me dead. They would not have done so, if I had indicated that I was not really religious or that I was basically critical or ashamed of my Muslim inheritance—that is how even a neutral statement like 'my parents are Muslim' is liable to be construed by some.

I refuse to give such people the soft option of not facing up to and acting on their own prejudices. I may not be religious, but I am not ashamed of my Muslim inheritance. I am not ashamed of being Muslim or Indian or coloured or anything else that has descended on me through time and as such carries with it the complexities—neither entirely good nor entirely bad—of history. So I say I am Muslim, and sometimes watch well-meaning Danes melt away.

Corresponding with Sanjay, my old classmate, I realized that such prejudices have always dogged my steps. Such is the fate of being part of a minority, perhaps. But still, it was easier in the past—because I grew up in a rhetorically-Socialist phase when both Islamic and Hindu fundamentalisms were unfashionable—and in a nation that remains a rich land of minorities. Perhaps because of those memories I still hope that we can overcome such prejudices, and the texts included in this book are tentative explorations of the ways forward, from the perspective of a Muslim who is also many other things.

I hope schoolmates have not started to walk away when someone says that he is Muslim, or Hindu, or Jew, or Christian, or any other of the many wonderful and confused ways in which human beings have experienced and understood time and space.

Tabish Khair

Part I

ONE

A Blessing for My Children

To be born into a minority is a blessing and a curse. I was born into a Muslim family in Bihar. But within the community of Indian Muslims, my family again belonged to a large minority—that of the middle class professional Muslims. My father is a doctor. His father had been a doctor, and his father's father had been a doctor too. Before that, my father's ancestors had been impoverished but independent and proudly literate farmers. My mother has a college degree in political science and, for some time, ran her own business. Her father had been a police officer and his father had owned a small tea plantation in Assam.*

When you are born into a minority, that too a minority within a minority, you learn to belong in different ways. I grew up as Indian and as Muslim. I grew up speaking three languages and writing two scripts. I was told or I read stories and poems from the West (especially Russian and British) as well as the East (especially Hindi/Urdu and from the Sanskrit and Persian-Arabic traditions). I was brought up on a concept of civilization and modernity that was not spelled E-U-R-O-P-E or W-E-S-T, for while my family members spoke English, they also spoke other languages; while they had imbibed Western education, they often also had a sense of other sources of rational thinking and possible modernities.

It is this that often makes me frustrated even with much of acclaimed post-colonial literature, for very often this literature is only

* Talk given at the Florence Poetry Festival, Italy.

concerned with the bridge of West-and-the-Rest. In my family, over centuries, we had crossed many other bridges. It is also this that made me feel—once my schooldays were behind me—that the India I had grown up in was a fragile entity—it was increasingly threatened by various kinds of fundamentalisms (Muslim, Hindu and 'Western'). There were other kinds of threats too such as Hindu-Muslim riots which were more threatening to secular Muslims like me and my family members than to religious Muslims living in ghetto-like colonies. There were constant attempts to bracket our identity. Are you Muslim or Indian, we were asked—as if one could be only the one or the other. So, when the time came, it was not too hard for me to leave the geographical space of India, for the India that mattered to me was there in my mind and memories.

Not that the questions got better. I was, after all, again part of a minority—the minority of coloured people in Denmark, the minority of immigrants, the minority of Indians, of Muslims. I was complimented on being taller than 'most Indians'; I was praised for more liberal habits than 'most Muslims'. And again and again I had to—I have to—read largely ignorant articles and letters in Danish newspapers denigrating Asians or coloured immigrants or Muslims. That is the curse of being part of a minority.

The blessing is that one belongs in different ways, one learns to see different perspectives, one speaks many languages, one is aware of many histories, one is both this and that. If you only stop to listen, you are blessed with so many stories. If you only shut out the screaming of those who will not listen, you recognize the blessing of a coherent identity—for the identity of a person from a minority does not depend on a piece of cloth or a ritual; it is a part of his or her own lived being. It is not external; it is internal. And with it comes the blessing, in my case, of having a cause to write.

And so, in spite of the curses and the threats, in spite of the screaming and the swearing, this is what I wish for my five-year-old son and my two-year-old daughter—may you learn to belong to a multiple minority, to the minority of minorities. For then you will also learn to see—and feel.

TWO

9/11: Conscience and Coffee

There are moments that cleave Time into two. Everything that happens afterwards seems to happen in a different world. World War II and the Holocaust was one such moment for Europe. The Vietnam War was another for America and Vietnam. The suicide-hijack-crashing of four passenger planes and the destruction of the World Trade Center on the morning of 11 September 2001 was such a moment for the entire world.*

A world we know appeared to have come to an end. Or so it seemed then. We stood poised on the margins of two new worlds, one of heightened hatred and violence and other of serious peace and equality. It is a choice we had to make. I won't write about the five thousand lives lost in a senseless and criminal act of violence. Such human loss escapes the limits of language and representation. One can only stand silent in front of the monuments of sorrow that tens of thousands—relatives, friends, colleagues—will carry in their hearts for the rest of their lives. It is a sorrow the rest of us can only share in silence. I cannot write about that silence.

And I should not for, in Copenhagen, I was deluged with sound—the opinions of ordinary people, the film-like coverage of the tragedy by TV stations and the voices of commentators and politicians. Much

---

* This was originally written immediately after the New York terrorist-strikes in 2001. This article has appeared in the *South African Guardian*, in *Information*, Denmark, etc., and been put online by the *Lawyers' Committee on Nuclear Policy*, USA. It has been updated for the purpose of this book.

of this sound had a certain tone to it which set me wondering. Is there much of a difference between the terrorists who struck back at a group of politicians by targetting tens of thousands of innocent people and those voices that seem to be using the cruel act of a handful of Islamic terrorists to tarnish and blame entire populations of Muslims and Arabs? Don't both the acts demonstrate the same type of abstract hatred and prejudice? But the questions never end. On the margins of time, in the split space between worlds, one is always deluged with questions. For example, the first Danish person who brought me news of the tragedy—a person I respect in many ways—said that he was against violence of any kind and added that he would understand if Americans decided to hit back.

Why is it that we always justify our own violence and consider violence by the enemy to be sheer sacrilege? Isn't this where it all begins? Isn't that why there were shocking pictures of embittered Palestinian youths celebrating the tragedy in the occupied areas—youths who have become so used to the idea of missiles being launched at their own buildings by Israeli security forces and the notion of reciprocal violence that they could not feel the inhumanity of their inane celebration?

But, then, is this what we can write about—this gyre of violence and inhumanity? Is this immense tragedy going to remain at such a general level of discourse? The answer seems to be 'yes' if various media discussions in the West are to be believed. But it has to be 'no' if we are to salvage some sense from the wanton destruction—if we are to do the necessary honour to the needless deaths of those thousands of innocent people.

It is easy for us to sit here in our cosy sitting rooms in Copenhagen, holding a cup of coffee, munching a biscuit, watching the tragedy unfold almost as fluently as a film on the idiot box, and speak in general and ineffectual terms. What we are doing is celebrating our own humanity, and all human beings—even terrorists—are convinced of their own superior humanity. Many of the most inhuman acts known to humanity have been the consequence of such a conviction. We need to go beyond it. We owe it to the victims of the tragedy to go beyond it.

The second person who called me with news of the tragedy was my father—a semi-retired, devout Muslim doctor who has lived most of his life in a small town in a backward part of India. He was shocked by the news. How could anyone do this, he asked again and again. The word he used was 'anyone'. I went back to the TV and, in spite of the fact that as yet no one knew anything about the identities of the terrorists, I did not hear too many people say 'anyone'. I heard 'Muslim', 'Islamic', 'Middle Eastern', 'Arab'. These were people who had already decided to exclude entire populations from the circumference of their definitions of humanity. My father's 'anyone', which pointed an easy finger at no one, had been reduced by many of these contributors to 'Arab' or 'Muslim', even to the very type of an Arab or Muslim. I could feel the non-conformist 'Muslim' in me cringe every time I heard the expert discussions (with some honourable exceptions, such as Anders Jerichow in Denmark). I could feel my father—his voice heavy with sorrow for people (Americans) he has never known—I could feel him being put in the dock.

It is so comfortable, this celebration of our own humanity. All it requires is tea or coffee, a candle-lit room, some cakes or biscuits and live coverage of a tragedy at some distance from us. It can be so inhuman, this celebration of our own humanity. But what about violence? Way back in the late 17th century, Thomas Burnet, the English divine, wrote about apocalypse, or rather the tendency in the established Roman Catholic church to postpone, persecute or reason away those cries of 'apocalypse now', those cries of sweeping violence that reverberate through the Bible. But while an apocalypse followed by a millennium of Christ's rule is what the Bible had prophesied, the Roman Catholic church—which ought to have welcomed the prospect of the Second Coming and a truly Christian millennium from a theological perspective—took a dim view of promises of the dawn of the millennium. It regularly countered or hunted down the self-appointed prophets of apocalyptic violence. Why? This is what the Reverend Burnet had to say:

> "The Church of Rome hath been in prosperity and greatness, and the commanding church in Christendom, for so long or longer, and hath ruled the nations with a rod of iron. And the Millennium being properly a reward and triumph for those who have come out of persecution, such as have lived always in pomp and prosperity can pretend to no share in it, or benefit by it. This has made the Church of Rome have always an evil eye upon this doctrine, because it seemed to have an evil eye upon her."

Violence, in other words, is not a free choice at social level. It has never been a free choice. It is predicated upon some individuals by circumstances. These individuals are usually those who feel that an injustice has been done to them and theirs, those who labour under an overpowering feeling of deprivation. However senseless it might be—the perpetrators of violence against the innocent should always be tracked down and brought to justice as criminals, neither more nor less—however shocking an act of violence might be, behind it lies the rubble of shattered hopes, of real and imagined injustices, of human desperation and, consequently, inhuman hatred.

Let us not take refuge in the easy excuse that the angels that we are, we are against violence. For all of us, given certain circumstances, are capable of violence or sympathy with violence. Let us wipe that smug smile off our faces. Let us learn to see the rubble of other buildings behind the rubble of the World Trade Center. While a thousand candles have been lit in Copenhagen for those who died such a shocking death in New York, let us also light a candle or two for the approximate 10 thousand or more who starved to death in Afghanistan almost every month, the approximate five thousand children who died in Iraq every week because of lack of medicines due to an embargo put into place by us. Let us not keep our tears only for those who are like us. Let us not traffic in the worth of human lives.

No! General and large descriptions such as 'violence' or 'inhumanity' do not help if we stay confined to that general level. Neither does the kind of cry for vengeance that one heard in the voice of the American who wanted the Middle East levelled under asphalt. It is true that we have to take a stand against violence. Not just violence of one kind, we have to take a stand against all kinds of violence, the violence of terrorists as well as the violence of state agencies, physical violence that leads to the death of innocent bystanders as well as economic violence that leads to the starvation of millions in a world that has enough to go around.

Post Script

It is time we in the West think a bit before we bite into the cake of our affluence and drink the coffee of our civilized condemnation. If general sentiments will not do, then what about the specific lessons that we can draw from the unimaginable tragedy? Do these lessons relate to heightened security or the bombing to rubble of some other country, as has been suggested by some? Does this outrage mean that the US actually needs a missile shield, for example?

One of the things that this criminal outrage has demonstrated is the final ineffectiveness of any kind of physical or military shield. The only shield that can be effective is that of a more equal and just world.

And for the world to be made equal and just, it not only needs some of the resources of the affluent, it also has to be made democratic. One hesitates to point this out in circumstances as sorrowful as these, but the US has made itself the target of extremist groups partly because it has tried to go solo or exert undue influence in certain international quarters. The working internal democracy of the US almost never gets translated into international democracy. Had certain decisions been taken through the channels of the United Nations (not a military alliance of the privileged, like the NATO), the US would have been only one nation among many. The burden, the 'blame' and the risks would have been shared. There are advantages to democracy at the international level, but it has to be true democracy. As in all democracies, this means that sometimes some members would have to accept unfavourable decisions taken by the majority—what is important is respect for the spirit of democracy and the process of law.

And the final lesson is that of the dangers of abstract hatred and prejudice. The terrorists who caused the horrible tragedies in Washington and New York had made themselves blind to the fact that people have names and faces. The act of one person or a group cannot be blamed in a generalized way on an entire country or people. And this is a lesson that we should remember every time someone uses the dastardly act of a handful of Islamic terrorists to implicitly or explicitly blame entire populations of Muslims and Arabs. For, this has too often been the case in the West, as the post-9/11 attacks on 'Arabs'—including Indian Sikhs—in the US show.

The crashes that reduced the World Trade Center to rubble and the two terror-inducing plane crashes elsewhere have cleft our age into two. On the other side of this smoking chasm of blood and bitterness, lies another world. It can be a world in which all the mistakes of the past-global inequality, socio-economic exploitation, lack of international democracy, lack of national democracy and literacy in some nations, prejudice and hatred—are consolidated into a system of greater violence and suffering. Or we may learn, finally, to work towards a world, a very different world, where we will tackle not the consequences of senseless tragedies but the reasons for them. A world in which we will condemn not only a certain kind of violence but all violence—a world in which we will love not only our humanity, but all humanity. It is a choice that our politicians, editors and commentators will not make for us in the rooms of conference halls or the pages of newspapers. It is a choice we have to make ourselves. And in order to do so, we have to look deep into our own hearts before we tidy away the tea dishes and swap the channel in places like Copenhagen.

THREE

Placebo for Pain

Suffering, death and terror. What do these words evoke? There can be only one obvious answer to this prescriptive question on the 'occasion' of the 'first anniversary' of the tragedy of 11 September 2001. And yet there is at least one other answer—the Plague. Let us then observe the 'anniversary' of that sad day, but let us observe it under the sign of the plague.*

For there is much that it shared (and shares) with the plague.

In folk consciousness in most countries—and not least in Europe and European-settler countries like the United States—the word 'plague' remains associated with suffering, death and terror. With growing awareness of the causes and better medical treatment, plagues no longer sweep across countries as they used to in the medieval period. And yet, plagues are not irrelevant to our times.

A plague is a "disease or other condition causing high mortality or morbidity and often accompanied by social dislocation." But the plague is also spread by "social dislocation." So much so that outbreaks of the plague often led to segregation of the poor and the stranger, especially in communities that felt themselves exempt from this "scourge of God."

This is how the plague was seen as in medieval times—the scourge of God, divine manifestation and divine chastisement. And connected to it was the independent implication of suffering as atonement

---

* First published in *The Hindu*, India.

and pain as redemption. As many folk traditions still have it—pain cures pain.

What, the reader might still be wondering, does all this have to do with September 11?

Much as I would answer—suffering, death and terror, obviously. But also 'the scourge of God' and 'social dislocation' and segregation and prejudice against strangers. And, above all, pain—the myth of pain as a cure.

One can never really write about suffering. But it is not as hard to write about death, which by definition, takes us into the realm of wordlessness. That is why death is simpler than suffering. One can count and record the thousands of needless deaths due to the terrorist strikes on 11 September and the thousands of needless deaths due to war, disease and starvation in Afghanistan. It is more difficult to write about sufferings, for how can one write of the concrete sufferings of the families and friends of those who were killed on that fatal day. And then there is a kind of abstract suffering—that of many Americans who felt powerless in the face of the terrorist strikes and that of many Muslims of the third world who continue to feel powerless in a US-dominated world order. Such suffering may be abstract but it should not be overlooked, for it gives birth to the concrete crimes of those who, like Bin Laden, want to be instruments of the 'scourge of God'.

Who said the plague was a thing of the past?

For here we have 'the scourge of God' again. And we have it in two versions. First, and most blatantly, the kind of scourge that people like Bin Laden wish to visit on those they don't like—on Gays or Marxists or Feminists in their own regions and on 'Americans' everywhere. But perhaps there is another 'scourge of God'—a subtler edition—that informs the general feeling of disinterest many Europeans, Americans and Australians show in the face of death and suffering in the third world.

Is this version called the 'scourge of the God of free market'? The unseen God that 'third worlders' are always being asked to worship and who is also the unseen God that protects 'first worlders' with agricultural subsidies, trade monopolies and political hegemony? Is this, finally, a battle between Bin Laden's unseen God and the unseen God of the free market? Is it only a minor skirmish between the terror of the plague of the past and the plague of the terror of the present?

That is part of the answer, but not all.

Another part of the answer brings us back to other aspects of the plague—'social dislocation', and segregation and prejudice. The terror of 11 September was itself an index of social dislocation. Entire populations have been dislocated from traditional ways of life that ordered their universe. Many of them, especially in the third world, have realized that political independence is either not forthcoming, or that it is a severely limited factor in the face of the economic domination of the 'global' world by businesses and politicians of the rich nations.

9/11 has its roots in this vast dislocation of people, compounded by the fact that 80 per cent of the wealth of the world is still controlled by 10 per cent of its population, mostly living in the rich 'West'.

The dislocation in itself is not necessarily bad, but the vast socio-economic gulf that exists between individuals and societies turns it into a negative experience for a large number of people. That is the real plague—not terror, but poverty and inequality.

But all plagues have a cure, we are told. This particular plague will be cured if we, in third world countries, cut down on state expenditure and open our markets to global capital. Never mind the fact that all rich capitalist countries went through phases of heavy state expenditure and continue to protect their own 'weak' sectors.

Some pain, we are told, that's all you need—some pain today to cure a painful future. It is called restructuring. There is a long list of countries in South America, Asia and Africa that have taken this treatment. You can hear them howling with pain. The September tragedy was also the story of this medieval penchant for present pain as a cure for future pain.

And no wonder September 11 unleashed another story of pain as cure. They hit us, we have to teach them a lesson—as an American told me. He had no idea who 'they' were and, ignorant as he was of most of American culture and all of American Indian and Black American history, he did not even have much of an idea of who 'we' were.

But he had his medieval belief—pain cures pain. So had the Muslims who justified 11 September by referring to the atrocities committed by American-supported forces in other parts of the world.

So today, on the eve of the anniversary of the plague that hit the US on 11 September and continues to sweep in various forms—American or Arab, Islamicist or Neo-liberalist—across the world, today that is what I want to say—pain is never a cure for pain. Those who recommend pain for others, those who traffic in pain, those who glorify pain and those who justify pain—those are the people to distrust. There is only one human response to pain of any kind—alleviate it.

FOUR

Tony Blair and the Intentional Fallacy

Perhaps the biggest myth of 'Iraq War II: Operation Freedom' relates to Tony Blair and the role played by the UK. It is the myth of the well-meaning English gentleman. This myth goes back to at least the Afghanistan war when a senior British gentleman interviewed on TV had given the following reply to the question whether Britain should be marching into Afghanistan with the Americans—Yes, he had said, because the Americans don't know what they are doing. The humorous implication was that Britain was there as the more experienced and humane partner.*

This implication has other shades as well. I have often come across well-informed Europeans expressing either surprise at the British involvement or segregating Blair from Bush. An astute and highly experienced Danish editor recently wrote an essay claiming that while Bush was not to be trusted, Blair was on to another (more civilized and humanitarian) ballgame altogether. Even those, who were against Blair, seemed to be surprised at the British involvement and saw it as an anomaly. This is what Julian Barnes said in an otherwise excellent article in *The Guardian* "This war was not worth a child's finger"(11 April 2003):

> "In the past three weeks, I've had emails from friends in different parts of the world. Almost without fail, they have expressed incredulity at our prime minister's position. 'We can understand Bush, we see exactly where he's coming from, we aren't surprised by his gross limitations and gross ambitions. But what is your Blair up to? He seems a civilized, intelligent man. What does he

* Published in *The Hindu*, India.

> think he's doing? And what on earth does he think he's getting out of it?' Oil? Reconstruction contracts? Hardly. As for what he thinks he's doing: it seems, I explain, to be a mixture of deluded idealism (finding a moral case for war where neither the Anglican bishops nor the Pope—moral experts he might acknowledge—can see one) and deluded pragmatism: he really does believe the military conquest of Iraq will reduce the likelihood of terrorism."

Barnes was not making excuses for Blair. He was, like many others, genuinely bewildered. And this bewilderment owed to the fact that Barnes and others had been misguided by the popular media regarding British foreign policy. Blair's and the UK's involvement in this war was *not* an anomaly or due to misguided idealism or deluded pragmatism—it was the logical result of British foreign policy in general and the British foreign policy on Iraq and the Middle East in particular.

The truth is very different from what is being suggested in the popular media in the West.

As Mark Curtis documented in *The Great Deception: Anglo-American Power and the World Order* (1998), Anglo-American power perceptions in the global arena have been remarkably similar and consistent at least from the 1920s onwards. These perceptions have been oriented towards the protection and expansion of a global order conducive to British and American (Northern in general) economic interests. The only main change here has been that while in the 1920s, Britain was arguably the dominant partner globally, from the 1940s onwards various British governments have agreed to accept junior partnership status under US aegis. In the colonial half of the 20th century, the US generally supported the continuing control of colonial territories by European powers (of which the greatest was Britain); today, the UK generally supports the control of post-colonial economies by superior American military power.

Anglo-American collaboration goes back many decades—it includes the coup in Iran in 1953, organized jointly by the CIA and the British MI6. This coup, which brought the tyrannical regime of the Shah to power and finally led to an Islamic reaction against the Shah, was organized explicitly in response to the nationalization of British-controlled oil industry by the soon-to-be-toppled Iranian government. All through the Cold War, British governments explicitly or implicitly backed US interventions or operations all over the world—in Guatemala in 1954, Cuba in 1959, the Dominican Republic in 1965, Vietnam, Brazil, Chile, Nicaragua, Combodia etc. Britain was the only major nation to support the 1989 US invasion of Panama. There seem to have been only two occasions when the invasion or manipulation of a state by the US was not strongly supported by the UK, or vice versa.

Actually, Curtis points out that "the pattern of postwar US military intervention in Latin America... was begun by Britain. A long-forgotten British intervention occurred in British Guiana (now Guyana) in 1953, when Britain overthrew the democratically elected government of Cheddi Jagan," who threatened nationalization of the country's foreign-controlled economic resources. Curtis goes on to note that "Britain was, and remains, especially active in the Middle East," where once again the policy has been to cement Anglo-American dominance and prevent national control of the oil industry. Force or the threat of force is seen in many British and American governmental documents as a legitimate option in this regard. History, too, backs this interpretation—the invasion of Egypt in 1956, British involvement in Oman from the 1950s to the 1980s (sustaining a regime so stupidly repressive that it banned football and the wearing of glasses in 1970), etc. Keeping this background in mind, it is only 'natural' for Britain to be America's closest sidekick in the Iraq War.

Again, it has to be recalled that Britain was the country that first envisaged an invasion of Iraq when the Baathist regime came to power in 1958 and threatened the nationalization of various economic resources. Britain, writes Curtis with reference to recently declassified governmental files, was worried about the spread of anti-colonial nationalism following the 1958 revolution in Iraq, which overthrew a very pro-British monarch, and seriously considered invading Iraq from Jordan around the time. There is also evidence that the alleged threats to the Jordanian regime in 1958 and the Kuwaiti regime in 1961 were deliberately fabricated by British planners to serve as excuses for intervention.

Of course, we know by now that crying wolf does finally lead to the appearance of a wolf—even if, in this case, it was as toothless in international terms (no matter how vicious to local Kurds) as the Saddam Hussein regime. And what happened with the invasion of Kuwait by a brutal dictator who had been, until then, pampered and allowed to bomb Iranians and Kurds, is (I hope) too recent to have to be recalled. Britain was US' staunchest ally in 'Iraq War I: Desert Storm' too. So, please, do not tell me that Blair and the UK came on one platform of Iraq II by mistake. It might feel nice to believe so if you are a decent British or European citizen, but all of 20th century history indicates otherwise, as do the economics of globalization and global war-making in recent years. As a matter of fact, in some ways this war was first dreamt up by British planners way back in 1958. Blair's intentions, true or not, have very little to do with the matter.

When someone as experienced in matters of foreign policy as Lars Erslev Andersen (*Den Amerikanske Orden)*, unwittingly or wittingly reinforces this intentional fallacy, one is forced to face the fact that large sections of the well-meaning public in the West have chosen to turn a blind eye to aspects of the colonial experience. Not surprisingly, this has coincided with the dominance of politicians like Blair on the so-called Left. After all, Tony Blair was probably the first British Prime Minister after Winston Churchill (who, by the way, justified using chemical weapons against 'barbarous peoples', meaning Asians and Africans) who unabashedly defended Britain's colonial past in major election speeches.** Claiming that Britain "has been a major force in world affairs for several centuries", Blair has noted with nationalist pride and no trace of colonial embarrassment that "no British patriot should be willing to give up that status." This from the current leader of the state with the biggest colonial empire in the period between 1750 and 1950—the period that saw ratio of the Gross National Product between the South and the North increase from 1:1 to 1:40 (Today it stands at 1:60).

No matter what Blair might or might not *intend*, colonial and neo-colonial history attest to the fact that foreign policy considerations in both the UK and the US will finally ensure the protection of privileged Anglo-American and, at a secondary level, Northern economic interests and that these interests have been and continue to be opposed to the interests of the vast majority of people in the South. If some good comes out of this war, it won't be because of US or UK governmental decisions or Blair's 'Christian' intentions, it will be due to the (circumscribed) ability of ordinary people—whether American, British, Palestinian or, even, Iraqi—to create a space for themselves in spite of the constraints of Anglo-American policy considerations and the nightmare of neo/colonial history.

** This launched a trend that led, by the middle of the first decade of the 21st century, to sophistic 'justification' of empire from everyone ranging from Niall Fergusson and Ian Jack to the next-door European hack.

FIVE

The Colour of Passports

I spent most of 4 November 2003 at Kastrup, the shiny, efficient international airport of Copenhagen, trying to board a flight to an academic conference. I had a valid ticket, a valid (Indian) passport, a valid (Danish) permanent visa and the usual letters from my employers in Denmark and the conference organizers in Munich. I had taken the cheapest route—as is expected of scholars flying to academic conferences—via Heathrow, London. I had been to England many times for readings and lectures and I had also caught connecting flights from British airports in the past.*

But this time I was not allowed on board the flight. Someone had changed the rules in London a few days ago. Now, I was politely and sympathetically informed at Kastrup, people with certain kinds of passports need to have a transit visa even in order to catch a connecting flight from the same airport in England. In the past, transit visas were required only if you had to leave the airport. Not so, any longer. The colour of my passport was wrong.

Finally, giving up my plan of going to Munich, I returned to my university in Aarhus and was asked, by concerned colleagues and friends, the question that I had expected. "Why don't you apply for a Danish passport? After all, you became eligible for one about four years ago."

It is a difficult question to answer. There is much I am proud of in India, and there is much I am ashamed of. So, I am not a nationalist

---

* Published in *The Hindu,* India.

in the sense in which parties like the Shiv Sena define the nation. Being born a Muslim, I have grown up on the margins of that nation; I have grown up having my identity, my past, my languages questioned and subtly discredited in such "nationalist" circles.

And yet, I have no desire to opt for a Danish (or any other) citizenship. Yes, it would make my life in Europe easier (and cheaper): I have given up on some conference invitations simply because they came too late or I did not feel like penetrating, with my wrong-coloured passport, the fortifications of the US embassy in Copenhagen to apply for a visa.

But is convenience and cash enough of a justification? Or aren't they the very core of that heart of whiteness, as Arundhati Roy puts it, that we often get to know as global capitalism? Aren't the evils of capitalism finally reducible to two formulations: that financial profit (cash) is the final end of human existence and that we can conveniently murder, manipulate or ignore those who are different and less privileged?

If I hang on to my Indian passport, I hang on to my memories. But these memories are not of the sort that one hears canted in popular *ghazals* about paper ships and the shade of trees in the ancestral village. My memories are of difference, of alternatives. Not necessarily their celebration, but their existence. And strangely, every time I travel with my Indian passport, I am reminded of what I share with people travelling on Nepali, Algerian, Nigerian, yes, even Pakistani passports. Out in the world, the colour of all our passports is the same. Our difference is the same.

No number of nuclear devices being tested by India and Pakistan can change this defining "global" reality. The nuclear bombs we explode are little more than firecrackers in the hands of children. No, I am not under-estimating the damage they can do. I agree with Roy that nuclear bombs are "man's challenge to god". I agree with Amitav Ghosh that it is preposterous to justify their use. But finally, it is more than likely that our nuclear bombs will go off, like firecrackers do, in our own hands.

Perhaps because while we have the ambition and the hatred to develop these devices, we do not have the cash to keep them at the highest levels of maintenance. There are too many pressures on the means available to our states. Someone will cut corners some day and then what will be blown off will be Pakistani or Indian hands.

And the world—the heart of whiteness that claims to be first in the world—will remain largely unaffected. At the most, it will turn to us and repeat a colonial prejudice: what else can you expect of children and barbarians, it will ask. At best, it will give us pity and dubious aid; at worst, it will shower us with scorn and dubious legislation. The bomb has not and will not redefine our relationship to this world of whiteness. It will not make a change where it matters: our relationship to this world. But it might help us to forget further the relationship that we share with another world, the so-called third world.

So, I hang on to my passport for I do not want to forget both these relationships. My passport reminds me how marginal I am in the global heart of whiteness, and how childish and superfluous are the squabbles of our (third world) governments. My passport reminds me of what I share with Nepalis, Algerians, Nigerians, yes, even Pakistanis. My passport reminds me that Bin Laden and his ilk are little more than excuses. The new rule for transit visas has little to do with terrorism and everything to do with terror of people with the wrong colour of passport. Europe and the US—and their satellites like Australia—have long been frightened of those who have little cash and cannot be conveniently ignored. This fear goes back a long way: it did not grow out of the foolhardy act of a handful of young men flying planes into buildings in New York and Washington. That tragic event simply provided the excuse to take legislative and other action that many have wanted to take for decades in the 'West'.

And so, I hang on to my passport. For, I was born in India. If I were to relinquish my passport, I would do so in favour of a country that I found superior to India. But while there is much to be admired in places like Denmark and England, there is also much to be ashamed of. The heart of whiteness is lit with lamps of blood.

And today the heart of whiteness is closing its arteries. It is doing to people with the wrong colour (of passport?) what it tried to do to its own poor in the 18th and 19th centuries. Even the discourse sounds familiar: undeserving poor, accountability, violence, criminality, free market, etc, we have heard all this before. But this time the struggle will be longer and more bitter as the poor cannot be deported and settled in 'newly-discovered' continents, where they can get rich by their own sweat or the blood of the aborigines and slaves. Today the poor of the world can only be attracted like moths to the rich heart of whiteness. And hence the arteries of Europe and US are being closed with new rules and regulations.

Medically, of course, we know that the choking of arteries to the heart leads to a heart attack.

SIX

The Death of Rumi

There is something missing. I sit at the table surrounded by about a dozen distant relatives. They are mostly doctors and engineers and we are in the banquet room of a posh hotel in London, celebrating a wedding. Almost all the people in the room have lived in the 'West' for decades—though they have lived in different countries, mostly England, US and Canada, but also occasionally Germany or Denmark.*

The table is loaded with delicious Indo-Pakistani food. Conversation flows. It reminds me of many such occasions I have had in India or Denmark, with Muslims and Christians, with atheists and believers. And yet I keep feeling that there is something missing, at least on my table. It is not the food. Waiters keep us well-plied with that.

It is only later that I manage to put my finger on the lack. The conversation on my table was different from what I am accustomed to in my circle of writers, artists and academics, Muslim or not.

The conversation embraced professional matters: salaries, jobs, prospects. This was not unusual or surprising. Academics love to complain about their jobs; writers worry about royalties. What was surprising was that whenever the conversation moved away from professional matters, it got stuck in Islam.

There were people of my parents' generation and people younger than me at my table. They came from at least four 'Western' countries. They had seen many different things, for they were educated and reasonably successful in their fields. They also shared a lot, as all of them belonged to a larger and culturally-rich Indo-Pakistani

* Published in *The Hindu,* India.

Muslim community. But when they stopped talking jobs, they ended up talking religion.

Only one of them was politically religious and felt that Islam was under threat, and even he was frank in his admiration of what he called the 'tolerant and decent Englishman'. Most of the others only discussed religion in humane terms: one of them, for instance, narrated the common story about Prophet Mohammad and an old woman who would toss garbage on him every morning when he passed her house. His companions noted that he never protested. One day when the woman failed to throw garbage on him, he went into the house to discover the old woman lying ill and alone. He nursed her back to health.

I remembered this story from my childhood, and appreciated it. Many of the other stories were similar. They were religious, but not necessarily fundamentalist. And yet something disturbed me. I was shaken by the fact that in a group of a dozen educated Muslim professionals, the conversation stayed stuck in religious areas, quotations from sacred books and narratives of admirable actions by admired religious personalities.

I was not used to such insular conversation. For example, among the Muslims I knew in India, conversation could veer into religion on such collective occasions, but it was more likely to encompass local politics, social gossip and banter, fashion, films (Bollywood), TV programmes, cricket, even literature at times. But since then I have remarked this tendency, especially among professional Muslims in the West, to end up talking religion.

Not all of this is due to the rise of political Islamism. In fact, the people I have in mind are not really Islamists, even though they might be religious. They are people with technical and professional education: rich enough in material terms, but sometimes greatly impoverished in cultural terms.

Some of this has to do with the kind of education they chose, or had forced upon them. In places like India, Pakistan or Egypt, you do not choose to study history or literature or film. You study those subjects only if you have no other choice. If you have the choice, you study medicine, engineering, computers or at least business management. The 'Muslim' world—and actually all of the 'East'—is in a rush to catch up with the 'West'. And the 'West' has long told us that our cultures and literatures are worthless—as Babington, later Lord, Macaulay put it in the recent 19th century, one shelf of a European library is worth more than all the literatures of India and Arabia. Our modernisers and conservatives share the realization that the Maxim gun—and its later avatars—speaks much louder than any book can.

Hence, the desperation of the 'East' to seek 'modern' education—that means medicine, engineering, computers and management techniques. Who cares about handicraft and sculpture, paintings (yes, there are Muslim paintings) and literature, dance and drama? As long as we stay in our own cultural spaces—unless they are being blasted by the Taliban or the US marines—we still retain some sense of our complex and changing cultural heritages. But once such modern professionals move to the 'West', they are confronted with a greater impoverishment. To their professional training is added the self-centredness of the 'West', the fact that 'non-Western' cultural heritages are even less visible here (especially in public discourse and basic education) than in their home spaces. They flail about for some identity to hold on to, and the branch they often grasp is the branch that is thrust at them both by Islamic fundamentalism and dominant 'Western' discourses—it is the straight and narrow branch of textual Islam, with its socio-historical leaves plucked and its cultural blossoms crushed almost out of existence.

If on the one hand, 'Islamic fundamentalism' is the result of a certain kind of Islamic education (as among the Taliban) and a genuine, if at times exaggerated, perception of Western imperialism and double standards, on the other hand it is also a consequence of this sort of cultural impoverishment. This is part of the explanation why Abdel Bari Atwan, who interviewed Bin Laden in 1996 and stayed with him, had this to say in his recent book, *The Secret History of Al-Qaida:* "I found it remarkable that so many of the mujahidin possessed the very highest academic qualifications. There were doctors, engineers and teachers among them."

Remarkable perhaps, but given the uneven commerce between the West and the rest and the almost constant dismissal of non-Western cultures and heritages, not all that surprising. It is this factor that complicates and adds to the other main branch of Islamic fundamentalism—best typified by the Taliban, those students of Muslim madrasas who have a very different educational and class background from the doctors and engineers depicted above. Even here though, the West plays a part—for madrasas are basically schools of theology that did not, unlike so many European 'universities' in the 17th and 18th centuries, develop into places of secular learning as well. Partly due to European imperialism, so great a gulf was created between 'secular-modern' and 'traditional' branches of learning in Asia and Africa, that madrasas appear to have reduced the secular content of their syllabi, such as classical Greek philosophy, from the 18th century onwards.**
But then that is another story, and just as sad.

** But there might be good news too: the parental demand for modern education, if only in a limited technocratic way, has induced some madrasas in places like India to again begin introducing secular components in their syllabi.

SEVEN

Murder of the Divine

You do not need to be religious in order to have a sense of the sacred.*

And for me, Varanasi—or Benaras, as we called it—is one of the few places I have known that are seeped in the sacred. It is not the sacredness bestowed by devotional verses that I read in school, or the sacredness of the main temples of Varanasi, which will never admit me because I am a Muslim. It goes beyond that kind of ritualized holiness. Varanasi is imbued with sacredness in a deeper sense: the sense of human possibilities and limitations, of human hopes and aspirations, of human continuity and connections, the majestic flow of the Ganga that, in spite of the clogging and pollution, still communicates a sense of all that exceeds the limits of humanity and all that makes us human. Raja Rao's excellent collection of fictional sketches, *On the Ganga Ghats,* captures some of this.

For, you do not need to believe in the God of any religion in order to have a sense of the sacred. Perhaps, if you believe too literally in the God of any religion, if you believe that a book or a holy man can reveal to you the very mind of God, you fail to sense the sacred. The sacred is a sense of the vast possibilities of life, of which human experience forms a major but by no means the only part. Just as God is an index of human possibilities and limitations, we are only human to the extent that we are not divine. But we are also human only to the

---

* Written after a bomb exploded, probably placed by some Islamic militant, outside a Hindu temple in Varanasi in 2006. A number of devotees were injured or killed. Published in *The Hindu,* India.

extent that we have in us that which can comprehend the divine, or conceive of it. It is not, as some militant atheists believe, that human beings create Gods; it is more that human beings become human beings because they can conceive of God.

In our humanity, we are both much less than God and slightly more than mere animals. This realization is essential to a true sense of the sacred.

Which is why when we, in the name of some God or the other, appropriate to us the powers of God, we betray the sacred. Perhaps the people who are most irreligious are those who use religion to justify murder and genocide. Perhaps, it is a greater blasphemy to claim that you are doing the work of God than to claim that you cannot believe in a God—for the person who claims to be the will of God claims that he knows the mind of God. But who except God can know the mind of God?

You do not even need to believe in God in order to realize that the man who claims to be God, or do the direct will of God, appropriates to himself more than human possibilities and limitations can ever allow. But if you believe in God, how can you take a human life that was never in your power to give? How can you plant bombs outside sacred places in India or drop bombs on sacred places in Iraq that take the life no human being can give back?

But if such acts of violence can be seen as unholy acts, acts that deny the sense of the sacred that is essential to all religions, they also need to be condemned from a pragmatic perspective. For violence, contrary to what Bush Junior and Bin Laden say in their different ways, is never an answer to violence. That is so because violence spreads through violence. To react to violence with violence is to spread violence. Violence is not a wound; it is more like a virus. Gandhiji was one man in the 20th century who saw this with absolute clarity. Violence came to him too. Even before his violent death, violence came to him again and again. And every time he stopped it by refusing to succumb to it. By refusing to catch the virus of violence, he managed to prevent it from spreading.

That is all we can do too, because that is the only effective antidote to violence and because that is the only true expression of a sense of the sacred and of our humanity. For, it is not enough to say that the person who planted the bomb outside the temple in Varanasi committed a heinous crime. We have to add that by that act of mortal violence he killed the human in himself—and the God he had believed in.

EIGHT

Crown of Scars

Mahesh Patel, a Hindutva supporter, said to a reporter in the summer of 2002, "We have broken a mosque and made a temple." He added, "We used hammers. Muslims should not live in India. They should go to Pakistan."*

But the building that was torn down by Hindutva fanatics on 1 March 2002, one of many demolished during the BJP government-supported anti-Muslim riots in Gujarat, had not been a mosque. It was the tomb of a 17th century poet, sometimes called the Chaucer of Urdu poetry. Vali Mohammed Vali, also known as Vali Gujarati, had died in Ahmedabad in 1707 and the tomb had been built for him by the residents of the city. It must have been a tribute to his popular poetry as well as recognition of his love for the region of Gujarat and Ahmedabad, which he once celebrated in these lines:

It shines among cities, who would not make
A world to house it simply for its sake?
It's known by the name of Surat; its sight
From human hearts all animus does rake.
Numberless creeds and countless are the faiths
Of its inhabitants: Adam's mistake
Has bred so many colours of skin here,
Beauty pervades its people like a lake.
Such beauty that the court of Lord Indra
Would trail behind, abashed in its wake.

---

* Published in *PN Review,* UK.

If Vali had been told that Ahmedabad was not his city, and that he actually belonged—because he was a Muslim—to a land that lay hundreds of kilometres to the North, he would have laughed in derision. No Hindu of Ahmedabad would have told Vali that in the 17th century.

The destruction of Vali's tomb is an index of all that has gone wrong in India in recent years. It reflects not only mutual ignorance—willed ignorance that fails to distinguish tomb from mosque—and intolerance, but also the dominance of a colonial discourse that has divided a rich, composite culture into the warring 'nationalities' of 'Hindu' and 'Muslim'. It is not that Hindu groups did not fight Muslim groups in the past. They did. They also fought together, with Muslims supporting Hindus against Hindus, and Hindus supporting Muslims against Muslims. However, it was only with the coming of colonial modernity in the 19th century that such differences came to be seen solely or primarily in terms of two newly monolithic and homogenising faiths: 'Hinduism' and 'Islam'.

In recent decades, the heterodoxy that enabled Hindu singers to attract Muslim disciples and Muslim poets to attract Hindu followers has been threatened not as much by the rise of 'irrational religiosity' from the bog of the past as by the steamrolling of a rationalist-colonial 'nationalism' in the present. The Hindu fanatics and the Islamists who see themselves as custodians of custom and tradition against the influence of the 'West' are in this sense guilty of aping the 'West' more than anyone else. Their very categories of self-perception were mapped out by colonialism and Western nationalism. Vali, way back in the 17th century, was much more original and revolutionary in his 'modernity' than many of these defenders of faith and tradition:

Don't waste your life in sloth: arise, arise!
How long will you sleep?: time's awake, it flies.
The face of Truth if you desire to see,
Escape from where the slave of custom lies.
If you learn to wear the crown of your scars,
You'll lead the suffering far beyond their sighs.
That promised spring of love awaits like dawn,
Awake from dreams to what it signifies.
This opening line by Vali learn by heart:
Don't waste your life in sloth: arise, arise!

But who was Vali? We know and don't really know. His poetry has survived almost in its entirety, but personal information about him is sketchy at best. In his magisterial history of Urdu literature, Muhammad Sadiq comes to the informed conclusion that "Vali was born in Ahmedabad and completed his education in the seminary attached to Shah Vajih-ud-Din, but like some other members of his family, he migrated to Aurangabad [in the Deccan] and, for all practical purposes, settled down there and came to call himself a Dakkani... But Gujarat was dear to him for his early associations with it, and he longed to be there, as his *Qitat dar Firaq-e-Gujrat,* indicates." He evidently returned to Gujarat in his later years and was buried in Ahmedabad.

There is much that seems contemporary about Vali. He travelled across cultures and places, while retaining an emotional attachment to his homeland of Gujarat. He was cosmopolitan in his literary influences. He was a multilingual writer, writing in Dakkani as well as Urdu and Farsi. Unlike some other Urdu poets, he was a man not given to lamentation and despair: there is an optimistic, fighting quality to much of his poetry. He comes across as a man who loved life, though it seems that he was never affluent. But joy in friends and in the world appears to have compensated for this lack of money.

Vali was a man of strong social ties, including a lasting relationship with a 'graceful young man'. (Sadiq uses 'the euphemistic language of the day' to describe this relationship: it was an "attachment which rose to an unusual degree of admiration and love.") His social circle contained many Hindus, as is evident from his *ghazal* in praise of Amrit Lal, in which he compares Lal to the Cypress tree, a candle and the crescent moon, and ends with the homoerotic image of his lips full of nectar.

As a poet, Vali was radical in many ways. Being based in the West and South of India, he finally adopted Urdu as the language of his composition. While Urdu, in various forms, was part of linguistic culture in Gujarat and the Deccan by the 17th century, it was nevertheless the spoken language of Delhi and the North. Still, it was Vali who, for the first time, revealed to the poets of the North the poetic possibilities of their daily language, Urdu. He was also responsible for making the *ghazal* the dominant generic form in Urdu poetry, a dominance that has continued to the present day.

What strikes one most of all today about Vali's poetry is its strong erotic imagery. This erotic imagery can be understood in mystical terms, but often it appears that mysticism was not Vali's primary concern. He was above all the poet of earthly love in all forms, love that made existence bearable, meaningful and perhaps better. And, not surprisingly, he is remembered today for his love poetry. *Ghazals* like the one below continue to be sung in India:

My love has melted Cruelty drop by drop,
As bud is sunned to lily drop by drop.
My grief is quenched by faith in her and love,
As blooms cull humidity, drop by drop.
A strange delight there lies in lonely nights:
Her answers can then reach me drop by drop.

Her eyes have stolen me from my own self,
As wine removes clarity drop by drop.
The thought of reckless love visits my heart
As dreams visit the sleepy, drop by drop.

Vali was a poet who celebrated love and friendship and what we today call 'multiculturality'. He drew upon Hindu as well as Muslim traditions in his poetry. It was the tomb of such a man that was destroyed in one night by a handful of hooligans who could not distinguish mosque from tomb and knew nothing of the history of their own city. Love was not what they had in their hearts. They wanted to cleanse the city of exactly that multitude of colours and faiths that Vali had celebrated. On the night of 1 March 2002, they demolished the stone slab of his tomb with pickaxes and hammers. A road ran next to the tomb. The police commissioner's office lay only a few yards away.

Next morning a small Hanuman temple marked the spot of the tomb. It was a symbol of these Hindutva youths' notion of progress. But the government, of course, had its own notions of progress, of modernity that is finally little more than an aping of the West. Within months it extended the adjoining road, slapping a highway on top of the tomb. Now we can drive to the future on the tomb of Vali Mohammed Vali, slave to the customs of colonial mapping that have been absorbed by both modernists and revivalists, Islamists and Hindu fundamentalists. It might turn out to be a future, Vali would have averted his eyes from.

NINE

These are no Revolutionaries

At the heart of any profession of faith is doubt. Monotheistic religions are no exception to this. They tend to use the creative possibilities of doubt, accessed as ambivalence, and they also try to curb doubt from blossoming into disbelief.*

What, for instance, does one need to do to become Muslim? One needs to repeat two lines from the Quran with sincerity. A simple requirement, and followed widely in Muslim societies—so much so that 19th century European adventurers managed to enter Mecca (out of bounds for non-Muslims) by simply repeating these two lines in front of the local authorities.

But what are these two lines? Here is the most commonly published English translation till date:

There is no God but God;
Mohammed is His messenger.

The first line starts with a complete negation, the epitome of doubt: 'There is no God'. But then the line turns into an affirmation, a profession of faith: 'but God'. In other words, 'but (there is) God'. It is not just the meaning that is remarkable, the sounds (in the original Arabic) are just as significant: most of the sounds of the first half of this sentence are reversed in the second half. One starts with doubt and chooses to end in belief. One starts with negation, and is forced to find an affirmation. The philosophical dilemma of human

* Published in *The Hindu*, India.

existence is encapsulated in this line: the second line is an appendix that provides a specific social and historical basis for the negated negation of the first line.

If one has to simplify the complex histories of Muslim thinking in the world since these two lines were first uttered, one can say that some Muslim thinkers have focussed more on the first line and some have focussed more on the second.

It was in the spirit of the first line that Mirza Ghalib penned lines like these in 19th century Delhi:

> For God's sake leave the Kaaba's veil alone,
> There too may lie hidden a god of stone.

Or, to be exact, an 'infidel idol/love' (*kaafirsanam*). It was also in the spirit of that first line that the 13th century Persian-Turkish poet and Sufi saint, Jelaluddin Balkhi Rumi (born in Afghanistan) could claim, "the ways of worshipping are not to be ranked as better or worse. Hindus do Hindu things; Dravidian Muslims of India do what they do. It is all worship, and it is all right."

Such lines abound in the works of Muslim poets and thinkers, including Sufis who were and still are revered as saints by many devout Muslims. Such lines are often resented by jurists and Islamic traditionalists who would stress belief to the extent of erasing every trace of doubt.

It is these people that we often call 'Islamic fundamentalists' today. It's a new tribe, but it has descended from older ones: the tribe of traditionalists, the tribe of conservative jurists, the tribe of religious fanatics. But it is a new tribe, for one can be a 'fundamentalist' only in societies where writing has become so widely disseminated as to make it possible to reduce the multiple religious practices within any lived religion to some global 'fundamentals'. Islamic fundamentalists are at the same time the most 'traditional' and the most 'modern' of all Muslims. In that respect, they are like fascists (National Socialists, to be exact) in Europe and the Rashtriya Swayamsevak Sangh (RSS) in India. Islamic fundamentalists would have been as impossible in most Muslim cultures before the rise of modernity and widespread literacy as Fascists would have been in Europe before the cauldron of the 20th century had been set bubbling by capitalism and revolutionary opposition to it.

The aim of Islamic fundamentalists is not the exegesis of Islam. They would much rather skip the problems and potentials of the first line of their profession of faith. They want a social, political and economic order in which they can feel safe—and empowered. They want their message to be applied, and of course they would like to believe that their message is also Mohammed's message. Actually, they would like to believe that there could be no two opinions on Mohammed's message. And they would like us to believe that.

It *appears* that fundamentalists have chosen to freeze their Islam in time. In this too they resemble neo-fascists in countries like Denmark and France, and for that matter many Hindutva nationalists in India. These nationalists have also chosen to seem to freeze their Nationalidentity in time.

And in all cases, one is not really allowed to question the historicity of the time that is held up for emulation. In all cases, absolute belief is insisted upon.

For, in all cases, doubt lurks at the heart of this belief. Doubts about belief, doubts about the sacred and the profane, doubts about identities and doubts about the world we live in and might live in. Being unwilling to allow space for doubt, all these doubts have to be repressed into a unitarian belief, whether one calls it fundamentalism or nationalism or 'Nationalsocialism'. All pluralities have to be singularized—by force, if necessary.

The excision of doubt is always bloody, and incomplete.

Behind the doubt that Islamic fundamentalists, Hindutva supporters and National Socialists try to expel in different ways, lay the realities of a world in flux, a world in which all that is solid melts into air. Islamic fundamentalists see this world from one side, the National Socialists of Europe from another. One exclaims 'It's like a snake!' another exclaims 'It's like a pillar', but both fail to see the Elephant of capitalism that they are blindly groping at.

Islamic fundamentalists see the occasional historical overlap of capitalism with (largely Protestant) Christianity and confuse the two. They need to do so. For one can fight 'Christianity' with reference to some safely fixed idea of the past, while one would be forced to face the confusion of the present to tackle capitalism.

And then Islamic fundamentalists are seeking hegemony over people who call themselves Muslim. By definition, their 'fundamentalism' is a modern and literate element—it is imbricated in capitalism, just as the middle and upper class leaders of Islamic fundamentalism are themselves beneficiaries of a global capitalism that, in general, keeps most Muslims (and Christians, Hindus, etc., in the 'third' world) in various degrees of powerlessness and impoverishment. Their opposition to this capitalism tends to take symbolic shapes: they want to give it an Islamic face, they will not dismantle it. And the Bharatiya Janata Party (BJP) too would rather parade capitalism in 'Hindu' garb.

These are no revolutionaries.

The National Socialists and nationalists of Europe are not revolutionaries either. They want to control doubts about the future and some aspects of the melting down effects of capitalism. And they will do it. Oh yes! They will do it—in their own countries. They will do it by turning a blind eye to the fact that capitalism is global and that their countries are basically beneficiaries of capitalism. They would champion Capital, which has become global, without facing the fact that labour has not become correspondingly global. They would hide this fact by making a fuss about the very limited labour mobility that global capitalism has led to—less mobility today, in actual terms, than in the 19th century for example. And of course, they would defend the welfare state for their own 'people', or otherwise, they would have to face the prospect of extending it to the world.

TEN

Why do they Hate America?

We all remember the scene through several television replays. It is 11 September 2001 and a woman, anonymous and shell-shocked, emerges from the dust clouds swaddling the crash-bombed Twin Towers. She looks into the camera of the waiting reporter and asks: "Why do they hate us?"*

I had heard exactly the same question about five months before 11 September. It had been posed by an American poet—white, Democrat, much travelled and intellectually open—in response to a private discussion with some Asian and African writers at a residency in Switzerland. The Asians and Africans were fluent in English and held democratic and feminist views, and yet this well-meaning and intelligent American could respond to their criticism with only that subjective question: Why do they hate America?

Arundhati Roy has replied to the question from the perspective of Anglophone American-literature-reading Indians like me by pointing out how grossly misleading the rhetoric of hate is. Does 'hating America' mean hating Walt Whitman and Sylvia Plath, Hollywood films and the various kinds of American music that we listen to? That, evidently, is one side of the answer to that rhetorical question: America is many things and one can resist aspects of 'the American experience' without 'hating America'. In their book *Why Do People Hate America?*, Ziauddin Sardar (writer, editor and cultural critic) and Merryl Wyn

---

* Published as a review in *The Hindu Literary Review,* India.

Davies (writer and anthropologist) provide the other side in great detail. While highlighting the complexity of America and segregating official American policy from an easy correspondence with the American people, they nevertheless set out to illustrate why some people actually have reason to hate America. It is a brave attempt in a world where even historical allies, like France, are to be made—according to some US policy makers—to 'pay a price' for not kowtowing abjectly to American decisions.

Sardar and Davies debunk the 'Us-Them' thesis of the American Right that, as they point out, sees 11 September as a landmark in the battle between good and evil, with America monopolizing the former. They point out how spokespersons of the American Right routinely simplify complex issues and indulge in disinformation. While they highlight how the current villains, Islamic fundamentalists, have stepped into the shoes of the communists and socialists in the rhetoric of the American Right, perhaps Sardar and Davies miss out on a contextual opportunity by failing to highlight how the American and US-led persecution of the Left, in the USA and globally, created or consolidated the discourses and instruments that are now being used to justify a permanent state of controlled long-distance war that, after all, is not very different from the Cold War.

However, quoting extensively from other writers and scholars, they successfully dismantle the stereotypes of Islamism, Arabs, 'anti-Americanism' etc., being used to sustain largely undemocratic control of global resources by American governments. They also quote texts like Zoltan Grossman's *A Century of US Military Interventions from Wounded Knee to Afghanistan*, which lists 134 such 'interventions' between 1890 and 2001. Sardar and Davies illustrate how the "ascendancy of the hamburger culture has meant the eradication of indigenous third world cultures everywhere" and how American failure to see the 'obscene power' of their cultural hegemonies makes them many enemies, among native elites who fear cultural erasure and the poor millions who cannot afford hamburgers anyway. Of particular interest in the book are the chapters about the stories Americans tell (and have been told) about America and "the burden of the American (gunfighter) hero," both of which enable one to understand the widespread support that Bush's policies have gained in the USA. The book also takes up more specific issues for discussion, such as the US-support for Israel: "Israel receives 40 per cent of all US foreign aid…, roughly $500 per Israeli citizen."

Finally, Sardar and Davies try to understand why well-meaning Americans often take recourse to the 'they-hate-America' argument: "America is what we have termed a 'hyperpower'—a nation so powerful that it effects the lives of people everywhere. Yet, Americans are shielded from knowledge and debate about the actual consequences of US engagement with the rest of the world." As *Why Do People Hate America?* has been published in the UK and Australia, it is unlikely that it will enable ordinary Americans to dismantle their shield of comfortable ignorance in these days of hawkish 'missile shields'. Nevertheless, Sardar and Davies cannot be accused of either intellectual apathy or moral cowardice in the face of an increasingly tyrannical 'new world order'. Sometimes at the risk of simplifying complex economic matters, they provide highly readable and pertinent answers to the question: Why do (ordinary) people hate America?

And the simple gist of their answer is that people tend to hate powers that interfere in their lives in an arbitrary, heavy-handed and largely undemocratic manner (as the US has done from Guatemala to Indonesia, Nicaragua to Iraq)—and this answer should also be made available as a warning to Islamic fundamentalists.

ELEVEN

British Newspapers and Islam

Working on an anthology of African and Asian travel writing from before 1900, I was struck by the way in which perception of 'Muslim/Islamic' sexuality has changed over the last one thousand years or so. Until well into the 19th century, Muslim societies were mostly seen by Europeans as sensuous and sexually permissive. Even in the 19th century and early 20th century, this perception survived in some forms: Oscar Wilde, for instance, decided to leave a 'boy' companion behind before embarking on a tour of Turkey because, as he wrote, 'you know how the Turks are with boys'. However, from the 19th century onwards, this perception of sexual permissiveness was increasingly overshadowed by the discourse of Islamic conservatism, rigidity, intolerance and misogyny. Today, for instance, dominant or vocal discourses present Muslims as anti-female, anti-gay, sexually repressive etc., even though subterranean traces of the fear of 'Muslim' sexuality remain and are often encountered in perverted or demagogic terms: 'Muslims have too many children'.*

It had struck me that while such a significant twist existed in the European discourse on 'Islam', most texts on Europe and its relationship to Islam tended to give the impression that this relationship had hardly changed across the centuries. It redounds to John E Richardson's credit that he addresses exactly this change—and other subtleties—without wavering his focus on the (mis)representation of

* Written as a review for the *Journal of Language and Politics*, UK

Islam in Europe and, in particular, in British broadsheet newspapers. He points out that "the belief that sexual licentiousness was particularly linked with Islam, and therefore Muslims, has been a ubiquitous orientalist preoccupation, particularly of the earlier Christian writers." He highlights that Islam's acceptance of eunuchs, marital sex in various forms, divorce and widow remarriage—as well as the supposed or real acceptance of homosexuality in Muslim societies—were all viewed with abhorrence by early European writers. The fact that the same signifieds and signifiers (lines from the Quran, for instance) have been read in opposite and contradictory ways by European commentators—but annotated negatively in both the cases—illustrates the ways in which power operates. Unlike what some naïve multiculturalists and other well-meaning beings assume, power and hegemony are expressed not only in what is permitted or prohibited, what is said or not said, but above all, in the capacity to define (misrepresent) in favour of the elite whatever might or might not exist on the ground.

Such philosophical issues are not the central concern of John E Richardson's *(Mis)Representing Islam: The racism and rhetoric of British broadsheet newspapers* (2004). But Richardson's astute mix of qualitative and quantitative research assures that many such issues are highlighted or raised, even if they are not pursued further at times. Employing Critical Discourse Analysis and based on an interdisciplinary foundation, the bulk of Richardson's book deals with the data-set of 2,540 items of newspaper reports culled from British broadsheet newspapers (*Financial Times, Guardian, Independent, Daily Telegraph, Times, Independent on Sunday* and *Sunday Times*). With the help of a detailed coding instrument, which allowed him to tabulate 80 variables, chapters three to seven record, reflect and discuss prominent patterns in the broadsheet reporting of Islam and Muslims. These chapters are fascinating in many ways, and I will return to them. But before moving on to the bulk of the research reported in the book, it is pertinent to put on record the richness of Richardson's discussion of matters like racism and orientalism in the first two chapters, in spite of the contingency of space, and the connections that he establishes between 'racism' and the perception of Islam/Muslims. These discussions, highlighting the contradictions in the European perception of Islam across time, end in an accurate remark: "Whilst these co-occurring essentialising discourses of racism—physical threat and sexual allure—may appear contradictory, they are, in fact, based on the same presupposition: that 'racial and ethnic others' are closer to nature and instinct than to rationality; more ruled by the urges of the body than the thoughts of the mind." (p 19) How I wish a certain school of comfortable multiculturalists and post-colonialists could be made to read these pages and start every morning with a recitation of Richardson's pithy conclusion!

Another interesting discussion in the introductory first chapter relates to 'Islamophobia'. The discussion is indebted to the Runnymede Trust's report of 1997 and it engages intelligently with texts like Fred Halliday's paper, "Islamophobia Reconsidered" (1999). It discusses this new signifier (Islamophobia, the term, was first coined by the American periodical, *Insight*, in 1991) without losing sight of the long history of the signified. If there is a lacuna in this chapter, it relates to a lack of engagement with anti-Semitism. Today, anti-Semitism is less what the Nazis and similar 'European superiorist' groups espoused and more something Muslim Arabs tend to be accused of because of their tendency to be opposed to Israel. However, there is an interesting contradiction in this easy bandying about of the term, for Arabic is a Semitic language and the Arabs are probably more 'Semitic' than many Israelis (let alone Anglophone Jews living in the US etc.). What does it mean to accuse a 'Semite' of being anti-Semitic? An exploration of this issue might have added to Richardson's introductory first chapter.

Chapter two presents a discussion of the discursive representation of Islam and Muslims. It is based on the assumption—drawing from Critical Discourse Analysis—that "if racism is reproduced through discourse, then racism will be in evidence at all three 'levels' of discursive communication—social practices, discursive practices and the texts themselves..." (p 33). The chapter traces out a map of British journalism by setting out its backdrop, pressures and routines: finance, profit and advertising, employment of Black journalists, white management, the 'burden of representation' and the professional norm of objectivity. The discussion concludes by observing:

> "The alignment of journalism with the interests of the powerful is a combination of the (mainstream) media's corporate bureaucracy, the reliance on other corporations for funding (through advertising revenue), the institutional conservatism of white management and editorial staff, and apathetic, or self-serving and career-hungry, journalists." (p 47)

This is neither new nor remarkable, but it does help clear the ground. The chapter goes on to sketch the broad outlines of the critical textual analysis of newspaper reporting, with particular reference to the work of Norman Fairclough. With reference to Ghassan Hage's work (1998) on Australian multiculturalism, Richardson reads the discourse on Islam in British broadsheets as an 'elite discourse', emanating from the "agent's fantasy that they occupy a privileged position within ...[the] national space as 'the enactors of the national will.'" (p 67)

Over the next chapters, drawing on Teun A Van Dijk's ideological squares, Richardson documents how broadsheet reporting of Islam and Muslims projects 'Muslim negativity' and the 'West as civilizer'. With reference to many reports, he illustrates that broadsheet reporting of Muslims is dominated by a twin process of 'division and rejection':

> "The broadsheet approach to division and rejection suggests that its success is based upon a three part process: first the identification of a 'space' (which can be political, cultural, social, mental, physical or metaphorical) separate from 'Our own' space; second, explaining the workings or composition of this space in contrast to 'Our own'; and third, placing a (negative) value on both this space and its composition." (p 69)

The discourses of 'Islamic' despotism, extremism and sexism—along with the perception of a military threat from Muslims (also as a 'fifth column' in Britain)—are central to the creation of this negativity.

This construction of 'Muslim negativity' in reporting leads to and is under-girded by the discourse of 'the civilizing influence' of 'the West' and 'Westernization'. Richardson provides dozens of examples of this. Many of these examples are so obvious—at least to a reader from a 'non-European' background—that I, for one, would be depressed by the necessity of annotating them, of revealing their discursive colourings. But it is necessary to do so, and Richardson performs the task with remarkable precision. Not only does he expose the more obvious statements, he even puts a question mark against some statements by commentators, like Robert Fisk, who have a well-deserved reputation for objectivity and even sympathy towards Muslims. Such question marks are necessary for they highlight not the ill will of the speaker but the subterranean tenacity of dominant discourses. Intention, it appears, is not enough in the face of the language used.

Richardson ranges across a number of topics that are featured in the media, excavating the language of each to uncover the skulls of 'Muslim negativity' and the bones of Western civilizational hubris. These topics include broadsheet reports of 'pluralism' in Iran, events in Israel, Algeria, Iraq, British Muslims (an excellent chapter), 'fanatical' Muslim violence in the public sphere, 'Islam-vs-the-West', etc.

If there is a significant topic lacking, it is the reviewing of 'post-colonial' and 'minority' literature, for it appears to me that the valorization, publicity and success of recent novels like Monica Ali's *Brick Lane* have at least something to do with the civilizational myth vis-à-vis Islam. However, book reviews are not news items or editorials, and one can understand why Richardson does not devote a section to them.

There is also an interesting discussion of how newspapers reacted to the publication of Runnymede Trust's report, *Islamophobia: A Challenge to us all* (1997). Richardson illustrates that central to the majority of reporting on the report was 'a rhetorical management of this criticism' by deflecting the Runnymede criticism on to others, subtly countering the criticism, directly refuting it and, on occasion, ignoring the criticism altogether.

It is almost impossible to illustrate how interesting and relevant the book is—in spite of some, at times, inelegant 'sociological' writing. Much of the punch of the book lies in the excerpts that Richardson excavates and annotates, and to annotate an annotation is to do it signal disservice. As such, I have concentrated on the issues raised and the inferences drawn in this review. I have also been unable to draw attention to the tables and diagrams employed, often to good effect, by Richardson.

In conclusion, Richardson points out that the findings of his book emphasize:

> "The need for any future research on broadsheet journalism to adopt a context-sensitive analytic position, and take into account not merely the product(s) of reporting, but also the ideological, the contextual and the structural controls on reporting...In embracing such an approach, future research will not only foreground broadsheet newspapers' location in the social and political world, but should also illustrate the way journalists are marshalled by capitalism, manipulated by powerful social/political elites and the manner in which journalism is used to maintain racist global inequalities." (p 232–3)

This is sage advice at the end of a very useful, competent and sensitive study (and one that yet again illustrates the strengths of Critical

Discourse Analysis) and Richardson's tone is generally optimistic in his conclusion. It is an optimism that I am hard-pressed to share, given the evidence marshalled in the book, the general lack of self-reflectivity in the media and the gap between the media and academia. As Richardson notes earlier on in the book, there is probably no book-length study of broadsheet newspaper coverage on any issue in any national or reporting context in England. Add to this the complications and blind spots introduced by the 'spectre' of Islam, and one is hard-pressed to hope for any perceptible rise in 'context-sensitive analysis' by the mainstream media.

TWELVE

Muslims in the 'Wild West'

It is assumed by many educated Americans (and Europeans or Africans or Asians) that Muslim Americans are a recent phenomenon, at best going back to the rise of the Nation of Islam movement among Black Americans in the USA in the 1920s. This is a myth. Various records show that there were Muslims on the American continents at least as early as the 16th century. There survive written records—including autobiographical texts—by Muslims who were taken to the Americas as slaves in the 18th and 19th centuries and accounts by free Muslim travellers as early as the 17th century.*

In particular, there was a substantial—and subsequently obscured—presence of African Muslims in North and South America from at least the 16th century. As Allan D Austin puts it in one of his books, African Muslims were "a proud people, influential beyond their numbers on both sides of the Atlantic Ocean," who until recently have been "almost completely neglected by modern America's eagle-eyed historians and storytellers." So much so that American critics criticized Alex Haley for making his African ancestor in *Roots* (1976) a Muslim.

One could, of course, go further back than the 16th century, and scholars like Ivan Van Sertima *(The African Presence in Ancient America: They Came Before Columbus)* have done so. While Van Sertima is particularly anxious to prove that Black Africans—and not

---

* Published in *Information,* Denmark

Arabised ones—had reached America before Columbus, his evidence and arguments point to a sequence of African arrivals—ranging from those of Ancient Egyptians to the half-Muslim Black Africans of the glorious Mali empire to Arabised Western Africans and Moors. Actually, the controversial and on-going discovery of African presences in pre-Columbian America is fascinating in itself. The first mention of Africans and Muslims (Moors) in America occurs in early accounts by European explorers themselves. But the first academic study came about, in a round about way, when a professor of linguistics at Harvard, Leo Wiener, discovered what appeared to him to be clear evidences of African and Arabic influence on Native American languages. Weiner was a white American and the books he wrote in the early decades of the 20th century, propounding Arabo-African influence on American languages, were largely ignored by the academic community. This, as Van Sertima indicates, seems to have been the fate of much research in the area—done in different fields and not taken up by a broad community of scholars. Not only have the evidences in fields like linguistics, art and historiography been rarely examined and combined with scholarly rigour, supporting evidences from African, Arab and Moorish historical sources (and texts) have not been fully explored yet.

However, as much of this research has to do with areas in which I can claim little or no expertise (linguistics, art history and archaeology), I have decided to leave out this debated pre-history of the African and Muslim presence in pre-Columbian America. Moreover, I feel that while the evidence is strong, it still has to be substantiated by a broad and objective body of scholarship. Instead, I have chosen to focus on uncontroversial records—written and historically recorded—of the Muslim presence in America.

If we ignore the pre-Columbian era, we are nevertheless faced with European records dating from the first centuries of the colonization of the Americas—there are 16th century documents that show the presence of Turks and Moors in not only America but also on the islands of the Caribbean. Many of these Muslim Africans, Turks and Moors must have been brought to the Americas as slaves—In *Turks, Moors and Englishmen in the Age of Discovery,* Nabil Matar points out that by the 17th century, American Indian slaves were being sold not only in Europe but also in Africa and that European slave-traders were also selling Muslim captives as slaves in the Americas. Some Muslims in 16th and 17th century America might also have been sailors or traders: the earliest extant Arabic account of the sojourn of a free Arab in South America goes back to 1668.

It should also be kept in mind that in the 15th and 16th centuries the Muslim empires of Asia and Africa had not been colonized, though some European 'bases' had come into being in Asia and Africa. Muslim rulers could, and did in many cases, interact with European powers on a basis of political equality. Queen Elizabeth I, in particular, was on friendly terms with the Ottoman Empire and major West African kingdoms, specially Morocco. Diplomats were exchanged, royal letters went back and forth, mutual trade was permitted and, at least until the Jacobean period, Muslims from Africa and the Arabic lands retained the reputation of being intrepid sailors and traders. Contemporary European writers even urged their countrymen, in terms of Christian admiration or Christian frustration, to emulate the travel-based trading of the Muslims. There is overwhelming evidence of the presence of relatively free Moors in Spanish America as early as the 16th century: for instance, Matar notes that in March 1586 some Moors deserted the Spaniards to join Sir Francis Drake during English attacks in the Caribbean.

Apart from accounts of Arab travellers from the 17th century onwards, there are also records—a greater number, in fact—of African

Muslims in South and North America from at least the 16th century. The evidence of the existence of African Muslims in North America exists in many forms: slave records, cargo lists, newspaper articles, portraits, regimental records, transcribed texts, interviews, reports, autobiographies etc. The stories these records tell are varied—though many seem to echo the sentiments of the African-born Lamine Kebe who wrote, in 1835, that "there are good men in America, but all are very ignorant of Africa." All these men—and, at times, the women with them—undertook arduous journeys, often under taxing circumstances, and survived under conditions of servitude. In this, they were not any different from thousands of other African slaves. What, however, made them conspicuous at times was their knowledge of writing and always their knowledge of Biblical stories (through the Quran). Both these 'assets', Austin suggests, enabled some African Muslims to weather the assaults of servitude and, what is more interesting, leave behind written accounts. Many of these accounts—in Arabic or in a native African language written in the Arabic script—are yet to be translated or made available to a wider readership, though Austin has tried to do so in two of his books and other scholars have started publishing in the area.

Job Ben Solomon's is one of the early extant stories of these Muslim 'pioneers': he was brought to the British colony of Maryland in 1730 and later returned to Africa, where he seems to have set up as an agent for European trading companies. Another contemporary Muslim, a slave who probably arrived around the same time as Ben Solomon, was Yarrow Mamout, immortalized in an oil portrait by Charles Peale, one of America's first great artists. Mamout, who claimed to be more than 100 years old when he sat for Peale, had been set free by his owner, after he made the bricks for the owner's large family house. Often praised as a good worker, he twice survived losses of his earnings to whites and finally bought a house. He was said to be a good-tempered man, refusing to let the heckling of local boys provoke him when he said his Muslim prayers.

Unlike Mamout, some Muslim African slaves were not 'good-tempered' towards whites and slavery. In the 1850s, we come across accounts of one such slave, Osman, described in newspaper reports as "a famous African chief, who was sold into slavery and escaped." Hostile to slavery, he 'obtained firearms' and 'led a reign of terror during the early fifties'. Posses were sent to find him but failed to do so, and he reportedly died of snakebite in the swamps. It is a story that ought to fit well within the established annals of the 'wild West', but it has been left out as the outlaws and cowboys of the American wild West need to be white in the American imagination (with, of course, a few 'Red Indians' in sidekick roles or getting merrily shot off galloping horses).

Many Muslim slaves—partly because of their literacy—rose to positions of power within the slave hierarchy.** One such was Salih Bilali, who not only persuaded fellow slaves to stay with the Americans (and his American owner, Spalding) during the war of 1812, but also received 80 muskets to defend the plantation. According to Austin, this is the only known incident of slaves being provided with guns by their owners in the region. Bilali—who told his owner that he would "answer for every Negro of the true faith [Islam], but not for the Christian dogs you own"—kept his word, at least to the

** This was not confined to the US. The famous Haitian slave revolution—the only fully successful slave revolt in the new world—was probably led by a Black Muslim man, whose very name highlighted his literacy. However, unlike today's 'revolting' Islamic fundamentalists, this man spoke up for all suppressed slaves in a demotic language, and did not confine himself to Muslims or the idiom of Islam.

extent that no Spalding slave fled to the British. During the terrible hurricane of 1824, Bilali is reported to have saved 'hundreds of slaves' by his presence of mind.

Another African slave, a Muslim who converted to Christianity in the USA, Umar ibn Said wrote the only extant autobiography by an American slave in Arabic on the continent (another such autobiography exists, written by a slave in Jamaica). It was written along with many other extant manuscripts, published or written between 1819 and 1864. Umar ibn Said was taken up by Christian evangelists as one of the 'saved': this probably accounts for the fact that so many of his writings were also saved. Like many such conversions, Said's adoption of Christianity appears to have been partly a matter of convenience or the result of a more syncretic sense of religion than that available to the evangelists. After conversion, Umar ibn Said continued to transcribe Quranic extracts in his autobiographical text, focus positively on his past as a Muslim and refer to Jesus as the Messiah (which is how the Quran sees Jesus) rather than the Son of God. Austin argues that Said probably did not see acceptance of the Christian God as severing him from his Muslim Allah, and in this he was not altogether unique. Muslim slaves who accepted Christianity mostly continued to retain a predominantly Muslim identity: some of them probably saw no contradiction in calling a recognizably similar deity by another of his many Quranic names, others probably converted as a political necessity. At least eight such converted slaves 'reverted' to Islam as soon as they returned to Africa or gained freedom. One such person was the six-foot-tall and imposing Ibrahim Abd ar-Rahman Jallo who not only managed to protest his way to freedom but also to buy the freedom of much of his family, largely by morally browbeating white liberals.

Autobiographies written in English by Africans taken to the USA as slaves also exist: the most well known being the one by Olaudah

Equiano (who was not a Muslim) in the 18th century. This book was a bestseller when it came out and has remained widely read. Much less known is Mohammed Ali ben Said or Nicholas Said's shorter autobiography that first appeared in *The Atlantic Monthly.* Said was born in 1833 in present-day Nigeria and he came from a prosperous military-merchant family. He was captured by Taureg raiders in 1849, marched across the Sahara Desert and sold as a slave in Tripoli. Lucky in the masters he found, Said was released by a Russian aristocrat in 1859, after traversing much of Europe. He travelled of his own volition to South and North Americas. Fluent in seven languages, he became a teacher in Detroit, Michigan, in 1862, and joined the 55th Regiment of Coloured Volunteers in 1863. He was mustered out in 1865 and disappeared from sight after that.

Unlike Umar ibn Said, many Muslim slaves did not convert to Christianity. They tried, like Yarrow Mamout who said his prayers unprovoked by heckling, to retain their faith, often also transcribing extracts from the Quran by memory and passing them around. By the 19th century, Arab and other Muslim settlers had also started reaching the Americas. To recall all their scattered stories is to fill in a chapter left strangely blank in the history of America. It might also help restore a semblance of balance in a world where growing American hegemony seems to be based on the myth of the making of America by white Europeans.

THIRTEEN

The Closing of Doors

The title story of Attia 's 1953 collection of short stories, *Phoenix Fled*, creates a complex narrative space that, among other things, is defined by a sequence of walls and doors and their inter-relationship. Behind this complex space lurks the tragedy of the Partition of India in 1947.*

The short story, "Phoenix Fled", starts off by introducing us to an unnamed old woman in an unnamed village. It tells us that she is so old that people associate her with the existence of the village—if we trace out the narrated events of her life in historical time, the woman is definitely more than 90 years old. It also tells us that she is known in the village and the adjoining 'hamlets'. More specifically, it places this ancient woman—almost blind due to inflamed cornea—in the family courtyard of that unnamed village. This courtyard is connected to the village by 'a heavy wooden door' that creaks when it is opened, and it is often opened when people from the village/s or her grandchildren from the city visit her. Finally, the courtyard contains a doll's house. Not an unusual appendage in the courtyards and houses of many Indian villages until recently, a doll's house was not just a plaything for children, but also an object of decor and used, at times and in some regions, for certain socio-religious rituals.

The text can mislead us about the situation of this ancient woman if we are not careful. It would be a mistake to see her as isolated and

---

* Published in *Passage: Tidskrift for Litteratur of Kritik*, Denmark

walled in—a common tendency in Western readings of 'traditional' settings in non-Western literature. We are told that she had 'become static in time' and that she remembered the past better than the present. We are also told that she does not use sight but "time's familiarity for seeing and recognizing her changeless, circumscribed world." But this narrative discourse that tends to wall the woman in the past and the courtyard is also subtly contradicted by the story. Her courtyard contains a 'door to the world outside'; she can hear cars and locomotives and is aware that the world has changed; she remembers relatives in the nearest town; she receives regular visitors, even from far-away cities. Most significantly, she connects most effortlessly with the people who are in some ways—in terms of both time and space—most distant from her: her great-grandchildren, boys and girls born and growing up in distant cities. The narrative discourse also reinforces these elements of the story at times. This is what it tells us about her time with her great-grandchildren: "Then there was no conflict of worlds, they shared one created of their bright young love, not flat one-dimensional but given depth and form and colour by their curiosity, amusement and repulsion." The expression 'no conflict of worlds' is significant as it helps us avoid a common tendency in Western academia to see such 'Eastern' characters as torn between 'modernity and tradition'. Actually, in very different ways, both 'modernity' and 'tradition' sit quite easily on this woman and her great-grandchildren.

The space that contains this woman has its walls—it would not be distinguishable as a kind of space otherwise. But it also has its doors. If we were to map the spaces in the narrative, we would need to begin with a box titled the 'doll's house', with doors leading to the larger containing box of the 'courtyard', with a door leading to the larger containing box of the 'village', with doors (roads/rail-tracks) leading to the larger containing box of the vicinity (the neighbouring 'hamlets'), with doors (roads/tracks/flight routes etc.) leading to the larger containing box of the 'outside world'.

It may be the presence of these doors—permitting a two-way traffic of experiences—that enables one to understand the difference between Hosain's 'doll's house' and Ibsen's.

There are walls and doors of another sort in the narrative too. For instance, we are told about the 'invisible bond' of stories that the great-grandchildren share with the woman: a door through the wall of age and other differences. The doll's house itself appears in the nature of a door in this context: it is the 'invisible bond' between the woman and the children. What is interesting—but almost imperceptible—up to this point of the story is the ease with which walls are penetrated, differences overcome. The narrative does not evade the difference—the children even find the woman repulsive—but it indicates how doors (visits, bonds, shared interests and stories, language, even expectations of basic decency etc.) can be opened through walls of differences. In particular, it is the relationship between the old woman and her great-grandchildren that enables us to understand this achieved ability. As such, it is perhaps significant that the tragedy of the story is presaged by a 'misunderstanding'—a mixing of signifier and signified—between the woman and the children.

Soldiers have passed through the village. When the woman hears 'soldiers', she thinks of 1857 ("The red-faced ones, like monkeys in red coats. They whistle to bad women."); but it is 1947 and the children tell her that soldiers no longer wear red coats and that 'there are black-faced monkeys too'. Among other things, this handing-on of the possible beastiality of man—from red-faced monkeys to black-faced monkeys—is a telling commentary on the currency of male violence (physical, political, geographical) that British colonizers passed on to post-colonial authorities in 1947.

To begin with, the old woman had remembered the revenge exacted by British soldiers after the *Gadar* of 1857 (when suspected Indian mutineers were summarily hanged and used as cannon fodder by the resurgent British forces) and the children had experienced the soldiers in more benign terms—the soldiers had distributed sweets, probably to celebrate the independence of India/Pakistan. But this has changed by the time we reach the conclusion. The families have fled with the children and the old woman has chosen to stay behind, partly because she would slow down the desperate refugees and partly because her experience of the past makes her view this latest threat with a degree of knowing complacency: "You will return. In the Mutiny [1857] we returned and our fears were more cruel than reality." There is deep irony and pathos in this statement. The reader, burdened with knowledge of the Partition and its riots, knows that the families won't return. This is one phoenix that will not rise from its ashes.

Lonely and frightened, the old woman lies on her string bed and falls asleep. She is woken up by the smell of burning thatch and the creaking of the door. She can sense people approaching. She tries to sit up. The story ends with these lines: "'Mind,' she scolded, pointing her bony finger, 'mind you do not step on the doll's house.'"

Apart from the depth of the implied tragedy, and the significance of the 'doll's house' as a symbol of decency and the meeting of opposites, the narrative has concluded with a complete rewording of 'doors' and 'walls'. The walls of the houses in the village have been set on fire—they will probably collapse. And yet such a wall of hatred and revenge has been reared in the (un)known distances, that the door lapses from its prior function of the entry of life to the concluding role of the door of death. The door that the old woman has refused to barricade despite the emigration of her family has finally been closed on her—and this closure mirrors the closing of doors for all those who survived her and people like her in India and Pakistan.

In spite of the much touted death of the author, the narrative death of this old woman forces the reader to recall that Attia Hosain, the author, refused to choose between India and Pakistan after the partition of 1947,, preferring to live in London to make her home in the shut and barricaded rooms of partitioned India/Pakistan.

FOURTEEN

The Matter in 'The Matrix'

In a recent issue of *Le Monde Diplomatique,* Valerio Evangelisti argued that serious literature, particularly serious literature in Europe, no longer reflects the contemporary realities of new technology, globalization, the leisure industry, social conflicts, psychedelic weapons, terrorism, communications, etc.* For contemporary reality, added Evangelisti, one has to go to crime novels, science fiction (sci-fi) and, in particular, cyberpunk.**

When one thinks of polished and acclaimed novelists like Malcolm Bradbury or, until recently, John Updike, one is tempted to agree with Evangelisti's claim. Their novels seem to be caught in a time warp that has conveniently bracketed the most impressive and the most disturbing developments of the last two or three decades. Serious literature of a certain variety often seems to ignore or occlude such contemporary issues as those of governmental responsibility, power, the discourses of the market, extreme cultural clashes, political subversion, elitist hegemony, etc. These issues, however, provide the thematic skeleton of the best works of cyberpunk, such as *The Matrix* (film; part I) and the novels of William Gibson. Evangelisti's claim may be exaggerated, but it contains a solid kernel of truth. It is true that as the capitalist media reduces "the real tragedies of the world to a sequence of fleeting

---

* *Valerio Evangelisti:* "The truth is in here", *Le Monde Diplomatique,* August 2000, p 15.

** Published in *Biblio: A Review of Books*, India

images so rapid as to leave no trace," sci-fi, fantasy and cyberpunk help us counter various hegemonic manipulations in the inventive and relatively free realm of the imagination.

But if 'imagination' is the strength of cyberpunk (and sci-fi in general), it is also its weakness. Cyberpunk is a sub-genre that depends heavily on virtual reality (cyberspace+the matrix) and the computer world, thus constructing an alternative reality (or alternative realities) to the material world of human bodies and human agency. That is its basic difference from traditional sci-fi. It is not that computers or virtual reality did not play a role in traditional sci-fi, but their roles were circumscribed by and embedded in material reality. In cyberpunk, virtual reality becomes a parallel—often a superior—reality.

Traditional sci-fi would include HG Wells and novels like Mary Shelley's *Frankenstein,* which do not contain 'cyber elements'. However, a typical sci-fi movie with cyber elements would be *Blade Runner* or *The Terminator* and a full-fledged cyberpunk text will be Gibson's *Neuromancer* or *Virtual Reality* or most of the stories in the cult anthology edited by Bruce Sterling, *Mirrorshades*. The Larry and Andy Wachowski film, *The Matrix,* is also a late cyberpunk film but, as we shall see, with a revealing difference.

In a brilliant essay, "Just Gaming" (in his book, *Gargantua: Manufactured Mass Culture),* Julian Stallabrass makes some points about computer games which can also be made about cyberpunk. He notes that, in computer games, "as if previewing cyberspace, simulation takes the form of commodification which has arrived at a more rarefied stage, emptied of all materiality."[†] Apart from radically denaturalizing acts of extreme violence, this simulation creates a world

† Julian Stallabrass: *Gargantua, manufactured mass culture,* p 90–91.

that is more real than reality. Things happen faster in virtual reality. 'Players' have more agency there. They can move about at a superhuman pace and do incredible things. The reality of cyberspace—as we can see in Gibson's *Neuromancer*—ends up being more real than the reality of the material world. The former is where things happen; the latter is only an access to this virtual space of hyper-reality. In this relationship, the equation between reality-imagination and human-machine has been turned upside down. Imagination becomes more real. The machine is where reality resides, and the human world is only an instrument (machine) to access that hyper-reality.

One may argue with Evangelisti that such an 'escape' into a heightened 'imagination' can be a subversive act aimed against a material world that has been dragooned into the institutional and intellectual rigor mortis of high capitalism. This argument should not be taken too far because cyberspace dilutes the issue of material oppression and because, even in the imagination, cyberspace is more a replica of material space than anything else. Things do not really *change* in cyberspace: they just get bigger, faster, better, more evil, etc. The very imagery and language of cyberpunk illustrates this: power is suggested by size, evil is suggested with the help of the usual colour schemes and discursively significant terms like 'cyberspace cowboy' and 'hustler' proliferate: in future, I am sure, the issue of Islamic terrorism will not be 'solved' or even fruitfully confronted in cyberspace, it will simply be reproduced in a faster, more colourful distortion of the reality 'out there'.

It is interesting how cyberpunk uses contemporary fears while at the same time diffusing them into individual play. In a recent article in *New Left Review,* Frederic Jameson has commented on the "stark visibility [of] this destructive side of the new world economic order, in which instant transfers of capital can threaten to impoverish whole regions, draining overnight the accumulated value of years of national labour."[††] This description could be applied to the 'action' in cyberpunk novels like *Neuromancer*. In such novels and stories, cyberspace cowboys, hustlers, data thieves etc., strike out of the blue of cyberspace and create mayhem with other players or even corporations. In many ways, these cyberspace raids resemble the international capital raids that Jameson (among others) describes. But in cyberpunk, their effects are circumscribed to individuals and, at best, groups; they do not "impoverish whole regions." Or if they do, this impoverishment is hardly ever narrated and never sufficiently dramatized.

If this is what cyberpunk is, where does *The Matrix* fit in?

What makes *The Matrix* a fascinating film is exactly its use of cyberpunk conventions and its attempt to go beyond them. While much of cyberpunk depends on a contrast between a degraded, decaying material world and a cyberspace of greater colour, speed, agency, *The Matrix* subverts this equation. In cyberpunk speak, it ought to be pointed out, 'matrix' stands for the concept of virtual space, while 'cyberspace' (which is used synonymously with matrix in this essay) denotes only that part of the matrix that is occupied by data.

The Matrix starts in a 'real' world that seems to be quite well regulated. It proceeds to reveal the fact that this 'real' world is imaginary—it is virtual reality created by machines—and that the way out is to escape from this machine-controlled virtual reality and re-enter the world of physical bodies and material things. The escape route is reversed. While in much of cyberpunk (and computer games), there is an escape from the material world into virtual reality, in *The Matrix* there is a bid to escape from virtual reality into the material world. Of

[††] Frederic Jameson: "Taking on Globalization", *NLR,* 4 July/August 2000, p 56.

course, 'material' and 'virtual' are not opposed in a Manichean manner and they remain interconnected, but the plot does suggest that a privileging of virtual reality leads to loss of human agency.

Such reversed escape not only restores a modicum of privilege to the material world, it can also be read as an allegory of capitalism. As Marx pointed out, capitalism operates by locating value not in human labour but in capital. In many ways, then, under capitalism, an *abstraction* of human labour and agency assumes reality. It is this abstract and abstracted capital that seems more and more real with time, and human beings more and more unreal—in the sense, above all, that the needs of capital tend to take precedence over the needs of human beings.

This process is similar in many ways to the virtual reality depicted in *The Matrix*. The relationship between virtual and material reality in *The Matrix* also echoes aspects of the relationship between capital and human beings. But, given the fact that *The Matrix* is the creation of popular consumerist culture and was manufactured in one of the cultural centers of global capitalism (Hollywood), it is almost inevitable that this tangential (almost allegorical) diagnosis *cannot* lead to a credible prescription. Predictably, in *The Matrix* the dubious 'prescription' or 'cure' is that hybrid of bourgeois individualism, capitalist entrepreneurship and traditional elitist heroism—the lone saviour, played by Keanu Reeves.

But then the 'saviour'—whether as Keanu Reeves or the various 'heroes' of Islamic terrorism and the 'war' against it—is another story, and one that will be narrated not in cyberspace but historical time.

FIFTEEN

Welcome to the Bush, Mr Blair

It had to come. Mr Blair is on the way to joining a long list of supposedly left-leaning, or at least well-centred, leaders who have unleashed the tiger of the Right, ridden a dangerous ride on it, and then aired ghostly complaints when the tiger finished licking their political bones clean.*

I first saw it happen to Rajiv Gandhi in India. True, he was following in the footsteps of his mother, Indira Gandhi, who liked being seen in temples and mosques, and not his grandfather, Jawaharlal Nehru, who avoided all connections with established religion as the Prime Minister of India. Rajiv was not a particularly religious person, I am sure. But he tried to flirt with both sides: when religious fundamentalists wanted an antique and conservative law upheld, he obliged them. When religious fundamentalists wanted to get a long-locked mosque opened, he obliged them too. He did all this with the best intentions, and with an eye to the electorate. Things went out of hand; the reopened mosque was destroyed and Hindu fundamentalism was on its way to power.

The fact is that once you start speaking a certain language, you have to speak it fully. You cannot dabble in the language of religion, and expect to score over religious fundamentalists. You are speaking their language, however toned down. By speaking their language, you strengthen their voice. You need to talk to them, but not in their

* A shorter version published in *Daily News and Analysis,* India, as "The Roaming Tiger of the Right."

language. Moreover, even the ordinary objective voter—if there is any such animal—will see through it, and probably vote for the more honest, if objectionable, party.

Then I moved to Denmark, and saw it happening to Poul Nyrup Rasmussen and his Social Democrats, who were in power then. Today there are some Danes who object to the convenient xenophobia allowed by the neo-liberalist Danish Government at some levels and the obvious xenophobia preached by the rightist Danish People's Party, which supports the government from the outside. They sound so nostalgic about the Social Democrat years.

But to be honest, Nyrup's Social Democrats had long been whispering the language being spoken loudly today by the neo-liberalists and Danish People's Party. They were just as worried about 'foreigners'. They were just as prescriptive about immigrants. They were just as concerned about Danishness. Their worldview was almost as binary and Eurocentric. The only difference was that they still wanted to be decent about it all.

It is hardly surprising that Social Democrats lost the maximum support during the recent Prophet Mohammad cartoon controversy in Denmark. The rightist Danish People's Party gained in a big way, and some leftist parties increased their support to some extent. But Social Democrats lost their voters, mostly to Danish People's Party. After all, if you need to stand on a molehill, why not go directly to the mountain?

Clinton happened in between. I still hear my Democrat friends weeping about all the good that Bush put an end to. But what good, really? Apart from a couple of points, Clinton's administration sat on almost all progressive law-proposals, and passed many of the ones only on its way out. Even today if you hear a Democrat and a Republican senator on 95 per cent of the issues that concern us, you will be hard pressed to tell who is who.

And now Blair, who is in some ways still the humane face of the madness that is gripping Europe and the rich countries. He wants to save us, and the world. So what does he do? He blames our problems, or at least the existence of our fears, on the Human Rights Act. It is an act that makes crime and terror-prevention difficult, argue his supporters from England to Denmark.

Strangely, they were arguing the other way during Denmark's cartoon controversy. I recall them getting very angry when people like me argued that the cartoons were not necessary for freedom of speech and were an abuse of that freedom, but that one had to tolerate (under strong protest) such abuse for the sake of political democracy. And today I will say something similar about human rights legislation. Sometimes, a particular human rights law might prevent us from catching a criminal—for me terrorists are simply criminals—but that signifies its abuse. The slight chance of this abuse has to be accepted for the larger cause of human rights.

But the problem is not human rights or cartoons. The problem is that the so-called left-of-center and center parties—sometimes even strongly leftist parties in the West—no longer dare speak the truth. Sometimes, they claim to fear Bush, but actually—like the Right—they are ruled by a fear of 'the Bush', or their exaggerated estimate of the hold of this potentially xenophobic fear on their electorate. That is what makes them stop speaking their own language. That is what makes them dependent on a watered-down version of Rightist slang.

The truth they cannot speak is that we live in a capitalist world in which capital is largely free but labour is not. The truth they cannot speak is that 850 million people in the world are malnourished, almost all outside the rich Western nations; that the income of the richest one per cent of people in the world is equal to that of the poorest 57 per cent; that 115 million children in the developing world have no basic education; that commodity exports in places like Africa continue to be used to pay rich countries for increasing foreign debt; that four-fifths of total consumption expenditure is accounted for by just one-fifth of the world's population. The language they need to speak is that of international socialism and, at least in its absence, the free flow of labour. And they need the courage to speak it even if it costs them some votes in the rich nations.

SIXTEEN

The Loneliness of Arundhati Roy

Something huge and extravagant and sometimes even useful has come up in Delhi every time I return to India, and I do so about once a year. This time it was a swanky new metro station in Connaught Place, the concentric British-built core of New Delhi.*

As I emerged from the clean and cool interior of the metro station, rushing to get to the hotel where I was to stay for the duration of a literary festival, I witnessed a stream of immaculately dressed young men and women fan out into the more democratically-attired populace of the roads and paths on the ground. Here they mingled with the beggars and auto wallahs, the clerks, guards, Rajasthani women selling embroidered cloths, petty shopkeepers and hustlers. One of them caught my eye. He was young, dressed in an expensive suit, carrying a leather briefcase. Coming out into the light of the open ground, his shiny boots fell on some rubbish and for a second I noticed on his affluent, self-absorbed face an expression of deep irritation and impatience.

I didn't know that I would meet various equivalents of that expression again, very soon.

The organizers of the literary festival had, rather extravagantly, put me and many other writers up in an expensive hotel opposite Jantar Mantar, the famous 18th century observatory. Around the corner, in

---

* Written in 2006.

another world from the polished floors and air-conditioned rooms of my hotel, a different kind of literary festival was going on. Some local poets had gathered to read out their poems in support of a demonstration by the Narmada Bachao Andolan (NBA)—this was part of a decade-long attempt to, initially, stop the construction of a big dam in the Narmada Valley and then, failing that, force the government to provide adequate rehabilitation to the tens of thousands of people, mostly poor villagers, displaced by the project.

Medha Patkar, for some the main leader of NBA, had gone on hunger-strike a few days ago because, she claimed, rehabilitation had not been adequate or efficient. On the day our literary festival began, the police stepped in and arrested her, on the charge of attempting to commit suicide. She was taken to a hospital where, at the moment of writing this article, she was continuing her fast.

The next day I organized a petition that was signed by almost all the writers and editors attending our posh literary festival. Knowing that the matter of the dam is controversial—there are various arguments in favour of and against big dams—the petition was worded cautiously. It expressed concern and stated that, no matter what one feels about the dam, it is impossible to deny that rehabilitation should be given top priority. It added that a democracy can only thrive if things like 'development' and 'progress' are not experienced as being achieved at the cost of ordinary citizens.

When I went to the site of the NBA demonstration to submit the petition of support, I was offered an introduction to Arundhati Roy, author of the Booker-winning *The God of Small Things,* who has staunchly and consistently backed the cause of the poor villagers and the NBA. Much as I admire her work, I declined the offer, for I was there for a different purpose. But I came away troubled. Why was

Arundhati Roy here and not at the literary festival? And why were we there and not at this demonstration?

Some time back, Roy wrote an essay titled "The Loneliness of Noam Chomsky", in which she noted how Chomsky's non-ideological but unwavering critique of the myths of our world and American policies has made him a beacon of hope—and also a lonely voice in the world. Something similar has been happening to Roy. With her unrelenting critique of not only the liberalist 'development' of India but also the expansive double-standards of USA, Roy has isolated herself from many people of the sort who go to literary festivals. What they want is some soft criticism that does not make them feel too uncomfortable. What Roy and Chomsky provide is something much harder, less digestible to the young men and women with leather briefcases and self-absorbed faces. Even the media space Roy sometimes gets for her politics in India is tinged by the irritation of such fast movers.

For these men and women are on their way somewhere, a place that they believe, and are told, is the natural destination of all history. Suddenly they meet the critical glare of Roy's writing, or the protesting voices of the NBA. It is like having a bit of garbage land on your shiny shoes. They have no time for it. They shake it off with a look of impatience and proceed.

Even my feeble attempt to ease my conscience by floating a petition of support was shaken off by the Delhi papers. Hardly any of them reported it, though it had been signed by some prominent writers, scholars and editors of India, Pakistan, the USA and UK. And the next day, a major national daily from Delhi hardly reported the NBA demonstration either—the reporter focussed on a smaller demonstration by victims of the Bhopal gas leak, another piece of shit on the shiny boots of progress, while privately (in a conversation with me) blaming NBA for hogging all the limelight.

As if two wrongs make a right. As if we can justify one crime by condoling with the victim of another. As if the loneliness of Noam Chomsky in USA has nothing to do with the loneliness of Arundhati Roy in India.

SEVENTEEN

The Prophet Cartoons: No Space in the Middle?

When I first saw them, I was struck by their crudeness of perception and execution. Surely *Jyllands-Posten* could have hired better artists? And surely, decades after Edward Said's *Orientalism,* cartoonists and editors ought to be able to spot the difference between, say, Indian turbans and Arab ones? Because in many of those controversial cartoons of Mohammed, the Prophet of Islam, the turbans looked more Indian or Pakistani than Arabic.*

In some ways, that was the essence of the problem to begin with. Not just the fact that there are educated people in countries like Denmark who cannot distinguish between Arab and Arab, but that they sometimes cannot even distinguish between Arab and Indian. It is this patronizing and generalizing tendency—much stronger in Denmark than in more self-aware countries like England or Canada—that decided the initial course of the controversy and has coloured the Danish reaction.

One could see that the matter would take a turn for the worse when, late in 2005, the Prime Minister of Denmark brusquely refused to meet a group of Arab diplomats who wished to register their protest. His explanation, later on, was that the diplomats had demanded action

---

* A shorter version of this article appeared as "We Have Lost our Voice" in the *Guardian,* UK. This longer version appeared in *Pausing to Reflect: On Europe's Culture Wars,* Ed. by Rosemary Bechler and published by the British Council, 2006.

against *Jyllands-Posten.* This is a lame argument, for such meetings are meant to discuss such differences and demands, if only to decline them; they cannot be held only on the basis of premises set out by the government.** If you refuse to talk, the matter ends up where extremists want to take it—on the streets.

In most other countries, these diplomats would have been received and their protest accepted. Then the government would have expressed 'regret' and told them that it could not put pressure on any media outlet as a matter of law and policy. In their turn, having done their Muslim duty, these diplomats might have helped lessen the reaction in their respective countries. By not meeting them and their like, the Prime Minister of Denmark just as effectively silenced all 'moderate Muslims' as they would be later silenced, in January and February 2006, by the shouting and burning of mobs of fundamentalist or militant Muslims in various countries.

Like many other 'moderate Muslims'—practising or not, religious or not—I too have been silent on the matter of *Jyllands-Posten's* cartoons of Prophet Mohammed and the ensuing protests. Not because I do not have anything to say or because I am fighting shy of the controversy. But because there is no space left for me to say anything in either Denmark or in many of these Muslim countries.

This does not appear so to many Danes. Here the local controversy seems to be raging between two 'Danish Muslim' public figures: Abu Laban, the Copenhagen-based Imam who has co-ordinated much of the protest against the offensive cartoons, and Nasser Khader,

** It also turned out—as was revealed in a series of *articles* (mostly ignored by the government) in *Information* and *Politiken*—that the supposed demand to take action against the cartoonists or *Jyllands-Posten* was, at best, a very slanted (some experts said 'incorrect') reading of the text of the letter by the Muslim diplomats.

a member of the Danish Parliament. Khader, liberal, democratic, clean-shaven, is posited against the bearded Abu Laban and seen as standing on the side of such 'Danish' values as freedom of speech and democracy. He is supposed to represent sane and democratic Muslims. On the other hand, there is repeated talk of kicking Abu Laban out of the country.

In actual fact, of course, both Khader and Abu Laban make it even more difficult for moderate Muslims to be heard. Abu Laban is not afraid of being kicked out of Denmark—he might even try to provoke such an action—because Denmark is not his political territory. He is setting himself up as a 'leader' or 'voice' of Muslims—and he can do that as well or better from France or Syria with a Danish expulsion in his baggage. Similarly, Khader, in spite of what he might say or believe, does not depend on 'Danish Muslim' votes for his survival in Danish politics. He depends on the votes of mainstream Danes and his politics is inevitably geared towards that end. Though I sometimes agree with Khader's socio-political views, I must say that both Khader and Laban end up, consciously or not, deriving political mileage from their Muslim backgrounds—though in opposite directions.

In some ways, the Danish prime minister's refusal to meet the Arab diplomats was also partly the result of local political considerations. Political commentators have wondered at the abruptness of this refusal, but of course what else could he have done as the head of a government that is supported by the xenophobic Danish People's Party and as a politician who came to power on basically a 'no-nonsense from the migrants' platform?

So much for Denmark, a land in which complacency and smugness have reached extraordinary heights in recent years. Now let us move to the Muslim countries. Here too we meet a similar string of local considerations. Surely the tensions between Hamas and Fatah, which had just lost the elections, played a role in the disturbances on the West Bank? Surely, some of the reactions—especially in Syria—were the working out of Islamic and pro-Iraqi frustrations on one of the two staunchest allies of the USA's invasion of Iraq? And so on, and so forth.

If on the Danish side, such local considerations were compounded by the larger aspect of orientalist and semi-colonial 'superiority', the Islamic reaction had its more abstract elements too. I won't mention the Islamic injunction (Quranic or not) against portraying Allah or even Mohammed, which is logically in keeping with the Bible's occasional opposition to graven images of divinity—though it is surprising that so many Danes do not see the connection. One could, of course, have this injunction and follow it—as every believing Muslim would—without forcing it on people who do not share one's faith.

But then, the question arises: why should people who do not share one's faith bother with images of one's prophet? For the sake of freedom of expression, said *Jyllands-Posten* and, implicitly, the Danish prime minister. Yes, sure, but what is it that a cartoon of Mohammed with bombs in his turban 'expressed' that could not be—and had not already been—expressed in other ways? Actually, the more I think about it, the more I come to the conclusion that the only thing that was expressed by the cartoons was contempt for Muslims. In that sense, it is not surprising that so many Muslims expressed their reaction to such contempt.

Wait a minute though. Isn't it surprising that the Muslims who took to the street angrily demanding 'respect' from the 'West' were sometimes Islamic fundamentalists? Why, one wonders, should Islamic fundamentalists be worried about 'respect' from a region they find unworthy of emulation? The answer to this lies in the histories of Islamic fundamentalism and European imperialism, both of which have aspects that are horribly inter-linked with each other. As a reaction to European imperialism and, later, a political development of the West's fight against communism and (at least in the Arab countries) socialism, Islamic fundamentalism is a quintessentially modern phenomenon. Hence, in their own way, Islamic fundamentalists are much more bothered about the opinion of the 'West' than a person like me would ever be!

Yes, the Danish government should have apologized long before it did, for not taking into account the sensibilities of so many of its own citizens. And yes, the Danish government was right in not acting against *Jyllands-Posten.* But it is not sufficient to answer that there is 'freedom of expression' in Denmark. Freedom of expression is not a mantra—democracy does not oblige people to 'express' sexism, anti-Semitism (which is not the same as opposition to Israeli militarism) and racism.

Indeed, it is a condition of human existence—and not just democracy—to be able to express oneself without pressurizing others violently by language, image or gesture. And freedom of expression is necessary not because it is a god-given virtue, but because once you allow the authorities to start hacking away at it piecemeal, you are liable to be left with nothing at all. But as all expression takes place in a social context, along with the right to express comes the duty to consider other people's rights. This applies as much to *Jyllands-Posten* as to the rampaging mobs in Beirut.

This brings me back to the larger aspect of the Muslim reaction. All the shouting and burning has simply submerged all moderate voices again. Perhaps even the vast majority of Muslims are silent now. They are silent because, no matter how much they dislike the activities of Islamic mobs on the streets, they cannot defend the cartoons carried by *Jyllands-Posten.* That is so because they know, as every intelligent and honest Dane would too, that *Jyllands-Posten,* a conservative, provincial paper, did not carry the cartoons because it was fighting for freedom or democracy. It carried the cartoons simply to provoke and ridicule, in keeping with a certain discourse that has come into existence in Denmark.

For many moderate Muslims, the matter was not about abstract notions like 'freedom of speech' or 'blasphemy' but simply about the sort of human decency that we display when we do not ridicule a child in the presence of her parent, or her parent in the presence of the child.[†] Much of Danish public discourse on Muslims and migrants has lost the last shreds of this human decency, and the *Jyllands-Posten* cartoons were and are a symbol and consequence of that.

So between the Danish government and Islamist politicians, between *Jyllands-Posten* and the looting mobs in Beirut, between Laban and Khader, the moderate Muslim has again been almost silenced. She has been forced to take this side or that, when actually she can take neither without ceasing to be moderate. She has been forced to stay home, and let others crusade for a cause dear to her—freedom—and a cultural heritage essential to her—some version of Islam. She sits there watching TV, watching the bearded mobs rampage and the clean-shaven, blue-eyed white men preach—she is unnecessary to both sides. In the clash of civilizations that is being rigorously manufactured, she is in between. And she can feel it getting tighter. She can feel the squeeze. But, of course, she cannot shout. She cannot scream. Come to think of it, can she really express herself at all now?

† For Muslims, sometimes even those who do not practise their faith, Mohammed is a parental figure to whom they are as deeply attached as they would be to their own children.

EIGHTEEN

Aarhus Diary: Screams, Murmurs, Silences

6 February 2006 (Monday)

Snow everywhere in Aarhus. I wake up and get dressed to go to work, though I am not teaching today and have decided to catch up on my reading. I get my children ready. But then the snowfall increases, the wind picks up. I decide to let my children stay at home. I need a day off, I tell myself. And I can always read at home, with the children playing in their room. So that is what I do.*

Except that I feel the urge to check my e-mail. There are two from Indian writers I greatly admire, Amitav Ghosh and Pankaj Mishra. Amitav is settled in New York; Pankaj is spending a few months in India. But both of them have written to me about the same thing. As one of them puts it: "We are missing your voice in this cartoon controversy. You have to write something."

So I sit down and write something. I send it to the *Guardian* in London, for I sometimes review books for them. The *Guardian* publishes a shortened version of it the next day. It is a simple, non-controversial piece to my mind, in which I try to explain how moderate Muslims feel pressed to take sides in a controversy that, for many of them, is not simply or only about 'freedom of expression'.

---

* Published in *Third Text,* UK; a Danish version appeared in a book published by the leftist daily, *Information.*

7 February 2006 (Tuesday)

My article has come out in the *Guardian.* I go to work and open my office computer. There are already about 30 responses to the article. Over the next few days, I will receive another 100 or so. For the first time, the extent of the polarization I had written about comes home to me. While many of the e-mails are positive, there are some critical voices too. And there are some rabid voices as well. All of these rabid voices are by Europeans who want immigrants out of Europe, or who simply want me out of Denmark for not toeing the government's line. Almost all the mails I receive from Danes in Denmark are negative, but all the mails I receive from Danes abroad are positive.

If this is how believing Danes are reacting, how is it that believing Muslims must be reacting? There were voices of paranoia in some of the more extreme mails. Someone screams at me in one of the e-mails about Muslim migrants turning Europe into 'Eurabia'. If such paranoia can be heard in Europe because of the presence of individual Muslim migrants, what must be the extent of the paranoia in Muslim countries, almost all of which have US military bases or Western occupational forces? I am shaken by the extent of the horror unleashed by some ill-conceived and at least partly dishonest cartoons.

I had realized the cartoons would be controversial when they were first published in September 2005. I had also started suspecting that the Danish Government—motivated by its links to the Danish People's Party, its own 'hard-on-migrants' attitude and simple 'Western' arrogance—was perhaps incapable of tackling the situation with diplomacy. The fact that Anders Fogh Rasmussen had turned down a meeting with diplomats from some Muslim countries in October had struck me as a tragedy—partly because I was not convinced by the excuse given. It later turned out that the excuse—that the diplomats had demanded action against *Jyllands-Posten* was as much of a convenient 'twist' as the claim, made by the same government earlier on, that Iraq had chemical weapons. I was afraid that, having closed the doors of dialogue, Anders Fogh had provided Islamic fundamentalists with exactly the excuse they needed to take the matter to the streets.

Isn't it ironic that Anders Fogh's government is just as responsible for Danish embassies being burned and Danish goods boycotted, as militant Imams are responsible for Muslim youths being shot in the protests? I am surprised by the fact that Danes let their government slip away from this just as easily as religious Muslims seem to absolve the Imams responsible for the needless deaths of their sons. (For, after all, as was the case with *The Satanic Verses* controversy, while press reportage and public opinion in the West consolidate the image of Islamic militants on the rampage, it is usually the semi-literate believing Muslim youth who is shot by paramilitary forces when Islamist demonstrations get too virulent or inconvenient.)

8 February 2006 (Wednesday)

My parents call from India. They have finally heard of the controversy. Over the past few days my family-members, spread across the world, had appeared unaware of the controversy. I had called some of them, but they had never brought up the matter—and some of them are people who love discussing political issues. I had felt that the Danish media was making the controversy seem bigger in the Muslim countries than it actually was. But now all my relatives seem to have caught up—even my parents. And my parents have called to ask me *not* to write anything about the controversy.

I feel tempted to tell my father that I have already written an article and that this time it has provoked people who are against the 'Imams'. It would surprise him. He has always seen me as a social radical and leftist, and he knows that in the past I have made fundamentalists—both Hindu and Islamic—angry. Perhaps it would even reassure him, for he is a religious man, though modern in his own way, extremely tolerant of other views and, like many Muslims, convinced that religion is a private matter. But I decide not to tell him much, partly because I am afraid I might end up telling him about the anti-Muslim hate mails that I have received—and that would worry him too.

The hate mails continue to trickle. Some are incapable of listening to reason. When I try to reply to some of them, I only receive insults—aimed at me as an immigrant and a Muslim. But four or five of the negative—but not rabid—correspondents are carrying out a debate with me. I try to answer these critics, even as I try to thank those who have written in support.

In general, though, I avoid discussing the matter with people I do not know too well. But I overhear statements, the most common being the claim that Danes are so used to caricatures that they would not even care about Jesus being abused. I have my doubts about such statements. Like almost everything in this controversy—on both sides—they appear to be only half-true. For I remember the 'Jesus sandals' being taken off the racks in Danish supermarkets only a few months ago. I recall the reason given by a *Jyllands-Posten* editor for not carrying cartoons of Jesus: that they were not funny and would have offended their readers. It appeared to me exactly the reason why many Muslims were protesting against the Mohammed cartoons.

The thought crosses my mind that perhaps the best thing to do on such occasions is to copy Gandhi—move on fast and stop talking. For it appears that, on such occasions, people talk across each other. I go to bed wishing for silence.

9 February 2006 (Thursday)

I make an early morning resolution. I will turn down all requests for comments and interviews on the issue. I break the resolution quite soon because I receive a call from Pernille Bramming of *Weekendavisen*. I feel happy she has called, because no Danish publication appears to have reacted to my *Guardian* article despite the fact that media from about a dozen countries have called or e-mailed. A suspicion has been nagging me. Is it that the discursive space in Denmark is even narrower than I had assumed? Does the fact that I occupy a moderate and democratic position without agreeing with Nasser Khader, the liberal Danish MP, make me a suspect in the eyes of even ordinary Danes?

For I disagree with Khader because I feel he makes it too easy for supporters of anti-Muslim lobbies to avoid facing their own prejudices—one cannot accept the claim that the cartoons were an expression of 'freedom of speech' even if one has to accept the democratic requirement that media should not be muzzled by any government. The two are different matters, and the 'freedom of speech' brigade has been stubbornly conflating them, just as Islamists have refused to accept that democracy requires a free media, even when it is abusive and irresponsible. In any case, the discourse of 'freedom of speech' as it has been formulated in recent weeks seems to share a central feature with the Islamic (or religious) discourse of the 'sacred' against which it is often pitted—both operate in the realm of idealist abstraction. Moreover, I feel that Khader has made it too easy for a paper like *Jyllands-Posten* to gain credit for its half-true explanations: for instance, the claim that the cartoons were a response to the problem of finding illustrators willing to draw Mohammed obliquely avoids the fact that *Jyllands-Posten* commissioned *cartoons* and not *illustrations* of the Prophet of Islam.

However, when one is contacted by what is basically a 'borgerlige' (conservative) paper like *Weekendavisen*—a paper whose political views differ from mine—one sees grounds for hope. I promise *Weekendavisen* the full version of my *Guardian* article.

The drawback is that it sends me back into the cartoon controversy.

I am by now tired of it. I want more time for my children and my books. I had never wanted to be embroiled in the cartoon controversy. I had felt that it was the sort of controversy in which you cannot take any clear position without being partly wrong, or at least wilfully blind to one side of the controversy. Even the moderate position, I am discovering, could be offensive to some Danes.

I am teaching Byron and Keats today. And Poe. The Romantics. Always a great fan of the Romantics, their poems still move me but their personal antics have started to bore me today. There appears to be a bit of the juvenile rebel in some of them, the teenager with a spray can 'expressing' himself on public walls and train compartments. They appear to have struck too many postures. I agree with many of their views, but I am getting tired of heroic postures. I am surprised by this response.

10 February 2006 (Friday)

I receive an e-mail from a good Danish acquaintance who informs me that my moderate position in the *Guardian* makes me sound 'more Muslim than usual'. In some ways, this irritates me more than the hate mails I have received.

Why is it that the 'Muslim' in order to be moderate has to distance himself from his religion? I have met hundreds of Christians who consider themselves irreligious but call themselves Christian. I have also met hundreds of Christians who call themselves atheists but practice

Christian traditions and celebrate Christian festivals. No one would dream of questioning them. But people like me are always forced to choose: if you do not shut up and accept the excuse of 'freedom of expression', you end up sounding 'Muslim'.

Actually, I think in some irritation that moderate Muslims, religious or not, have been harmed more by the West than by religious fundamentalists in their own countries throughout the 20th century. There was a time when moderate and progressive Muslims were being isolated, jailed and murdered by dictatorial (but mostly not fundamentalist) regimes in many so-called Muslim lands. Western governments looked the other way and sometimes supported the murderous regimes because, in those days, they were fighting 'the communist threat' and moderate Muslims often happened to be leftists.

Things have changed since then. The vacuum created by the premature abortion of leftist alternatives in these nations was filled by the genie let out of the bottle of the Cold War, when Islamic fundamentalism was encouraged as a counter to the communists in countries ranging from Egypt to Afghanistan and Pakistan. Now the genie of Islamic fundamentalism refuses to go back into any bottle. And Western governments and media are, now, very sympathetic to 'moderate' and 'progressive' elements in the Muslim world. As such, the moment any movement favouring secularism, democracy and modernity arises in the 'Muslim world', it is immediately covered—and described as 'pro-West' in the West. This even happens to moderate *mullahs*—as in Iran recently!

This has three consequences.

1. It obscures the legitimate grounding of the movement.
2. It strengthens the feeling of 'clash' between 'East' and 'West', as the internal debates in Muslim societies—some going back centuries and all with their own inner dynamics—are seen simply as mimicry

of the 'West'. This reinforces the self-defeating and false assumption that all such changes stem from the 'West' and are, as such, from the reactionary perspective, alien to Islam.

3. It makes the moderate movement suspect in Muslim countries—not only in the eyes of fundamentalists, but also in the eyes of ordinary conservatives and people who are suspicious of Western imperialism.

So, 'Western' sympathy does not make a difference to the moderate Muslim—who is again isolated, jailed or murdered. To get on from here, the 'West' will have to learn to see the 'rest' not simply as monster or mirror. To get on from here, the 'West' will have to accept the moderate (practicing or not) Muslim as someone who is distinct both from the 'West' and from 'orthodox' Muslims. Failure to do so results in moderates making themselves invisible—thus strengthening extremist positions on both sides—or actually falling into a more religious position in cultural defence.

The Weekend

I have dinner this weekend with some friends who have joined Nasser Khader's *Moderate Muslims.* They are from Egypt, and they think like me on these matters. Like me, a few years ago, they might not have seen any need to identify themselves as 'moderate Muslims'. But now they feel that this space in the middle has to be made visible to extremists on both sides—to xenophobic Danish nationalists and to Islamic fundamentalists. We owe it to our children. We owe it to our ancestors. We owe it to the world.

I envy my Egyptian friends the comfort that must come from joining an organization of like-minded and democratic citizens. I feel tempted to join 'Moderate Muslims' too. I know the ordinary members of the organization mean well. But I am afraid that the political climate in Denmark is such that 'Moderate Muslims' will be used for propaganda purposes by the government. It will be used to marginalize other Muslim voices and discredit them in Danish eyes, even though my friends do not want that to happen. They are democrats; they want all legitimate voices to be heard. But I remain suspicious: I have seen similar well-meaning and committed groups being put to propagandist uses by 'greater forces' in various countries.

I am not altogether wrong. CNN carried a snippet that weekend or on Monday. It shows Nasser Khader and other leading members of the group beaming around a grimly smiling Anders Fogh Rasmussen. The Danish Prime Minister met with Danish Muslim leaders, CNN informs the world.

I switch off the TV. I would much rather read out *Kaj siger hej* to my daughter. I prefer to read out *The Little Mermaid* to my son. I want a break from this world of cynical posturing. I want to be reminded of the common decencies that make life possible—and worthwhile.

I feel isolated and lonely, but I know I am not alone. No, I am not alone. There are other parents too reading or telling stories to their children. All over the world they murmur below the shouting of crowds and the hectoring of leaders, they murmur out their insubstantial stories in Danish and English, in Arabic and Urdu. I join my murmur to their murmur.

NINETEEN

Israeli Attacks: Delegated Aggressions

I am writing this article at a time when Israel is shelling Lebanon with the sort of freedom from human and civic concerns that would be heavily—and perhaps militarily—chastised if it was practiced by an Arab country, and more so against a people who belong to another religion and are considered by many Israelis as belonging to another ethnicity or race. But I have not written a single article about this shelling. Come to think of it, I have not written a single (full) article on the Palestinian issue, apart from a high school essay on Palestinian poetry.*

If I were an Islamic fundamentalist, or perhaps even a deeply religious Muslim, I would probably be apoplectic at the shelling. And perhaps with good reason. This, finally, is the reason why an ordinary Muslim is more likely to listen to and admire an Islamic fundamentalist than someone like me. After all, the shelling affects ordinary Muslims, as do various other equivalents of the shelling in other parts of the world.

Islamic fundamentalism arises from an elitist and narrowed reading of the Islamic texts by groups of mullahs. But it also has its demotic base in the effort to bring religion to the people (and its other side: people to religion) and, above all, in a spontaneous *emotional* response

---

* Published in *The Hindu Sunday Magazine,* India.

to the sufferings, real or perceived, of ordinary Muslims.** The usual liberal-secular dismissal of fundamentalist politicians—whether Hindu in India, Muslim in Pakistan or Christian in the US—as simply Machiavellian characters remains blind to this complexity, and as such cuts little ice with ordinary Hindus, Muslims or Christians, especially in periods of real or perceived threat.

Similarly, religious fundamentalism in countries like India, Pakistan and Egypt is not simply a throwback to the Dark Ages of the past, as some liberal-secular commentators seem to imply. Both Hindu and Islamic fundamentalisms are not only revivalist in their tone but also deeply modern—even at times 'Western'—in the structures of their perception.

It is not a coincidence that four out of the five *sarsangchalak,* or supreme leaders, of the Hindu nationalist-fundamentalist RSS had a background in modern science: KB Hedgewar was a doctor, MS Gowalkar was a zoologist, Rajendra Singh was a physician, and KS Sudarshan, the current head, is an engineer. Similarly, the two 'founders' of Islamic Pakistan—though both were not Islamic fundamentalists—Jinnah and Iqbal, were highly Westernized people with European education. Even the rise of groups and ideologies, such as that of the fundamentalist Muslim Brotherhood, had a lot to do with visits to Europe by their founders or leaders. Even the

** This also applies to the neo-Right in many European countries, such as the Danish People's Party (DPP) which combines xenophobia and subterranean racism with a seemingly heartfelt response to the problems, real or perceived, of the 'real or authentic citizens' of the nation. Pia Kjærsgaard, the leader of DPP, often stresses that she thinks from her heart when it comes to issues concerning ordinary Danes. This is not always borne out by the policies supported by her party, but it remains a convincing argument even with many Danes who do not vote for her.

most reactionary of Islamic fundamentalists are distinguished by their dismissal of European cultural and educational forms, and their respect for (even awe of) technology and, sometimes, forms of organization stemming from Europe and the US: hence, the gadgets and guns with which even some very austere Taliban leaders are said to have surrounded themselves.

While it is common to note that the Hindu RSS based itself on Mussolini's fascist Black Shirts and that Bal Thackeray is a great admirer of Hitler, it should also be noted that Islamic fundamentalist groups share almost as much affinity with European thinking of a certain sort. Their very claim that Islam is not compatible with democracy echoes the worst and most empty-headed of the various rhetorical chants of the right in Europe. So does their tendency to subscribe to the 'clash of civilizations' thesis of shallow and largely ahistorical thinkers in the West. In actual fact, perhaps this theory is a good indicator of a kind of contemporary fundamentalism: while Hindu nationalists might burn Valentine Day cards, Islamic militants might suicide bomb American installations and American rightists might advocate levelling the Middle East under asphalt, all three—Hindu, Islamic and 'Western' rightists—agree on the fact that we are witnessing a clash of civilizations. Their degree of agreement as well as their terms of definition in these matters are surprisingly similar—being rooted in a 'modern' European fascist-rightist tradition—and they only differ in their preferred aim. Or in other words, members of all three rightist/fundamentalist streams agree on the inevitability or necessity of genocide of some sorts—it is just that they have different 'target groups' in mind.

One area where the 'European' influence on Islamic fundamentalism is increasingly visible is the growing anti-Semitism of Islamic ideologues and their followers. This anti-Semitism is new to Islam. While Muslim cultures did have their conflicts with other peoples, Jews were generally safer in Muslim countries than in Europe until the 1930s, or the foundation of Israel. It need not be pointed out that the Christian re-conquest of Spain not only meant the expulsion of the Muslim Moors but also the expulsion of Spanish Jews: we remember the year when Columbus sailed on his discovery of the new world, but we forget that two shiploads of Jews were also forced to leave Spain in the same year from the same port.

Not only was there less persecution of Jews in the Muslim countries, the conflicts that took place had to do with real politick or economic factors: they were not based on the demonization of all Jews as murderers of Jesus/God (the influential Christian concept of Deicide) or as cabbalistic intriguers who performed human sacrifices and esoteric rites in their synagogues, as was often the case in the Middle Ages and even later in Europe. Neither was it based on pseudo-scientific 19th century theories of racism—for instance, pitting Aryans against Semites—as it often was in Europe and America until the fall of Nazism. As such, anti-Semitism of the sort that one hears from religious Muslims today is a recent development. Actually, even Bin Laden started focussing on Jews as the prime scapegoats/culprits quite late in this demagogic career.

That finally is the reason why I hesitate to write about the latest Israeli misadventure in the Middle East. I remain as staunchly opposed to Israeli militarism and lack of compromise, verging on a blatant kind of racism, as anyone else with an objective mind. But, as a Muslim, I cannot turn a blind eye to the fact that the justified and necessary opposition to Israeli militarism has in many Islamic circles become an opposition to Jews and, hence, potentially or actually anti-Semitic. Despite the fact that this is an anti-Semitism borrowed from

European traditions and that Islam in the past had little or nothing like it, and in spite of the curious fact that the Arabs are themselves a Semitic people. Is it a sign of the latent self-hate of colonized and semi-colonized people, as Frantz Fanon might have seen it, this growing anti-Semitism among a Semitic people?

And finally, is this sort of religion-based definition capable of addressing the main issues? For instance, it is easy to see the current Israeli misadventure, with effective US support, as another attack on a Muslim people. But by doing so, one relegates the matter to the kind of ahistoricity that makes it impossible to address more pressing matters. For instance, the current Israeli misadventure is a direct descendent of the National Security Strategy (NSS) announced by the US in September 2002. As Noam Chomsky has noted in *Doctrines and Visions,* the NSS undermined the Westphalian system of international order and the UN charter by enshrining and legalizing the right to aggression in response to a perceived or real threat to a country, or even in anticipation of it. The first part of this strategy was played out immediately with the US-led invasion of Iraq. The second part is being played out with the Israeli aggression in Lebanon. When the NSS had been passed, Henry Kissinger had welcomed it but also noted that the right to aggression cannot be "a universal principle available to every nation."† As Chomsky pointed out some time back, this meant that, in effect, "the right of aggression must be reserved to the United States, perhaps delegated to chosen clients." The Israeli aggression is an example of his delegation. The world order half-envisaged by Bush and his cronies will depend on both USA's right of aggression and its ability to delegate it to some cronies. To condemn

† Quoted by Chomsky in *Doctrines and Visions*

the Israeli aggression in merely 'religious' terms is to miss this larger picture, with consequences leading to further isolation and failure of the opposition to US imperialism.

Islamic fundamentalism very often runs against the inclusive trend in Islam, a trend that was the dominant factor in the richest and most successful phases of Muslim histories. By isolating the suffering of Muslims simply in terms of religion, it leads to paranoia of a very narrow sort—and this paranoia leads to more isolation. This creates a vicious circle of impotency and potential failure, hidden in the verbiage of grandiose gestures (including those of terrorism) and emotional rhetoric.

The way out is to break away from narrowly-defined religious perspectives. One can continue to be a Muslim and do so, because Islam—with its various theories about 'peoples of the book'—was originally an adventurous attempt to formulate a strong identity for disparate peoples, but to do so in non-exclusive terms. Hence, the various lines in the Quran and the stories in the Hadiths about the need for peace and compromise between people, about the necessity to accept other religious faiths as historically 'true' and authentic (the peoples of the book), the careful reworking of almost all the known (Christian and Jewish) prophets and saints into the Islamic tradition, the legal rights given to women (once so progressive), the encouragement to feed the poor (not from charity but as a duty) and to free slaves, the story of the first Muslim call to prayers given by a freed Black slave, etc.

In defining the world in an exclusive, religious way—'Muslims' versus or y or all—Islamic fundamentalists run against this inclusive trend in Islam. This is a pity for Muslims, because history illustrates that it was this inclusive trend that made Islam the religion of leading and progressive societies in the past.

TWENTY

The Smile of Post-modern Fascism

On 11 October 2006, a correspondent of a Danish newspaper went out to interview Muslims in an immigrant-dominated section of Copenhagen. She wanted to get their reactions to film footings of a fancy-dress party at the annual 'summer camp' of the youth wing of the *Danske Folkeparti* (DFP), a major rightist-nationalist party that supports the ruling liberal-conservative coalition from the outside. In this fancy-dress party, young DFP members had dressed up as Mohammad, the prophet of Islam, garnishing their fancy with demeaning connotations. She wrote an article later, headlined "Muslims silent about the DFP-affair."*

The journalists and much of Danish media have read this relative silence (especially in the wake of the recent cartoon controversy, in which Danish Muslims had voiced their objections democratically) along conservative lines—for example, her article implies that these were footings from a 'private' party and as such not offensive to Muslims. But this silence needs to be listened to more carefully than that. This silence is the prelude to post-modern fascism, just as 'marking' the Jews of Germany was a prelude to the worst of modern fascism.

The fancy-dress party itself, and the general trajectory of DFU, is a good example of how post-modern fascism works. Unlike modern fascism—of which certain versions (though not all) of Islamic fundamentalism form a variety—post-modern fascism does not appear to take itself too seriously in some areas. It is eminently playful about

---

* First published in *The Hindu*, India.

its prejudices, the core of the non-ideology that informs all fascism. Hence, the fancy-dress party in which young DFU members dress up as Mohammad in demeaning shapes. It is all a big joke.

Or take, for example, this TV advertisement from the last elections. A well-known rightist politician, whose first name is Christian, is shown as getting down from his car at a gas station. He is accosted by an elderly woman who says, Are you Christian? Yes, he replies. The woman continues: What is this we are hearing? They are letting Turkey into the European Union. Don't worry, assures our Christian, as long as we have a say in the matter, this won't happen.

Does this make you smile? Should it make you smile? Would it make you smile if you lived in Denmark and were not from a Christian background?

Part of the humour in Charlie Chaplin's *The Great Dictator* stemmed from Chaplin's comic parody of the stern seriousness of Hitler and his non-ideology. But such a parody would be ineffective against post-modern fascism. It can only be used against the stale mimicry of modern fascism that one comes across n the third world at times, not least in some anti-democratic Islamist movements or among the more conservative supporters of India's Hindutva brigade. Post-modern fascism—either because it is post-modern or because, unlike Hitler's nazism or Islamic fundamentalism, it is located in politically dominant nations—is capable of laughing, though more at others than at itself. (DFP is not actually renowned in Denmark for its internal democracy!)

But the laughter does not reassure me. Perhaps when the smile finally slips, we will get a glimpse of the skull that lurks underneath. Perhaps that is why Danish Muslims have been silent—not just because they know that you cannot get angry at post-modern fascism, but because they can see the skull underneath.

Part II

TWENTY-ONE

Heathcliff as Terrorist

Apart from prophecies of doom and similar 'religious' texts, the Gothic novel is the genre in English literature that depends most heavily for dramatic tension on both displacement and terror. At the heart of the Gothic text there hides a fundamental ambiguity: nothing is as it appears to be on the surface, the holy is intertwined with the demonic, the space between the Beautiful (also as the 'moral' or the 'rational') and the Sublime (also as the 'amoral' or the 'non-rational') is measured and narrated in screams of terror.*

Holy Terror

This perception starts off in Gothic novels as a narrative of what Terry Eagleton has recently called 'holy terror': "...the word sacer can mean either blessed or cursed, holy or reviled; and there are kinds of terror in ancient civilization which are both creative and destructive, life-giving and death-dealing. The sacred is dangerous, to be kept in a cage rather than a glass case." (Eagleton 2) The book widely considered to be the first Gothic novel in English, Mathew Lewis's *The Monk* (1794), is fully aware of this: it tells the story of an extremely virtuous monk, a holy man seduced into committing acts of terror by the Devil and his own inability to recognize the thin line separating the divine from the demonic. The monk of Lewis's novel is so enamoured of the glittering body of his own erudition, goodness and blessedness that he overlooks

* First published in the *Journal of Postcolonial Writing*, UK.

to recognize its shadow side. This is in keeping with the definition of wickedness and evil that Mary Midgley formulates in an excellent meditation on selves and shadows: "The acknowledged shadow may be terrible enough. But it is the unacknowledged one which is the real killer." (Midgley 126) It also recalls Jung's observation, quoted by Midgley, that "I must have a dark side also if I am to be whole; and inasmuch as I become conscious of my shadow I also remember that I am a human being like any other." (Jung 40)

Lewis's monk is shockingly unaware of his own 'shadow'; so convinced is he of his erudition and goodness that he believes that he is incapable of committing a sin, or doing evil. This is what lets the 'devil' in. Something similar takes place in Robert Louis Stevenson's *The Strange Case of Dr Jekyll and Mr Hyde* (1886), a later Gothic text. Dr Jekyll believes, as Midgley points out, that he can, so to say, separate his shadow from his body, the evil from the good at will. He finds out that he cannot. This play of shadow and body continues all the way through Gothic narratives, until in Bram Stoker's *Dracula* (1897) it has almost been reduced to a generic fetish, so that the interplay of body and shadow evokes horror but does not really convey a clear meaning.

However, to revert to my original observation, *Dracula* again returns us to the 'holy terror' that underlay the earliest Gothic texts, such as Lewis's *The Monk*. This was terror that depended on the ambiguity of the 'sacred', a deceptive plant sprouting from the seed of a word that could mean both 'blessed' and 'cursed'; it depended on the ease with which the divine and the demonic could be interchanged, the knowledge that, after all, Satan was a fallen angel. In this Gothic strain, what had been banished—Satan or the Devil to Hell, Dracula to his coffin, the dead to the other world—returned to evoke terror. It was a bit like Dr Jekyll realizing that, actually, he did not have the power to banish—to separate from—Mr Hyde; Hyde could come back almost at will.

Plastic Surgery on God

True, at a certain philosophical level, this stressed a concept of God that was being forgotten under the utilitarianism and voluntarism of Western capitalism, the narrower kind of enlightenment rationality and the pragmatism of Protestantism. All these different developments were tending to reduce God to a thing of rationality, beauty, order, a being or concept that could be dealt with at a rather business-like level, even if the currency of that transaction was less cash and more ritual. Against this, in a confused, half-conscious manner (a symbolic manner which was in keeping with something happening in the symbolic realms of literature), the early Gothic texts stressed the terror of God. This was not God as Sunday churchgoing, a stylized representation of Jesus, Santa Claus, vague Christian feeling for the suffering of the earth, a coin to a charity, or brotherly love. If God was love, it was terrible love, impossible to be humanly imagined. If God was mercy, it was mercy so unconditional that it could wreak havoc on all the moral and social structures of humanity. Even as the plastic surgeons of capitalist-Protestant thought operated on the God of polite circles in the 19th century and turned Him into a thing of beauty, the God of Gothic literature retained some sublime features, if only in 'demonic' forms distorted into a mirror image of the divine.

This development can be understood with reference to Edmund Burke's distinction between the Beautiful and the Sublime:

> ...[S]ublime objects are vast in their dimensions, beautiful ones comparatively small; beauty should be smooth, and polished; the great [sublime], rugged and negligent;... beauty should not be obscure, the great [sublime] ought to be dark and gloomy...They are indeed ideas of a very different nature, one [sublime] being founded on pain, the other on pleasure... (Adams 306)

As is obvious from the extract above, the Beautiful is humanly encompass-able, perhaps even partly or wholly man-made, for Burke: it is small or tractable, smooth and polished, clear and comprehensible. The Sublime is all that goes beyond such human limits of the Beautiful. The Sublime is that which exceeds the human, that which comes or comes back from 'elsewhere'. In the Gothic texts of the 18th and 19th century, this aspect of God—largely being reduced to the beautiful and the "love-ly" in polite society—comes back to haunt human beings and maim, cripple, kill them, to terrorize them in the negative forms of the demonic: the Devil, vampires, monsters, ghosts, the living dead.

But if terror comes back or comes from 'elsewhere'—thus revealing the terror of the sacred—in many early Gothic texts, by the end of the 19th century its return has started shadowing the trade and military routes of European empires. The Gothic protagonist is not just an orphan of obscure or hidden origins (as in Lewis's *The Monk* and many other early Gothic narratives); he is increasingly from the East or at least the margins of Europe. One can see this happening throughout the 19th (and early 20th) century in texts by Edgar Alan Poe and Rudyard Kipling, in Joseph Conrad's *Heart* of *Darkness* (1899), in novels with Gothic elements, such as Charlotte Brontë's *Jane Eyre* (1847) and in perhaps its richest complexity in Emily Brontë's great novel, *Wuthering Heights* (1847).

Heathcliff as Terrorist

Imagine an intelligent dark-skinned person, slipping into the countryside of a peaceful European country from somewhere disturbingly 'post-colonial', lying dormant for many years and then snaring the families that harboured him in a net of violence, revenge and terror. It might sound like an account of the so-called 'sleeper agents' that organizations like Al Qaeda are said to send into the heart of Europe, but actually it would be one way of describing Heathcliff.

Emily Brontë's *Wuthering Heights* is a novel of terror. In this it is not very different from other Gothic texts or from narratives influenced by the Gothic genre. *Wuthering Heights* is also a novel that brings the Empire into the heart of England, thus interlinking Gothic terror with imperial displacement and power. In this too it is not entirely different from the odd work by Kipling or Conrad. What makes it exceptional, to my mind, is its difficult and complex analysis of the relationship of terror to displacement, dispossession and power, its unrelenting narration of the colonial center as haunted by ghosts from the colonial margins, its examination of the tensions between the Beautiful-as-colonized/civilized and the Sublime-as-always-beyond-colonization/civilization. In this it prefigures some later novels, written by colonized or post-colonial subjects, such as Jean Rhy's *Wide Sargasso Sea* (1966) or Erna Brodber's *Myal* (1988).

Terror creeps into the narrative of *Wuthering Heights* even before the main story begins. Lockwood, the limited but well-meaning narrator of the novel—who would, in turn, be given much of Heathcliff and Catherine's story by the limited but well-meaning nurse, Nelly—has just experienced some of the minor horrors of Heathcliff's household and been forced by a storm to spend the night there, sleeping brokenly over his experiences and the dream-echo of names and accounts read in some mildewed books lying about in the room. Lockwood has a confused nightmare, which ends with the image of the dead Catherine, a waif-ghost, trying to enter his room from a window that has been unlatched by the storm:

> "The intense horror of nightmare came over me; I tried to draw back my arm, but the hand clung to it, and a most melancholy voice sobbed, 'Let me in – let me in!'

> 'Who are you?' I asked, struggling, meanwhile to disengage myself. 'Catherine Linton,' it replied shiveringly (why did I think of Linton? I had read Earnshaw twenty times for Linton.) 'I'm come home. I'd lost my way on the moor!'" (42–3)

Lockwood writes that 'terror made me cruel': he rubs the 'creature's' wrist on the broken glass pane, until blood 'soaked the bedclothes'. But still the 'ghost' maintained its 'tenacious grip', almost 'maddening' Lockwood with fear.

It is a disturbing scene—both terrifying and intensely moving in the thwarted humanity of the 'creature', the dehumanized instrument of terror,—and it is followed by another disturbing scene. Heathcliff, on waking up and being told of this experience by Lockwood, rushes into the room, wrenches open the lattice and pleads to no avail into the howling storm: "Come in! come in!...Cathy, do come. Oh do—*once* more! Oh! My heart's darling! Hear me *this* time—Catherine, at last!" (45)

The terror of this scene is intricately connected with displacement. In an almost banal sense, Lockwood is a traveller, sleeping for a night in the house. In a more immediate sense, Catherine is displaced, banished from her house and love, so to say, an exile for 'twenty years' as the 'ghost' puts it. In an even more key sense, Heathcliff—the current owner of the house—is a displaced person, a person who has usurped the house but only by using the legal and social rules that, in the first place, left him (and Catherine) on the margins. (Significantly, Heathcliff's way out of the margins and into brutal power leaves him displaced in a deeper way—estranged from his love, Catherine, whose 'waif-ghost' fails to enter his house and does not respond to his entreaties. It has to be borne in mind that both Catherine and Heathcliff see each other as their own true selves—and in that sense Heathcliff becomes estranged from his true self.)

It is from here that the narrative leads us back to the 'origins' of Heathcliff. Decades ago, Mr Earnshaw, came back from a trip to Liverpool bearing not only the presents that his children, Catherine and her brother, Hindley, had requested, but also a bundle tucked into his great coat. He handed this bundle to his wife with the comment, "See here, wife; I was never so beaten with anything in my life; but you must e'en take it as a gift of God; though it's as dark almost as if it came from the devil." (51) This bundle was Heathcliff, described by Nurse Nelly as "a dirty, ragged, black-haired child; big enough both to walk and talk… yet, when it was set on its feet, it only stared round, and repeated over and over again some gibberish that nobody could understand." (51)

Faced with this mini-alien in their midst, Nurse Nelly is 'frightened', which is in keeping with her well-meaning but limited—domesticated and normal, if one may say so—character. So intense is the 'otherness' of Heathcliff, often described as looking like a 'gypsy', a 'moor' or being a 'lascar's child' by people like Nelly in the novel, that no effort is made to decipher his gibberish. His otherness is not only illegible, but it is considered to be incapable of any other meaning, of being simply 'gibberish '. The only sentiment that he evokes in Nelly at that moment is the feeling of fear.

It is not incidental that Mr Earnshaw had returned from Liverpool. As Susan Meyer points out, "...in 1769, the year in which Mr Earnshaw found Heathcliff in the Liverpool streets, the city was England's largest slave-trading port, conducting seventy to eighty-five per cent of the English slave trade along the Liverpool Triangle…"(481). Liverpool was also, like almost all major ports in European imperial states, a place that contained various non-European peoples, including Black sailors and lascars (Indian sailors whose numbers rose steadily in the

18th and 19th centuries partly due to the fact that they were paid only one-sixth of the European rates of pay).

Throughout, the novel highlights Heathcliff's 'otherness' and suggests—without ever making it explicit—how his difference is negotiated by 'normal' people. On the one hand, we have Hindley, who hates Heathcliff in a deeply visceral manner, a class hatred permeated with elements of what Anthony Kwame Appiah has termed 'intrinsic racism'. Then there is the more common kind of fear that people like Nelly display: this is fear that situates Heathcliff's physical difference on a moral plane, thus divesting him of all positive attributes. For instance, Nelly fails, right from the start, to see anything good in Heathcliff: if he complains less than other children, it is just because he is 'hardened'. Being a decent, kind woman, there are moments when she softens, but then faced with something in Heathcliff that she cannot comprehend, she lapses into seeing him as diabolical and devilish. This is something she does even when she discovers Heathcliff lying dead, a strange expression of 'exultation' on his face; this largely positive word 'exultation' soon disappears in the usual terminology employed by Nelly to explain Heathcliff: 'frightful', 'sneer', animal or vampire-like ('sharp, white teeth'). etc. (285–6).

Finally, there are people like Isabella who move from a fascinated dislike of Heathcliff's otherness to a romantic idealization of his difference. That in Heathcliff which indicates all that is other, not-fully-colonized and not-domesticated in his nature, and in human nature in general (of which he is one example), is reconstructed into something else by Isabella, something more 'normal', such as a dark Romantic hero: much to Heathcliff's irritation (though he takes full advantage of it), Catherine's chagrin and Isabella's own subsequent suffering. One way to understand Isabella's error would be to return to the concept of the Sublime as something vast, non-rational, non-human, something always exceeding the 'now' and the 'here': Isabella's romanticization of Heathcliff is similar to an attempt to force the Sublime into the narrower and more decorous garments of the Beautiful.

One can argue that this intruding foreigner in the cosy Earnshaw household is basically liked only by Catherine and her father, Mr Earnshaw, in the novel—and later by the faithful Hareton. Mr Earnshaw dies soon after bringing Heathcliff to his home and, as such, it is not feasible to discuss his reaction to Heathcliff, except to point out that he recognizes Heathcliff's difference but does not see it in primarily negative terms. Catherine and, much later, Hareton do something similar.

Of course, as some critics have already noted, Catherine is the member of the family who comes closest to being an outcast. Her rights as daughter and wife are limited: for instance, she cannot and does not inherit property. In this, she comes closest to Heathcliff: a 'member' of the family, but without the privileges afforded to other members of the family. Hareton, it can be argued, comes to share a similar marginalized position due to the later mechanisations of Heathcliff. The acceptance that Heathcliff meets with from Catherine and Hareton does not suggest some sort of socialist solidarity of the oppressed, but it does indicate that perhaps one needs to stand somewhere on the margins of power before one can begin to see the working of power as determinate, lop-sided and oppressive (as well as constructive).

Heathcliff learns this in different ways, from the maltreatment and prejudices he faces after Mr Earnshaw's death, as well as seemingly innocuous incidents like his capture by the Lintons.

It is worth looking at this scene. Heathcliff and Catherine, both wild children, orphaned by Mr Earnshaw's death, have been spying on their refined (and richer) neighbours, the Lintons, and they are taken for accomplices of burglars, set upon by guard dogs and caught by servants. Now they are being examined, like any colonial museum specimen, under the light, and finally Cathy is recognized:

> "'That's Miss Earnshaw! He whispered to his mother, 'and look how Skulker has bitten her—how her foot bleeds!'
>
> 'Miss Earnshaw? Nonsense!' Cried the dame. 'Miss Earnshaw scouring the country with a gypsy! And yet, my dear, the child is in mourning—surely it is—and she may be lamed for life!'
>
> 'What culpable carelessness in her brother!' exclaimed Mr Linton, turning from me to Catherine. 'I've understood from Shielders' (that was the curate, sir) 'that he lets her grow up in absolute heathenism. But who is this? Where did she pick up this companion? Oho! I declare he is that strange acquisition my late neighbour made in his journey to Liverpool—a little Lascar, or an American or Spanish castaway.'
>
> 'A wicked boy, at all events,' remarked the old lady, 'and quite unfit for a decent house! Did you notice his language, Linton? I'm shocked that my children should have heard it.'I recommended cursing—don't be angry, Nelly—and so Robert was ordered to take me off…'" (62)

This is an extract that reveals more than it seems to. It places Heathcliff (and, initially, Cathy, who being a daughter does occupy a position closer to the margins) under scrutiny, as if he were a museum specimen. In its one-sided, objectifying slant, this scrutiny replicates the colonial gaze. As Susan Meyer also points out, this scrutiny reduces Heathcliff to his otherness and explicitly deprives him of any real language, so that Heathcliff joins that position of the colonized other which has been best expressed by Caliban, the monster in Shakespeare's *The Tempest.* When Prospero accuses Caliban of being ungrateful in spite of the fact that he, Prospero, the civilized nobleman, has taught him his own language, this is what Caliban says:

> "You taught me language; and my profit on't
> Is, I know how to curse. The red plague rid you,
> For learning me your language!"
>
> (Act I, Sc. II)

Heathcliff, like Caliban, has learnt a 'language', but is finally reduced to cursing. Mimicry has its limits. So does language, when not under-girded by other structures of power. And both can be wielded like weapons. Heathcliff is learning his lessons of terror. He is soon to disappear—like all those terrorists in real life, whose CIA or FBI-documented histories present a gap, six months or a year, when the terrorist is supposed to have been receiving training in Afghanistan, except that there is also some evidence of him being issued some official card in the USA during the same period. What Heathcliff does in that period remains shrouded in mystery and conjecture to the same extent as the activities of these real terrorists.

But when he returns, Heathcliff has achieved much dexterity in the instruments of power; for the rest of his life, apart from the last few days of ecstatic self-absorption, he will turn these instruments into devices of terror. They are the same instruments—language, manipulation, legal deeds, marriage connections, money—with which his marginalization had been enforced in the past. Now he uses them not only to terrorize his enemies and the bystanders (which means anyone who stands in his way), but also to end up becoming the richest gentleman in the neighbourhood—the owner of both Wuthering Heights and the grander estate of the Lintons.

The instruments are the same that once empowered the Earnshaws and the Lintons, except that they are experienced—and not only by Nelly—as instruments of terror in the hands of Heathcliff. Does this literary terrorist then differ so much from real terrorists who turn the instruments of power manufactured, marketed and used by the West—guns, bombs, the desire for bio-weapons and atomic power, to name only a few—against the West and the innocent bystander?

Terrors of Elsewhere

The Gothic narrative had a point. Wonders take place 'elsewhere'; terror comes from 'elsewhere'. But terror, contrary to what some might claim 'here', is not born 'elsewhere'. Terror takes place when that which has been disowned, exorcised, banished, exiled, prevented entry, nevertheless crashes the barriers. The Devil tempts the most virtuous monk alive, Frankenstein's repudiated monster returns to stalk his creator, Count Dracula rises from his coffin, ghosts walk into the lives of the living, the gypsy-lascar-slave whose labour has contributed to the affluence of the Lintons and the Earnshaws arrives in Wuthering Heights—and is not allowed to be anything other than 'evil'. Deprived of love, acceptance, language, voice, turned into a 'hardened' child even in his forbearance, the very devil in his difference, a museum specimen or a thief, what can Heathcliff be left with except the fetishization of power—which coming from him who came from 'elsewhere' and hence coming from 'elsewhere'—can only evoke screams of terror from those who take their own empowerment for granted.

It is one of the strengths of *Wuthering Heights* that Heathcliff's terror, coming from 'elsewhere', is situated in the context of the sublime in the 'English' moors. The displaced may well become instruments of terror, like Catherine's 'ghost' when it tries to get back into her home and Lockwood's room or Heathcliff after he returns to exact revenge. But this terror does not lie in their nature; it does not even lie in sheer displacement. It does not simply come from 'elsewhere'. It also lies in the local: the sublime moors and mountains in *Wuthering Heights* are an indication of all that cannot be simply tamed, domesticated and beautified even in neighbourly nature.

Terror arises, to rephrase Mary Midgley, from our inability or refusal to see the shadows that we always cast. It arises from our refusal to recognize all that can exceed our beautified (beatified) and domesticated limits of the human, the natural or the divine. The Devil, in that sense, is the shadow of God; 'elsewhere' a shadow of 'home'. If the displaced become instruments of terror, it is as much because we, who have decided to stay home or who have the privileged option of making the entire globe our home, have for too long averted our eyes from those who are 'elsewhere' or who come from 'elsewhere'.

In a globalizing world, to choose to stay home—to stay 'local' (or even 'glocal')—and to be able to make the globe your home are very different acts—but, what tends to be forgotten, is that both are acts of the empowered. What happens to those who *cannot* stay 'local', those who are *forced* to stay 'local' or those to whom the 'global' is synonymous with displacement *and* loss? These three are very different kinds of predicaments, but their agents are united by a certain degree of disempowerment. The Moroccan who has to risk being drowned in the sea to get to the privileges of Europe because he would never be allowed to immigrate legally, the Indian villager who can achieve affluence only by emigrating and the mullah, priest or local politician who sees his traditions under assault by the 'global' (or the 'Western' or whatever): all these occupy spaces that are 'elsewhere'. But this is an 'elsewhere' that also lies at the very heart of the 'home' of those who are at home 'here' or 'everywhere'.

TWENTY-TWO

The Death of the Reader

I

Zadie Smith's *White Teeth* is a novel that a young writer can only admire, a double-decker of a narrative powered by real talent. It is also a novel that appears to make careful use of 'history'. And yet, if one reads it from outside the celebratory space of multicultural Britain, one notices intriguing gaps and silences. The one that I still remember relates to Samad Miah Iqbal who claims to be and is portrayed by the text as the great-grandson of Mangal Pande, the Indian sepoy who fired the first shot of the 1857 revolt. Samad is a firebrand—if not fundamentalist—Muslim much of the time and the sceptical reader in me could not reconcile this fact with the name of his historically authentic great-grandfather. For Mangal Pande is not just a Hindu name, it is a twice-born, pure-as-snow Brahmin one. It is difficult to imagine the descendants of the Mangal Pandes of India converting to Islam, let alone a firebrand version of it, and that too after the snuffing of the last symbols of Muslim glory in 1857.*

Of course this is not life; this is a novel. But because this is a novel, there ought to have been a spectacular story around this spectacular conversion.

A similar problem confronts the sceptical reader in another celebrated novel, Yann Martel's *Life of Pi*, which—in spite of its solid

---

* First published in *Wasafiri*, UK.

adherence to certain textual and mainstream definitions of religions (particularly 'Hinduism')—is rather shaky in the field of names. Take, for instance, this extract: "He was a Sufi, a Muslim mystic…His name was Satish Kumar. These are common names in Tamil Nadu…" It could be that, in the years I have been away from India, Tamil Nadu (in South India) has been invaded and colonized by people from North India so that North and West Indian names like Satish Kumar have become common there. I am willing to allow for that possibility. But I still find it difficult to imagine a pious Muslim, even a Sufi, with a Hindu name—for Satish and Kumar are both Hindu names.

One wonders what such omissions signify? Of course, one can choose not to notice them. One can also answer, as Salman Rushdie did when some historical errors were noted in his excellent *Midnight's Children*, that we are talking of an art form and an unreliable narrator. In Rushdie's case, the errors—intentional or not—did consolidate the general discourse of the novel. It was, after all, a novel about history versus 'his' stories. I am not sure the same can be said of Smith's or Martel's novel, and a host of other, less celebrated or less accomplished novels. One can of course 'explain away' these 'errors', but only by detracting considerably from the art of the novelist.

But this bothers me not because of what it says about the novelist, but because of what it does to the reader. It marks the death of the reader. The reader, not as a blank receptor of the intentions of the author or the text, but as someone who actually reads. The reader as the critic. Here the etymology of the word 'read' has to be kept in mind: to read is to "think, suppose, guess; discern the meaning of (chiefly in *read a riddle, a dream*); inspect and interpret…" Related, as the word is, to the Sanskrit *rādh* and the Old Slavonic *raditi*, it also includes the active sense of 'accomplish' and 'attend to' respectively.

Moreover, one of the original senses of the Germanic root is that of 'taking charge' and the act of interpreting written symbols is suggested by its Old English root.

All of this reminds me of the way in which, for example, Seamus Heaney sees the act of writing. In one of his early poems, "Digging", he depicts his father digging outside while he, the poet and scholar, sits at a table, writing. The poem notes the separate nature of the two acts, but also suggests that writing is a sort of digging: "Between my finger and my thumb/ The squat pen rests./ I'll dig with it." Reading is also an act of digging. A reader is not only someone who stays on the surface of the text, but an active thinker and interpreter. She attends to the text, but she also accomplishes and takes charge.

Is it then that we have moved from the death of the author to the death of the reader?

In 1968, Roland Barthes published the definitive obituary of the author. Writing begins, he noted, when the author enters his death. It is language that speaks, not the author, he claimed, which was not incorrect if rather hyperbolic. In proclaiming the death of the author, Barthes also proclaimed the death of the critic and celebrated the birth of the reader. The reader, he claimed, is "the space on which all the quotations that make up a writing are inscribed." The reader, he added, is without history, biography, psychology; she is simply that space in which the traces by which the written text is constituted come together.

It might be churlish to proclaim the death of the reader in the wake of Barthes's and other theorists' announcement of the return to life of the reader. But there is some indication that a chunk of contemporary fiction seeks to cast the reader in a rather passive and celebratory role. And it appears that it is often this kind of writing—suave, polished, talented at times—that is celebrated in many well-meaning circles.

I have avoided the obvious colonial allusion. I have not suggested that as the times get more and more neo-colonial, it is perhaps inevitable that some colonial tendencies return to novel writing. After all, there was a long tradition in the 19th century of British writers writing about India with scant regard to specific matters, to local identities, to nomenclature. I wish to avoid this line of argument, for it appears to lead to a statement rather than an analysis. And I concede that nomenclature is always a problem. More so, when one writes of other times or classes or cultures. What one expects in these cases—that is, if one wants to stay alive as a reader—what one expects is the presence of 'textual traces' that enable the reader to fill the gaps, smoothen the rough patches, justify the 'errors', 'authenticize' the fiction.

No, I am not talking of veracity. Take for example one other recent example: Philip Hensher's *The Mulberry Empire*. Hensher is by no means an Afghan and he has not, to the best of my knowledge, ever lived in the 19th century. But his novel narrates events that take place (largely) in Afghanistan around 1839. It features a number of Afghan characters, some based on historical personages and some blatantly fictional. Hensher was obviously faced with the problem of finding appropriate names for these characters. He appears to have solved it by taking recourse to a narrative device that highlights the artificial aspect of the novel and also fictionally authenticates its narrative. He introduces a short initial chapter—framed like a fairytale or a fable—that presents the (historical) Afghan king on his deathbed. He is surrounded by his 50 plus children, and Hensher lists their names. Then, as he moves on to the rest of the narratives, these are the historical names that he chooses for his fictional characters.

I believe that a device like this opens up a space for the reader to 'interpret', 'accomplish' and be active. This is obviously not the only option. Writers as talented as Smith or Martel can surely think up many others. But if this space is foreclosed—not just in the text, which leaves unexplained and uncontextualised gaps, but also in criticism, which refuses to note these gaps—if this space of active reading is foreclosed, then all one can have is a kind of celebratory echoing of dominant whims. The author might or might not be dead, but the reader is surely expected not to think much for herself—not to 'read' in other words.

Another celebrated and talented novel comes to mind: Monica Ali's *Brick Lane*. And with that the need to apologize to those passengers in Kastrup, the shiny international airport of Copenhagen, who might have been frightened away from boarding their planes some months ago by the sight of a terrorist-type Muslim-suspect laughing like a hyena.

I had just finished reading *Brick Lane* while waiting for the airport authorities to let me know whether I could board a plane to Heathrow in order to catch a connecting flight from there. In the past this would not have been a problem. But, unknown to me, the rules had been changed in London a few days back and now some passport holders were required to have a valid visa even to catch a connecting flight from the same airport in England. While I waited, I read the last pages of *Brick Lane*, where the main protagonist approaches a skating rink wearing a sari. But you cannot skate wearing a sari, her friend says. "This is England," the protagonist replies, "You can do whatever you like."

Perhaps. Perhaps.

I know that I laughed hysterically for about three minutes when I was informed that, in spite of many visits to England, in spite of a letter of invitation and valid tickets to my destination, I would not be allowed to board my plane. I wished I could be a protagonist in Ali's novel. My history, regardless of Barthes, did not set me free either as a reader or a person. I was bound to notice names, for my name is always noticeable. I was liable to be kept from boarding the double-decker of even multicultural Britain. I could not do what I liked. I could not even do what I had paid for.

Even though I have eschewed the easy neo/colonial explanation, I cannot help wondering whether a line does not run from Ali's un-ironic ending, Smith's and Martel's misplaced names and similar slippages in recent fiction to Barthes's and other theorists' critical midwifery at the birth of the Reader-without-History. While this is somewhat unfair to Barthes, one can only imagine the Reader-without-History as a non-reader, as a passive receptor, as a simple celebrator of the text, not as someone who interprets, guesses, digs. It is at best a reader—to the extent that she is brought into being—who wants to escape from history. It is a reader who wants to feel good about being who or what she is, and a knowledge of history—even one's own history—does not always cause one to feel good. The construction of this wilfully ahistorical reader might explain not only the upbeat ending of Ali's novel but also the slippages in Smith's and Martel's novels.

Such slippages are undergirded by the myth of multiculturalism in different ways: the sari and skating rink in Ali, London hybridity in Smith and a religio-aesthetic plurality in Martel, whose text chooses between two narratives on the basis of 'beauty' and contains lines like these: "...Hindus, in their capacity for love, are indeed hairless Christians, just as Muslims, in the way they see God in everything, are bearded Hindus, and Christians, in their devotion to God, are hat-wearing Muslims." Even as Martel's narrator essentializes the religions, he also reaches into the core—the essence—of 'all religions' to assure us of the basic goodness of being. Even the brutality of the 'natural world'—essentialized in many ways too—does not detract from the anodyne nature of the narrative. Moreover, the very structure of the fable in Martel's novel conforms to a common prejudice of the multiculturalist: Pi moves from a tranquil though limited 'traditional' (ordered) space through a journey of much conflict and upheaval to the safe domain of a more complete and fulfilling Western multiculturalism.

There is little doubt that these novels lead to a certain feel good experience, which is carefully calibrated against the horrors of existence outside the scope of the first world reader's immediate experience, and this experience appeals to readers on both sides of the political center. There are various reasons for this. While it connects to the general tendency to 'spiritualize' and 'symbolize' in the center and liberal right, it also appeals to leftist readers who are aware of the harms of 'do-goodism' (the civilizing impulse) in the colonial era. Not having the courage—or the desire—to do good, they have settled for the alternative of feeling good. Hence, novels clad as history and philosophy and a general distaste for history or philosophy in such circles. Hence, the 'multiculturalism' of spaces where everyone buys the same things posited against the 'uniculturalism' of some bombarded village in Afghanistan, which is actually ripped apart to reveal Islamic terrorists from a dozen different nations speaking 10 different languages. This 'multiculturalism' encourages a celebratory mode inducing one to forget that there is a world of difference between, say, the active and combative multiculturality of slaves and labourers that gave us the wonderful mosaic of the Caribbean and the passive and consumptive multiculturalism of a corporation dinner with dishes from 10 different national cuisines.

Finally, in their celebration of a specific philosophy of existence (cosmopolitan West-facing multiculturalism), their defence of 'beauty' as a criterion of selection, their scorning of matters of 'mere believability', as Pi Patel puts it in Martel's novel, and their carelessness towards matters of fictional authenticity, such novels reduce the reader to the role of a non-reader, to the role, at best, of a reader of pulp. This fact may be camouflaged by the brilliance of the language or narration of Martel or Smith or even Ali, but it is something that we, readers, need to cotton on to if we want to keep on reading. Otherwise, we might as well watch more TV.

II

I sit at home watching more TV.

I surf the channels. The usual suspects. Ads, soaps, films, news. In what ways does this act of reception differ from the reading that I do?

There are various answers to this, but for me the difference that matters relates to time and space. When I read, I can control my relationship to the time and space of the narrative. I can make it stretch out. I can turn the pages or delve into a single word. This is not really possible with TV, not even if you tape the programme and play it in slow motion. The time and space of the TV images are always dominant. You follow them; they do not heed you. Even if you stop a TV image and read it, you have at best a two-dimensional world. You either accept the image or you reject it.

Take, for example, the image of that huge and ugly statue of Saddam Hussein being pulled down by people at the proclaimed end of the latest Iraq war. I have it on tape. The voice of the commentators keep describing it as an epochal event, involving thousands of Iraqis, a spontaneous demonstration of the repressed anger of a people finally freed by the US-led forces. I freeze the image. The voice disappears. What remains on the screen is at best a handful of people—a couple of hundred perhaps—a completely insignificant crowd in a place like Iraq. There are huge gaps between the demonstrators; most of the background is shorn of people, except for a few casual on-lookers. If one notices these gaps, one can read the TV image in a different way. One can see the other side of the story, so to say, the 'other dimension': but one cannot go beyond that.

Some acclaimed fiction of recent years displays similar gaps. Take for instance, another talented first novel, Khaled Hosseini's *The Kite Runner*. There is a lot to be admired about this novel too, even though the narrator's Afghanistan is—as the text acknowledges—a particular kind of Afghanistan. It is the Afghanistan of people who watch Hollywood films, not of ordinary Afghans I met in my childhood, who used to watch 'Bollywood' films. But that is not the gap I have mentioned; one has to narrate from a particular point of perception, and the perspective of Hollywood-Afghanistan is just as valid (though less widespread) as the perspective of Bollywood-Afghanistan.

The gap I have in mind is much subtler. The narrative of *The Kite Runner* takes us to the end of the Zahir Shah period and the edges of the Soviet invasion of Afghanistan. Then it does something strange. Except for an occasional remark or two, it skips the entire period of the Mujahideen and the US-inspired 'Alliance', returning to Afghanistan only once the Talibans are in place.

Perhaps this gap was called for by the narrative, though I am not convinced about that. What strikes me as significant—regardless of whether the gap was demanded by the narrative or not—is that this gap makes the novel much more palatable to a Western, particularly an American, readership. That is because the West—and in particular Bush-USA, which hailed the Mujahideen as the equivalent of the founding fathers of America—had its hands deep in the gore and mud of what is Afghanistan in exactly that period. The Taliban grew out of branches of the Mujahideen. For instance, much of what the Taliban did to Afghanistani women had been propounded—and at times implemented—by the Mujahideen too. The Taliban were just better at it, partly because they were more unified and organized—given the informal structure of Islamic schools (madrasas) behind them—than the Alliance leaders, and partly because ordinary Afghans were tired enough of factionalism and lawlessness to accept any kind of order. (After all, as a not-religious Afghan refugee had explained to me when the Talibans were going strong, it is difficult to fight for human and political rights if the choice is between rape and total purdah, murder and thought control. Many people, he had added, especially vulnerable groups (such as women), might prefer total purdah to rape, dictatorial control to the constant threat of assault, robbery and murder.)

So once again, if you notice this gap in the narrative you begin to understand why *The Kite Runner* appeals to a certain kind of reader: it evokes sympathy without guilt, it retells 'history' as we would like to remember it in the West. This does not make it a bad novel, but it makes it a certain kind of novel.

To notice this gap is similar to noticing the gaps behind the commentary about those 'hundreds of people' assaulting and dismantling Saddam's statue. There is no doubt in my mind that the statue deserved to be dismantled, as did Saddam's regime (though from within the land), but I cannot turn my sight away from the gaps in that narrative. Just as I cannot turn my eyes away from the narrative gap in *The Kite Runner*.

But, as I remarked earlier, noticing the gap does not do anything other than reveal the other side of the coin. It keeps the equation more or less steady, based at best on a binary perception. That is so because TV—and novels that have assumed the breeziness of television—never allow you the independent space and time, your time, in which you can delve into the gaps and excavate a more complex narrative. At best, they hint at those narratives, and then they move you on.

Serious literature does more than that. Serious literature has always done more than that. Even when it is not conscious of its own intentions, it expects you to roll up your sleeves and get your hands muddy with meanings—meanings which are ambiguous and complex and contrary at times. I will try to illustrate this with reference to two very different novels from two very different 'colonial' writers: Rudyard Kipling and EM Forster.

III

A phantom rickshaw appears every ten years or so in the English-reading world. It haunts various literary journals and magazines for a few months and then disappears, only to materialize again after a decade or two, pulled by a different literary coolie this time. The man sitting in this spectral rickshaw is always Rudyard Kipling, though you would hardly think so at times because this is a ghost that appears, often alternately, in two very different forms.

In the usual course of events, Kipling is dragged out on his spectral rickshaw—pedalled furiously by a writer or critic (increasingly a native) and dressed up either as the White Man's Burden or as the Great Universal Writer. As the White Man's Burden, he is everything that we should never be: not only a patriarchal colonialist but also a racist. As the Great Universal Writer, he is everything we can never be: not only a genius able to understand and narrate all men, women and animals but also pure as well-driven snow. Usually, if Kipling is raised from the dead as the former this decade, he is liable to stalk the land as the latter in the next.

Recently, however, thanks to the *London Review of Books*, we have snapshots of Kipling's ghost in both its guises. If Amit Chaudhuri's review of Harry Ricketts' biography (*A feather! A very feather upon the face!*, *LRB*, 6 January 2000) contained elements of Kipling as the White Man's Burden, David Gilmour's rejoinder (Letters, *LRB*, 20 January 2000) presented a vision of Kipling, the Great Universal Writer.

Kipling's ghost is up and about again and the controversy rages: is it a beast or is it a superman?

Gilmour takes exception to Chaudhuri's statement that Kipling was 'a spokesman for a particularly unpleasant racial theory'. He concludes that '(d)uring two years' research into Kipling's ideas on race, politics and empire, I have found no evidence that he formulated any such theory or that he was the spokesman for anyone else's'.

Chaudhuri, on the other hand, has not been as harsh on Kipling as Gilmour's reaction might suggest. While (convincingly) accusing Kipling of at least implicit racism, Chaudhuri has called him a 'very great writer', considered his works complex and subtle and even stated that Kipling 'indirectly acknowledges the existence of a colonial India of intellectual collaboration between cultures'. Chaudhuri associates this India with the pre-mutiny, East India Company phase. He notes that the *Gadar* of 1857 "brought to an end a period of cultural exchanges between different races." He states that attitudes hardened on both sides after the 'mutiny' of 1857.

Chaudhuri is correct to a large extent. It is true that the first few decades of the Company's ascendancy in India took place largely under

Indian cultural colours. Company officials and associated adventurers adopted Indian (mostly Persianised) customs and married Indian women, as depicted, among others, in William Dalrymple's *White Mughals*. However, to mark 1857 as the cut-off point is a little inaccurate, because attitudes appear to have started hardening as early as the turn of the century, and, on the other hand, as AN Wilson notes in *The Victorians*, much individual sympathy survived the mutual mass brutalities of 1857–58. One can argue, with justification, that the mutiny of 1857 was itself a result of these hardening attitudes. Moreover, while 1857 did leave behind legends of barbarity on both sides, it also marked a progressive political shift in England: India was ostensibly brought under the crown because politicians in England could no longer afford to ignore the rapacity of the East India Company and its officials.

These reminders point out the limitations of the kind of statements that both Chaudhuri and Gilmour make about Kipling, though again it must be added that Chaudhuri seems more aware of these limitations than Gilmour. It is not just that Kipling, his contemporaries and his times were far more complex than such statements acknowledge. It is more that Kipling's writing—the very gaps and ambivalences of the narrative of *Kim*—force the reader to dig for more, and this digging for more sometimes takes place from a position outside the text. One can dig into fiction from the space of facts, one can dig into the novel from the space of history, and so on and so forth, without necessarily stepping outside the language of the narrative or the novel. Which is why (like gaps and ambivalences) errors, even such 'simple' ones as those of nomenclature, have to be noted.

I wish to clarify the above claim with reference to another writer, a writer whose ghost is often interlinked with Kipling's: EM Forster. The White Man's Burden versus Great Universal Writer debate also, at times, ends up in a simplistic contrast between Forster and Kipling. Though there are exceptions to this, and currently Forster seems to be out of favour, generally speaking, Kipling is contrasted unfavourably with Forster. While both are acknowledged as important writers, Forster is considered more liberal and humane than Kipling.

Such a dichotomy illustrates the failure of critics and commentators to address Kipling and Forster with instruments appropriate to them. For the matter is much more complex.

Let us start with Forster. *A Passage to India*, that great novel, is often held up as a better example of the English writer connecting to India than Kipling's work. After all, Forster is deeply critical of colonial structures of power and sympathetic to Indian customs and political aspirations in the novel. On the other hand, Kipling, we know, not only wrote about the absolute incompatibility of the East with the West and celebrated the white man's civilizing mission among peoples who were 'half devil, half child', his great novel, *Kim*, is full of stock native stereotypes. These stereotypes range from the noble savage (the 'pure' native, usually from the effective fringes of the Raj) to the effeminate, weak, untrustworthy Babu (the culturally-hybridized, English-knowing, urban native). Even Hurree Babu, firmly on Kim's side, comes across as a ludicrous figure for much of the novel.

There obviously is some truth in the above statements. It is true, for example, that even in *Kim*, there are various narrative and dialogic statements about the babu—who is seen as untrustworthy, obese (not sporty like the colonial sahib), slimy, comical, effeminate. On the other side, Forster's narrative and dialogues in *A Passage to India* make frequent attempts to connect, to present native viewpoints and to criticize colonial prejudices. The language of Kipling in *Kim* is undoubtedly colonialist while that of Forster in *A Passage to India* makes careful—often successful—attempts to escape the clutches of colonialist discourses.

But to leave the matter here would be to tell only half the story. For what happens in both the books does not happen only in language, though it can come into existence only in the gaps created by language. Contrary to post-structuralist assumptions, something seems to exist outside language, and that something affects the two narratives very differently when it breaks into language. In *A Passage to India*, for instance, we have two significant scenes which expose the material limits of Forster's humanist-liberal language of 'only connect': the cave scene and the ending. The cave scene is one of unresolved doubt or aporia: it is unavoidable because of Forster's language itself. Forster has avoided colonialist explanations of the cave scene: Aziz is not an untrustworthy, unpredictable native who does what natives do in colonialist narratives—rapes a white woman. No, Forster will not have such an explanation. But what explanation can he provide? If in broad daylight, decent Aziz cannot be the sort of 'typically unpredictable' native (though, of course comfortably predictable in his unpredictability) who turns rapist in the darkness of caves, why then, the land itself has to be made unpredictable. If Aziz is rational, then the ground and rocks have to be irrational. How else can you understand and narrate the obvious differences that exist between the native and the colonialist? If the difference is not in them, it has to be around them. The ending of the novel then, to Forster's credit, acknowledges this contradiction: Aziz and Fielding want to ride together, but the land itself forces them apart. Not here, it says, not now.

If that is what happens to Forster's language of equality and humanist universality in the colonial landscape, let us see what happens to Kipling's language of British superiority, the white man's civilizing mission and the Englishman's natural right to rule. Two things, actually. Firstly, Kim, no doubt, is superior to native boys because he is white. He is introduced tossing puny native boys off a great cannon in a game that is a prelude to the 'great game' (spying) that he goes on to play in the novel. He is born to rule. But later we realize that he is also different from other white boys because he can pass for native. So, already, the white man's natural superiority is rendered far more complex than in colonialist discourses: Kipling (or, what is the same in this case, his narrator) still believes in it, but the material presence of the colonized world interferes to demand a very different type of superior white man. Actually, a white boy who can pass for brown.

But more is to come. Hurree Babu—who is that detested thing in the novel, a hybridized urban Indian—comes in for his share of scorn from both Englishmen (including Kim) and 'noble savages' like Mahbub Ali. He conforms to the stereotypical Babu of colonialist discourses, the babu who was compared unfavourably to both the 'masculine' Englishman and the 'pure native' like the frontier Afghan and the mountain Gurkha. He is obese, potentially untrustworthy, comical and lethargic etc. But what does this Hurree Babu do towards the end of the novel—he not only saves Kim and his companions by a heroic (physical) and clever (intellectual) effort, he single-handedly saves the entire British empire in India from the devious machinations of enemy agents! The body of the babu has interfered with the colonialist discourse on the babu in Kipling's narrative, though only within the colonialist limits of the 'necessity' of British rule.

Perhaps the matter we have been addressing till now can be finally clarified if we focus on what Kim says when he learns of Hurree Babu's heroism. He exclaims, rejoicing, 'What a beast of wonder is a babu!'

What a *beast* of *wonder*: an exclamation that places Kipling better than his ghostly native or British literary coolies seem to. For, of course, Kipling is a colonialist: for him the native is 'half devil, half child'. He is a man of his times (who isn't?) and he speaks the language of his fellow contemporaries. But he is also an exceptional writer with first-hand experience of the natives. To stretch Kim's exclamation a bit, given the discourses that enable his speech, Kipling can only *call* Hurree Babu a beast, but he also *knows* that Hurree Babu can be an exceptional human (a wonder).

While Forster starts with the liberal-humanist language of universality and is forced to account for the *material reality of differences and inequality*, Kipling starts with the colonialist language of differences and naturalized inequality but is forced to address the *material reality of human universality*. Finally, of course, Kipling is a colonialist—he mostly *believes* that the twain can never meet—but he is also a man who has *seen* the twain meet at times. Forster is *not* a colonialist—he *believes* that the 'twain' can and should meet. But he has also *seen* how difficult it is for them to meet in the material world of bridge parties, horse rides and dark caves.

Moreover, even as a colonialist, Kipling is not only under the influence of one set of discourses. While the discourse of colonialist difference makes him claim that the East cannot meet the West, his own experiences and the discourses of male heroism and adventure make him concede, in the same poem, that East and West are empty words when two *strong men* meet.

In other words, it might be more fruitful to see both Kipling and Forster against their *discursive* and *historical* backdrops and read their literature as not just language but also as an expression of the material reality beyond language. If so, 'history' cannot be irrelevant to 'literature' after all; facts needs not be abandoned in order to enjoy fiction. Serious literature, perhaps, provides one of those rare spaces in which the invisible relations between language and reality, between the symbolic and the material, are condensed into the tension of art. And serious literature allows the reader to dig into that space, to excavate it to her own depth and at her own pace. That might be the reason why serious literature makes bad television.

TWENTY-THREE

Foreign Ghosts in Denmark: All White History

Apart from anticipation of near-zero temperatures, I knew exactly four things about Denmark when I arrived in Copenhagen. The first of them was cheese. This is a common prejudice of middle class Indians: they are convinced—probably due to some glitch in their semi-colonial education—that Denmark is "the land of milk and cheese." Well, sometimes also butter.*

The second was HC Andersen; the third, Hamlet.

And the fourth was, shall we say, the correct premonition that I would find an Indian or a Pakistani taxi driver outside Kastrup Airport in Copenhagen.

But actually I knew more about Denmark than I had realized—Karen Blixen and Søren Kirkegaard, for example, both of whom I thought of as vaguely 'Scandinavian', and Rasmus Rask whom, given the $18^{th}/19^{th}$ century Germanic investment in the exegesis of Indo-European languages, I had always considered German. With time and with experience I discovered these strangely familiar connections** in a land in which connections between people like me and 'real Danes' were not supposed to exist.

Visiting a new place is always a matter of strangeness and familiarity. The two go hand in hand, for as a rule we walk roads others have trodden before us. In Denmark, however, the familiar footprints can

---

* First published in *Information*, Denmark.

** Lego, for one

be hard to discover if you come from a place like India. In certain quarters there might be talk of Danish colonies in India in the past or Danish aid to some Indian NGO in the present. But apart from such talk one seems to land in a vacuum, saved only by that Urdu/Hindi-speaking taxi driver outside Kastrup Airport or the owner of some cluttered corner shop.

I remember one such Pakistani shop-owner on Falkoner Alle. That was a few years later. I was finishing my PhD at Copenhagen University. When I told the Pakistani shopkeeper that I was doing a PhD, he came around the counter to shake my hands. And he discovered for me another connection: "Like Allama Iqbal," he said, "You are doing what he did." It was embarrassing to be compared to one of the greatest poets of Urdu. But it was useful to be reminded that, in the early decades of the 20th century, Iqbal too had obtained a doctorate a few hundred miles from Copenhagen—in Germany.

I also remember two pieces of information generously offered to me by my first 'Danish' taxi-driver. He told me: "When you speak to Danes, make it clear to them that you are a tourist. They are likely to be much nicer to you then." I have had occasion to pass on that bit of advice to other people in the years that I have lived in Denmark.

The taxi-driver's other bit of information has lost its force with time, but perhaps more for me than for people around me. This is what the taxi-driver had said: "This is not London, you know. They did not have (coloured) foreigners here until 20–30 years ago."

And for a long time I believed in it. I looked around myself—and apart from the occasional taxi-driver or corner-shop owner, I did not see familiar footprints. For sometime I believed that there were hardly any. But just as I had known more about Denmark than I had realized, Denmark has had more to do with people like me than it appears. Over the years, I have met some strange ghosts.

For instance, way back in 1713, when European critics tended to dismiss the multi-headed, multi-armed, hybrid sculptures of India with Christian-aesthetic repulsion, Batholomaeus Ziegenblag, a Royal Danish missionary to Tranquebar in South India, wrote the first objective study of Hindu religion and art. The book, *Genealogy of the Malabar Gods*, was written in German and received with immense hostility by the author's colleagues. It has never been translated into Danish, though an English translation exists. Incidentally, two of the best collections of South Indian bronzes and sculpture from two different historical periods are in Copenhagen, though mostly not on display.

But that was not all. Indians had been in Copenhagen too, at least as far back as the 18th century. The taxi-driver's 30-year-old history of 'coloured immigration'—which is commonly echoed by Danes—was not correct. We know, for example, that Lascars (South Asian seamen who comprised five to 10 per cent of the British maritime labour in the 18th century—rising to 26 per cent by 1938—and were also employed on other European ships) had arrived in Copenhagen in the 18th century. It was common practice in the 18th and 19th centuries for European ships in South Asian ports to replace European sailors (who died or defected to take more lucrative employment with Indian kings and *nawabs*) with newly-hired Lascars, who were often abandoned once the ship reached its home port in Europe. The first time this became an issue in England was in 1782 when several Lascars—employed by Danish ships and abandoned in Denmark—arrived in England and applied to the British East India Company for relief.

In general, however, these are faint footmarks, ghostly presences that Danish historians are likely to dismiss—as is also the case of black slaves in Danish colonies (and, presumably at times, Denmark). I have come across them in nooks and corners of overlooked books. The only time I asked a Danish historian why these presences were not mentioned in Nordic histories, I was given this answer: "But they were so few; they are insignificant."

Not being a historian, I could not offer more than a dozen such 'insignificant' examples: ranging widely from the essay describing a Viking funeral left behind by 'a merchant of Baghdad' in 992 to Rabindra Nath Tagore, the Indian Nobel Laureate's visit to Copenhagen in the early 1900s. Some of these connections were tenuous —for example, the merchant of Baghdad was probably writing about Vikings further North in Estonian-Russian regions (but wasn't that where Danes were to find their heavenly flag in later centuries?). And some, like Tagore's visit—he had reportedly been received by hundreds of students and intellectuals and taken in a torchlight procession through Copenhagen—were closer to hand but still strangely difficult to imagine. Can one imagine any Asian or African—or, for that matter, European—writer being taken in a torchlight procession through Copenhagen today? Donald Trump or Bill Gates perhaps, but a writer?

However 'insignificant' these traces might be, I cannot help wondering why popular Danish histories skip them. There is even no real account of slaves in Denmark—once a leading slave-trading nation— even though we know that Europeans from Russia to England often brought home black slaves and coloured servants from the colonies. My wonder changes to worry every time I come across ghostly traces of Asians and Africans in Denmark before the 1950s—or connected to Denmark (for example, Indians travelling on Danish ships)—in scattered texts in spite of not being a historian. They might not have changed the course of Danish history, but their footprints across Danish history seem too frequent to be relegated to such a loud silence. One can argue that because no textual gravestones have been raised to such alien presences in the Danish past, their enforced absence has returned to haunt the Danish present in the shape of recent xenophobia. For this xenophobia is based on a 'clean'—or at least a clean white—concept of Danish identity and history.

Insignificant as they might have been to Danish historians, at a purely personal level my chance meetings with these forgotten ghosts have enabled me to relate to Denmark in a different way. Even such cursory connections as that of Mirza Abu Taleb Khan, the 18th century Indian aristocrat who travelled across most of Europe and wrote an account of his travels: Abu Taleb never came to Denmark, but he left India aboard a Danish ship. Is it difficult to understand the significance of such ghostly traces at a personal level? After all, the first question that most educated Danes put to me is about Tranquebar in South India, a place that can easily be called 'insignificant'. But then, what makes it *significant* for Danes, and rightly so, is the trace of its past connections: it used to be a Danish colony.

Much of the currently excessive debate about 'integrating' (coloured) foreigners (and 'Muslims') into Danish society would lose its coercive and artificial aspect in the present if Danes learned to see the 'foreigners' who walked with their ancestors in the past.

TWENTY-FOUR

The Race for Capital: A Perspective from Norrebro Riots

In his influential essay "Marxist Theory and the Specificity of Afro-American Oppression", Cornel West had rightly noted that "the time has passed when the so-called race question, or negro question, can be relegated to secondary or tertiary theoretical significance in bourgeois or Marxist discourses."* West's essay was written and prominently anthologized in the 1980s. Time and events have vindicated his statement since then. In fact, time and events have done more than that. Today the 'race' question—defined very widely and involving all sorts of 'ethnicities'—provides the cornerstone of many tendencies and theories in such productive fields as Cultural Studies and Post-colonialism. This visibility of those who had been whitewashed out of history and theory is to be commended and defended. Even more so, perhaps, from the pen of someone like me—a small-town Indian who would have had fewer opportunities to publish this sort of article in the past. But is that all the story? Has this change been only a positive one? Or has something else been happening too, something that as a person influenced by the relational thinking of Marxism—and regardless of my colour—I have to notice, address and perhaps oppose.**

I intend to answer these questions with the help of two tales from one city—Copenhagen. The first one took place in November 1999

---

* Cornel west, *Marxist Theory and the Specificity of Afro-American Oppression*, p 18.

** Based on separate articles published in Danish in Politiken and Information, Denmark.

and the second one is still unfolding at the moment of writing this essay, i.e., in August 2000.

On the evening of 7 november 1999, I was late for an important appointment and, as such, committed the rash and uncharacteristic act of catching a taxi. But instead of taking the shortest route to the destination, the Pakistani taxi-driver branched off into a circuitous detour. not having money to burn, I objected instantly—though in Urdu, to be polite. The driver explained (in Danish, probably because he hailed from a non-Urdu speaking part of Pakistan) that the short route, passing through norrebro, had been closed due to *indvandrer uroligheder* (immigrant troubles).*** Troubles of any public sort are not common—or at least not commonly visible—in Copenhagen. On the other hand, Norrebro is one of the two parts of the towns where occasional, largely contained demonstrations—such as throwing stones at McDonald outlets—do take place. I dismissed the taxi driver's terminology and attributed the disturbance to some such stone-throwing act by young Danes.

However, what happened on 7 and 8 November was larger than a stone-throwing event, and more complex. A group of 40 or 50 young men, most of them hooded, set off a train of violent demonstrations that left a number of cars and shops in flames and led to clashes with the police all along the main street in Norrebro. At its peak, between 150 and 300 young persons were reported to have been involved in the demonstrations.

Not only was the scale of the event larger than usual, even its triggering cause was unusual. The young demonstrators were osten-

***In Denmark, the work 'immigrant' has increasingly come to stand for 'Muslim', especially when used in a negative way.

sibly protesting against the extradition of 23-year-old Ercan Cicek. A Turkish passport holder who had been educated and brought up in Denmark, Cicek was ordered out of the country under a new law that allows the Danish authorities to extradite 'foreign nationals' with a criminal record. While this law had been implemented earlier, this was the first time that it was being applied to a person who—apart from that piece of paper called a passport—was a 'Dane'.

This 'trigger cause' probably explains why the 'Norrebro *uroligheder*' came to be seen as something caused by 'foreigners and immigrants'. Because, according to eyewitness accounts, the young demonstrators were often light skinned and light haired.† However, ignoring or downplaying this blue-eyed Danish presence, many newspaper reports concentrated on the '*indvandrer*' (immigrant) problem. The Norrebro riots were used to fuel the ongoing debate on 'second and third generation immigrants'—the very terminology of which reveals its racist and nationalist bias in implying that dark skinned persons born and brought up in Denmark would remain perpetual 'immigrants'. Newspapers were full of letters dripping with repulsion and hate—often aimed at both the 'violence' and the 'immigrants' supposed to have caused it. At the political level, the racist and anti-immigration '*Fælleslisten mod Indvandringen*' attacked 'criminal second-generation immigrants' and stated that 'the strangers have yet again caused violent troubles in Norrebro'. Such was the Danish outcry against the 'violence'—often worded in terms of 'we do not behave like that here'—that even the Labour Council of Enhedslisten distanced itself from the demonstrations.

† I am not suggesting infiltration or provocation by the right or by nationalists. These demonstrators probably belonged to very leftist fringe groups, angry at the government's policies in general.

The fact that the staunchly leftist Enhedslisten distanced itself from the Norrebro riots indicates the bankruptcy of the established left in social democratic Europe and its failure to redefine the class struggle in keeping with material changes. For what was remarkable about the Norrebro riots was its similarity to labour riots in the 19th century. Cars were set on fire, affluent shops (especially multinational chain outlets) were ransacked and police pickets as well as symbols of authority were attacked. But, by and large, individuals and small shops were left alone. There were no deaths or serious injuries. The demonstrators, in their own crude and untheorized way, were targetting the material symbols of current capitalist exploitation. It is this that finally reveals the nature of Norrebro riots—it was an act of protest against capitalist national authorities by a group that, in many ways, can be considered the new proletariat. This new proletariat is not 'factory workers' in places like Denmark where a hegemonic social democracy has provided these workers with huge benefits and much security in tandem with a capitalism whose worst exploitation has been largely exercised internationally. The 'workers' of Denmark have been artificially jacked into becoming part of the bourgeois, and this has been possible because of the convenient situation that such countries occupy on the crossroads of multinational inequality and exploitation. In places like Denmark, the new 'proletariat' comprises 'third world' immigrants and their children—who often do the meanest jobs and have the least security—and younger, unemployed or semi-employed Danes. And it was exactly a combination of these elements that participated in the norrebro riots.

Writing in the 1930s, George Orwell had made the pertinent—and often overlooked point—that the bulk of the 'British proletariat' live not in Britain but in Africa and Asia. This process has been further consolidated after the end of colonization, in direct proportion to the difference between the wealth of the poor countries and the rich nations which has grown from three to one in 1820 to 72 to one in 1992.[††] Not only are millions exploited in the so-called 'third world', those few who manage to get into the El Dorado of capitalist nations are—with very few exceptions—accepted at lower social and economic levels. Their exploitation continues.

Unfortunately, the 'racist/culturalist' critique has not been used, as Cornel West or (for that matter) Frantz Fanon intended it to be, as merely an empowering discourse. It has also been taken over, as Albert Memmi indicates in his recent book, *Racism*, to consolidate the 'politics of difference' that under-girded and explained away the inequalities of colonialism and racism in the past. For example, Danes and 'third world' immigrants who come to places like Denmark are defined not in active socio-economic terms but in (often fetishized) culturalist and ethnic terms. This has the advantage of preventing any kind of proletarian unity and, hence, of leaving the underlying structures of capitalist exploitation unchallenged. This is what explains why the Norrebro riots were seen as 'immigrant troubles' even though a large number of Danes participated in them, and why even Leftist parties largely distanced themselves from the riots instead of addressing them in terms relevant to the present stage of capitalism and 'globalization'. But that brings us to our second tale of the same city, Copenhagen.

The *Images of the World* festival was a big event in Denmark: its official purpose was to display not only the multiplicity of cultures

†† The United nations Human Development Report (2000), as cited in Victoria Brittain and Larry elliott, "Rich live longer, poor die younger", the *Guardian Weekly*, July 6-12, 2000, p 3.

across the globe but also to explore the tensions arising from 'globalization'. The festival, stretching across most of August and September 2000 and the big cities of Denmark (particularly Copenhagen), had showcased music, poetry, dance and art from about 50 different countries and focused on lectures and debates purportedly involving 'other' intellectuals and writers. As would be expected of such a festival, *Images of the World* was inaugurated with a glittering function, attended by several Danish dignitaries (including Princess Alexandra) on 4 August. The inaugural function was met with much applause in the auditorium and from the pages of Danish dailies—though looking at all of it with non-European eyes, I found more reason to lament the bash than to celebrate it.

The inaugural function took place in a large and centrally located sports auditorium in Copenhagen, decked with a stage in front of which stretched rows and rows of (mostly tropical) fruits. entering the auditorium, I found this image of colourful fruits—with their obvious exotic symbolism that only lacked a few hula-hula dancers—extremely disturbing. When Connie Hedegaard, journalist and chairperson of the organizing body, proudly mentioned that the fruits on display had come from various corners of the world, I ought to have been prepared for the worst. For, of course, fruits always come from various corners of the world—one can observe that much in any supermarket of the 'first world'. There is very little to be celebrated in this fact, as various African, Asian and South American labourers working for a pittance in the killing fruit fields of their respective lands would attest. To convert fruits, today just one of the super-marketed images of capitalist exploitation, into an image of multi-culturalist celebration underlines the uselessness of such feel-good bashes. But much worse was yet to come.

In between five to 10-minutes dances, plays and music from various countries, we were treated to a number of short speeches. Not one Dane in the audience seemed to have noticed that all the speeches were by whites. While black Africans or brown Asians were brought in to perform and gambol in the best traditions of colonialism, speech remained the prerogative of whites. Non-whites were unobtrusively denied speech at the inaugural ceremony. This would not have been so bad if serious voices—white, black or striped—had been heard. But even though the festival listed some committed activists like the Indian actress, Shabana Azmi, and even fewer brilliant intellectuals, like the American anthropologist Jonathan Friedman, such voices were relegated to 'debate meetings' later in August, attended only by the already initiated.

Even the one African who got a word in at the inaugural function was a white South African, Prof Charles Villa-Vicencio. Villa-Vicencio, research director of the South African Truth and Reconciliation Commission, is a familiar figure at such culturalist bashes and is (rightly or wrongly) reported to travel only by business class. In his apportioned five minutes, he highlighted three examples of 'problems' that the world has to solve: not surprisingly, all the problems were in countries on the euro-American periphery, in the Far east, in eastern europe and in Africa. we were faced with another colonialist trope: the white knight in shining armour riding to the rescue of non-whites who always manage to mess up their parts of the world. One was almost reminded of Kipling's lines from *The White Man's Burden*. no doubt Prof Villa-Vicencio, as an anti-apartheid campaigner, does not share the worldview of Kipling's poem, but then why wasn't he able to offer anything better than the jaded leavings of a colonial discourse?

Then Prof Benjamin Barber from New York, best known for that glib book, *Jihad vs McWorld*, came in for his five minutes, and started with a compliment to the Danes. Denmark, he noted in truly diplomatic fashion, is not a big economic or military power, but it is a power in exercising huge 'moral force'. He went on to implicitly suggest a Danish torpedoing of Euro and, hence, the EU.

Coming from an American scholar, these were shockingly un-self-reflexive statements and suggestions. I am yet to come across Denmark vetoing something in the United nations using its considerable 'moral force'. I also wonder how effective 'moral force' would have been in the Iraq war or the Bosnia crisis. Moreover, while there are reasons to be sceptical of an EU that might turn out to be another club for bureaucrats, politicians and businessmen, the fact remains that larger than national political organizations are necessary to counter the USA's global hegemony and address the problems arising from economic globalization, religious fundamentalisms (which are by definition not contained within national borders), etc. One can discuss what such political organizations should be like, but one can only dismiss their necessity if one is happy with the current unequal and the US dominated status quo.

The problem with ethno-culturalist bashes such as *Images of the World* is that they fail to focus on the complex materiality of the problems facing the world. By extracting cultures and problems from their complex and material contexts, they make them matters of global consumption. This is similar to what happens to the fruits or, for that matter, the 'other cultures' on display. Perhaps this process is best illustrated with an example from the inaugural function. A Mexican street theatre group put up a brilliant presentation, and met with much applause. But the presentation, while no doubt relevant in Mexico, merely provided the 'internationalist' audience in Copenhagen yet another culturalist excuse to feel good without being seriously inconvenienced. For the problem being explored in the play was violence and addiction among street children in Mexico. This is a problem that makes us in Copenhagen merely feel good and sympathetic. we know that we do not have street children in Denmark, but we feel 'morally and humanly' touched and we applaud. what we applaud is less the play and more our own comfortable humanity. we nurse our version of Barber's 'moral force' even as the real powers polish their missiles, their missile shields and their vetoes. For street theatre to be effective in Copenhagen we would need a play on those exotic fruits being displayed in the centre of the hall. But such a play would never be part of such a bash.

In their different ways, then, both these stories highlight the fruition of Cornel West's prophecy—not only the 'race question' but the question of all 'races' (ethnicities and cultures) has come to occupy centre stage in the capitalist world. But this has come with its own hegemonies and silences, its own resources for perpetuating capitalist structures and global inequalities. while at the material level, this has been used to often prevent effective anti-capitalist coalitions (as in the failure to conceptualize the Norrebro riots), at the symbolic level it has been used to propagate convenient and lulling 'images of the world'.

TWENTY-FIVE

Why I Cannot be a 'Secular Muslim'

The myths of colonial secularism and post-colonial cosmopolitanism are deeply implanted in the very soil of colonial, commonwealth and, ironically, post-colonial writings. From that soil they send out such miraculous shoots as those of Babu-bourgeois secularism, colonial multi-lingualism and versions of Bhabhian hybridity.*

Examples? Well, what do we make of the recent writings of Salman Rushdie, of novels like *The Moor's Last Sigh* where the silver of a Euro-Indian (read: colonial and post-colonial) multiculturalism is counterpoised against the 'jet black and horribly unravelling' tresses of Indian 'homogeneity'. What do we make of this statement in one of the few histories of the English language that is actually open to 'new Englishes': "The Raj *created* an essentially bilingual society [in India]"? (McCrum, MacNeil and Cran) (My stress) What do we make of Bhabha's placement of 'hybridity' not only in a particular corner of history but in the very obvious corner of colonial history: "Hybridity is the sign of productivity of colonial power..." or "Hybridity is a problematic of colonial representation..."?

What do we make of the frequent failures of sections of the anglicised national bourgeois classes—the Babus, so to say—to counter the various challenges of (often non-Babu) nationalism, regionalism and Hindu/Islamic fundamentalism in India today without falling back upon the discourse of, yes, colonial secularism and post-colonial

* Published in *Biblio: A Review of Books*, India.

cosmopolitanism? Faced with non-Babu threats, the gleaming literary instruments of such disparate and brilliant artists as Nirad C Chaudhuri, VS Naipaul and Salman Rushdie seem capable of playing only variants of an old and mushy song: "Those were the days…"

Gayatri Spivak, on the other hand, is too stringent a thinker to indulge in such tune humming. But even she, at times, echoes certain problematic implications regarding the links between secularism and cosmopolitanism on the one hand with colonialism and post-colonialism on the other. Take this statement: "…the political goals of the new nation are supposedly determined by a regulative logic derived from the old colony, with its interest reversed: secularism, democracy, socialism, national identity, and capitalist development…(T)here is always space in the new nation that cannot share in the energy of the reversal." (Gayatri Spivak: *Outside in the Teaching Machine*) Here, it needs to be noted, that Spivak's qualification 'supposedly' leads to a comment on the extent of the reversal and not on, what Aijaz Ahmad would term, "the historical adequacy of the referent". But we shall return to this later.

What, finally, *can* we make of the following statement by even such an important commonwealth critic as Bruce King: "Those who pull up their roots tend to become exiles, nostalgic for a now idealized culture of their origins, or cosmopolitans, like Christina Stead. Many well-known late colonial and commonwealth writers were conflicted by or tried to blend their internationalism and longings for home…Yet it was often returning exiles, such as AD Hope in Australia and Nissim Ezekiel in India, who led the new literatures towards international standards and modern intellectual concerns." (Bruce King, *New National and Post-Colonial Literatures: An Introduction*)

Critics and teachers less astute than Bruce King tend to make the assumptions behind the above quotation even more evident, assumptions accreted in 'colonial secularism' and 'post-colonial cosmopolitanism'.

No, these misbegotten terms are with us today and they have been with us too long. It is time to see what they signify and what they deny. In order to do so I shall treat them separately, and then go on to provide a somewhat theorized summing up. Let us begin with colonial secularism.

Colonial Secularism

Gauri Viswanathan has shown in *Masks of Conquest* not just the imbrication of 'English literature' with colonial power but also the ambivalent role that the teaching of English literature played in 19th century India. On the one hand, teaching English literature was used by so called secularists to counter greater demands for evangelical activities. On the other hand, English literature was itself seen as permeated with not only Christian values but with Christianity. As such, teaching English literature was seen as a subtle but effective way of propagating Christianity. A major strand of colonial education and administration was provided by moderate Christian evangelism. As James Thomason, appointed Lieutenant-Governor of North Western Provinces (NWP) of the Bengal Presidency in 1843, put it: "We want books written in a Christian spirit rather than Christian books."

This itself indicates the nature of the 'secularism' that we are discussing. It indicates that 19th century secularism was *not* necessarily the same secularism as it is understood by progressive intellectuals today. It can be argued on the basis of, say, European reactions to 'Hindu' art,**

** See Partha Mitter's *Much Maligned Monsters: A History of European Reactions to Indian Art.*

that even the few intellectual oases of anti-clericalism and revolutionary atheism created in the 18th century were largely erased by the puritanism of the 19th century. With the partial exception of some remarkable intellectuals, like Voltaire, Charles Dupuis or Karl Marx, 18th and 19th century secularism was not based on the concept of *Christianity as just one other religion*. To the extent that it existed, it was based on a conviction of the TRUTH of Christianity against the falsehoods and superstitions of OTHER religions. Let alone English language and literature (mentioned earlier), even Western sciences—such as Western astronomy—were introduced with the explicit intention of promoting 'Christian knowledge'. This tradition was particularly strong in England, Germany and other European states, compared to France, where anti-clericalism was more common in intellectual circles by the 18th century. As is obvious from almost any colonial text on the subject, science was itself seen as a manifestation of the TRUTH of Christianity—as was the best of European literature. The religious aspects of such 'rational' and 'secular' discussions are best evident in the 19th century debates between Indian astronomy and Western astronomy. While Indian astronomers scoffed at the short age of the world as given in the Bible and counterpoised their own estimate of the Earth's age (running into millions of years), Western astronomers called upon their own self-claimed mathematical superiority to dismiss the entire gamut of Indian astronomical and religious observations. Or, as a colonialist article in the *Calcutta Review* of 1844 put it, Indian tradition was valueless, but in introducing Western astronomy "we come with the authority of the very God of Truth." Here the 'God of Truth' was not the unambiguous god of rationality; his lineage went back to Christianity.

In this context, it must be noted that even within England, the secularist movement lasted only for about four decades in the 19th century. It did not have a predominantly atheistic character and drew much of its inspiration from a system of Christian morality. The secularist movement also had less support than many other radical movements (including its parent, owenism) and even its leaders tried to distinguish between Christianity and, as one leader, Henry Hetherington, put it in his book *Cheap Salvation*, 'Priestianity'. Moreover, one ought not to attribute the intellectual positions of a handful of intellectuals (including 'organic intellectuals') in the homeland with the positions of colonizers in India. For the former, Christianity could well have been an intellectual issue at times; for the latter, it was mostly one of the rationale justifying the colonizing mission either in terms of evangelism or in terms of a superior Christian morality and civilization. This difference can be highlighted with an example. In the 18th century, a few French radicals (such as Voltaire) sought to undermine the historical status of the Bible by showing that the earliest Indian observations predated the supposed Biblical date of creation of the world. This was countered by most orientalists and colonial intellectuals. Historian CA Bayly points out that, "over the next 70 years a whole host of British and European astronomers and orientalists in India and outside—including William Jones, Colebrooke and Bentley—sought systematically to undermine the authority of these Indian observations." (CA Bayly, *Empire and Information*)

Of course, that still leaves us with the issue of political secularism, which one can claim is what 'colonial secularism' was. Even here we have to tread with caution. The so-called secularism in colonial times could well have been a political act ensuring state protection to all faiths, provided they abided by the rules of the company or colonial state, but it did not render the state or its enforcers non-religious. This fact was evident not only in the above-mentioned use of English literature to propagate Christianity but also in the vigour with which colonial officers celebrated various European-Christian festivities in India in their official or semi-official capacities. A recent description of the latter has been given in Mukul Kesavan's brilliant first novel, *Looking Through Glass*.[†] To this literary example, I can append a personal footnote: in my small town in North India, which hardly has a Christian population, Christmas is still known as *Bada Din* (Big Day).

Finally, even in the delimited context of a 'political secularism', the British administration was never less than acutely aware of Indian religions as real or imagined sites of alterity, subversion and resistance. To quote CA Bayly again, "According to the political [colonial] mind, the mechanisms of... intrigues and alliances were religious connections. Pilgrimages were believed to provide important opportunities for seditious meetings. More insidious were the wandering holy-men who were revered by roving Indian irregular cavalry." (CA Bayly, *Empire and Information*)

And the 'political mind' did not merely observe and/or imagine mechanisms of subversion in religious garb, it took active steps—ranging from incorporation to police action—to abort any such possibility. In that sense, colonial secularism—if it existed—was *not* the same as current political secularism, which is mostly seen (at least in Europeanized discourses) as a complete non-interference in religious matters.

But the above nexus of relations is not the only one overlooked in discourses of colonial secularism. At least in the context of India what is overlooked is the pre-colonial roots of much of what is described

[†] Years after having written this essay, I came across a brilliant book *Indian Secularism* by Mukul Kesavan, the author of the novel cited here. It is a book I would recommend to the reader of this essay.

as colonial secularism. For it can be argued that the so-called quasi-secularism that the officers of the East India Company practised in the *18th century* had nothing 'Euro-colonial' about it. In that case, the term 'colonial secularism' attributes a perceived virtue to the colonial years that might actually have had little or nothing to do with colonization.

Here let us examine 'secularism' in the twin sense of (i) daily life and (ii) the non-religious. In the first sense, early Raj traders and officials were more 'secular': they adopted Indian life-styles, languages and even married Indian women. This involved them in Indian social and religious traditions as well. After 1800, however, European colonizers of various shades secluded themselves on a racial basis and gradually withdrew from involvement with Indian religious institutions. This meant that they participated less in both the secular and the religious lives of Indians, marking out a separate area for European-Christian religious practices. Seen from this perspective, 19th century 'colonial secularism' was a retrograde movement towards social, racial and *religious* exclusiveness. In those terms, then, it was not secular as we understand that word today.

In the second sense, again, one cannot assume that India was made politically secular by and during the colonial presence. As historians have noted, the early period of Raj dominance was marked by a continuation of policies of governance taken from Abul Fazal rather than Adam Smith. This involved political tolerance and, at times, encouragement of all religions. Pre-colonial Indians had a sense of religious (and other) differences, but this was rarely expressed in generalized communal terms. As Bayly puts it, "Indo-Muslim traditions of social enquiry and representation were never communal in the sense that they saw India as a field for the conflict of two irreconcilable faiths. This does not mean, however, that officials and writers were unconcerned with differences in religious tradition. Their governing principles were not 'secular' in the sense that religion could be seen as a matter of political indifference." (CA Bayly, *Empire and Information*)

But we have already seen that colonial practice was itself not 'secular' in the sense that religion could be seen as a matter of political indifference. As for a honed communal feeling—in the sense of seeing India as "a field for the conflict of two irreconcilable faiths"—such a belief is much more in evidence in later colonial texts and continues today in the writings of such centred post-colonial writers as VS Naipaul.

Post-Colonial Cosmopolitanism

I do not intend to dismantle the notion of 'post-colonial cosmopolitanism' by merely questioning the antecedents of its parent, colonial cosmopolitanism, in the manner of Aimé Césaire who posed the query, "has colonialism really placed civilizations in contact?" and replied in the negative by appropriately noting the exploitative nature of such 'contact'. I would like to take the matter a bit further. For if secularism cannot be connected to colonialism in the way suggested by a term like 'colonial secularism', cosmopolitanism cannot be seen *unproblematically* as a post-colonial attribute either. There are major areas of evasion and occlusion involved in the use of a term like 'post-colonial cosmopolitanism'.

The first area relates to the implication that cosmopolitanism is a colonial heritage. Post-colonial cosmopolitanism becomes possible only due to colonization, whether seen in terms of Rushdie's *chutney* English or in terms of Bhabha's colonialism-centred hybridity. This perpetuates the colonial myth of the essential divisibility of the margins. Two glaring examples of this are the pre-independence legend that India would not exist without colonial power as the glue sticking it together and the post-colonial myth of English as the first language enabling Indians or Asians or Africans to talk to each other. As if Indians or Asians or Africans could not talk to each other, did not share a rich cultural complex before English was introduced in their midst! It is the second fact that has to be kept in mind: that there was rich and (often) direct cultural commerce between various regions of Asia, Africa and even parts of Europe long before colonization. In this sense cosmopolitanism per se is *not* a colonial construct. It existed in pre-colonial times as well. Actually, Bayly attributes the relative ease with which the English colonized India to the cosmopolitanism of India—cosmopolitanism that allowed Europeans space within India as just another group in the early decades. As Bayly puts it, "One feature of all these [pre-colonial] intellectuals and servants of state was that they were used to receiving knowledge from abroad... Theirs was not a narrow or declining tradition, but a universal civilization..." (CA Bayly, *Empire and Information*)

But if cosmopolitanism per se is not a colonial or post-colonial gift to the margins, the type of cosmopolitanism that postcoloniality often champions is. This is the East-West anglophone cosmopolitanism in India whose perceived diminution has been lamented by Salman Rushdie in *The Moor's Last Sigh*. What often goes unremarked or is underplayed in such accounts is that this particular version of cosmopolitanism was constructed at the expense of various other versions of cosmopolitanism. English, for example, simply replaced Persian as the language of the North and Central Indian elite. What this meant can be illustrated with the help of the following account from Harish Trivedi's *Colonial Transactions*. The famous Hindi poet, Harivansh Rai Bachchan, whose family *Ramacharitamanas* was *not* in the Devanagari script used for Sanskrit (and Hindi) but in the Persian script used for

Urdu and whose maternal and paternal grandfathers had been fluent in Persian, had to take recourse to Fitzgerald (in the 1930s) in order to translate Omar Khayyam's *Rubaiyyat* into Hindi. And, on the other hand, contrary to the lament of Rushdie, political *independence* (not some theoretical *post*-coloniality) opened India to other influences: Harish Trivedi has remarked, for example, how vernacular short fiction in India has moved away from a limited anglophone model to greater international and inter-regional symbiosis. Keeping such facts in mind, one can claim that what is described as post-colonial cosmopolitanism marks, more often than not, the hegemony of Eurocentric and high capitalist discourses.

Finally, a few words on the economics of current 'cosmopolitanism', or rather on the economics that enables the rhetoric of post-colonial cosmopolitanism. It has become commonplace to see our 'post-colonial' times as denoting a greater global economic mobility. This perspective is partly flawed. While high capitalism has opened the world to first world capital, it has also divided the world into bourgeois high consumers ('developed countries of high-wage earners and relatively mobile labour') and proletariat consumers ('developing countries of low-wage earners and less mobile labour). The high mobility of capital controlled from first world sites gives the impression of cosmopolitanism and leads to some cultural hybridization as well, but it also obscures the harsh economic realities behind such perceived cosmopolitanism. For example, contrary to the popular belief there is today probably less trade between the *developed* world and the *developing* world in terms of *percentage of total trade* than there was in colonial times. In 1990, for instance, US imports from low-wage countries accounted for only 2.8 per cent of GDP. Much of value-laden economic traffic circulates *within* the developed world even while the impression is created that first world jobs are being threatened by imports from low-wage, 'developing' or 'third world' countries. This fact needs to be noted because, to my mind, its mechanism of a kind of fetishistic occlusion shares common elements with the rhetoric of post-colonial cosmopolitanism.

Summing Up

It seems that the rhetoric of colonial secularism and post-colonial cosmopolitanism cohere in certain ways. Firstly, they mark the colonization of possibilities and referents. By this I mean the colonial and neo-colonial tendency to annex not only signs but ontological possibilities and not only words but their variously constructed referents to the so-called European episteme. As such, we do not have *varieties* of secularism and cosmopolitanism within the colonial context: we have colonial secularism and post colonial cosmopolitanism *per se*. The very *possibility* of such concepts is appropriated by discourses of colonization and/or confined to the European episteme. This is one side of the coin whose other side bears the imprint of the rhetoric of reactionary elements in, say, India or Egypt who oppose the very possibility of democracy or secularism as European and, as such, foreign to the Indian or the Egypto-Islamic episteme. Therefore, it is important to see this entire issue in the light of Aijaz Ahmad's comments on the status of terms like 'secularism' or 'democracy' in India: "*Words* may have originated in Europe, but the historical adequacy of the *referent* can only be established through reference to practices undertaken within India by Indian political subjects." (Ahmad, in Mongia) These practices, I have argued, were not and cannot be restricted to a colonial or post-colonial referent when it comes to words like 'secularism' and 'cosmopolitanism'.

Secondly, the rhetoric of colonial secularism and post-colonial cosmopolitanism marks the severing of relations and connections from the constructed entity. So secularism or cosmopolitanism is not seen in its complex historical context. The implication is that modern secularism is a construct of colonization and that cosmopolitanism is post-colonial in the sense of being a gift or by-product of colonization. But modern secularism and cosmopolitanism, as I have indicated, cannot be understood within the colonial–post-colonial referent: their constituting relations are not primarily colonization, but industrialization, capitalism and the discourses of modern science, etc.

Thirdly, they mark or mask other areas of appropriation, such as those of 'modernity' or 'democracy' by discourses of European centrality. To use them uncritically and without appropriate footnotes is to replicate colonial structures of dominance, occlusion and hegemony. They, and similar myths, are rooted in the discourse of European centrality—of the *modern* world as becoming possible only or primarily via the agency of Europeans. That, of course, is a serious enough political and moral objection to such myths, but conceptually too such myths are flawed in being finally based on sealed ontologies, on notions of idealist essence. I, like many others, would argue that the world *can* only become possible for other peoples outside the legacies of colonization once such myths of European centrality are questioned and displaced. This displacement cannot be a simple overturning; it has to be a complex and difficult act of restoration and revision.

It is this that some post-colonialists forget when they make a fetish out of cultural forms of protest. However, this is easy to forget. The myths of European centrality are so powerful that they inform the very structures of our understanding of the contemporary world, defining the responses of not only secular and 'modern' citizens/thinkers but also, more perniciously perhaps, the reactionary adherents to Islamic and Hindu fundamentalisms.

TWENTY-SIX

Immigrants or Refugees in the First World

Human history begins with movement—the earliest text known to us, *The Epic of Gilgamesh*, narrates the travails and travels of a man. It seems almost superfluous to document the cross-fertilization that forced or voluntary human movement has caused in the fields of literature, art, music, social forms and rituals, religion, science, agriculture, food, etc. But, as is evidenced by the shrill voices of intolerance that seek to remove or bar some people from some regions, such documentation is by no means superfluous. Our history of mobility and the richness of our mobile present needs to be reiterated again and again.*

And yet, there is a danger in saying 'asylum' and 'migrant' in the same breath. Migrant is related to 'immigrant' and, for us, an asylum-seeker is a 'refugee'. But the two are not the same today. To be an immigrant is *not* to be a refugee. For, by definition, the refugee seeks shelter for a period—even if that period may stretch to infinity in actual fact—but the immigrant is, again by definition, someone who "comes as a *permanent resident* to a country other than one's native land." It must surely signify much about the world we live in, that in popular and public discourse the two are more often conjoined than seen as different concepts. In countries ranging from India to Denmark, we talk of the 'problem of immigrants and refugees'. The volume of this

---

* Adapted from an editorial written for the *Prince Claus Fund Journal*, No 11, The Netherlands.

talk appears to be directly proportionate to the affluence of the circles in which it reverberates.

But if the multiple courses by which ordinary people like us become immigrants or refugees are seen as threatening in relatively affluent societies, then there is also a counter-discourse that attempts to defend such 'dislocated people'. If the refugee or the immigrant is seen as disrupting the course of a natural progress of 'national identity' in places like Denmark and Holland, she is also defended by some Danish and Dutch scholars who point out that people have moved across spaces throughout history. If the refugee or immigrant is seen as diluting the purity of some cultural ethos, she is also celebrated in terms of multiculturalism and plurality by some artists and writers. If the refugee or immigrant is seen as bringing with herself the curse of penury, she is also justified by some economists as the only cure that will enable the ageing populations of first world countries to maintain a high level of production, welfare and livelihood.

It need hardly be pointed out that the immigrant and the refugee are the two most commonly employed scarecrows in contemporary political discourse. They serve to scare the voter in two major ways: One, by raising the spectre of a kind of gradual invasion that will lead to cultural, religious, linguistic, political and economic changes of an undesirable nature in the host country; and two, by making the host voter conscious of an 'outside world' full of grave dangers—the refugee and the immigrant being proof of these dangers—if the host voter stops being the obedient worker, citizen, consumer, soldier of his nation that s/he is. Both perceptions condition the voter—fix her relationship to the nation and the world in definite and lopsided ways—and can be generally used to protect the status quo.

This, then, is the broad discursive framework in which this issue—in spite of its selective concentration on the cultural aspects of migration and asylum—intervenes. What, one may also wonder, are the hard facts? We know that immigrants and refugees are contentious and controversial, but what are the data, the numbers and graphs? In other words, as a popular song puts it, though in a different context, *hungama hai kyon barpa* (What's the fuss all about)?

Let us start with the facts. About 150 million people in the world live outside the countries they were born in: these include immigrants and 18 million refugees. (Some estimates put the latter at 35 million by including 'displaced persons' who are not 'refugees'). But 150 million is only three percent of the world's population, as Peter Stalker states in *The No-Nonsense Guide to International Migration.*

It is important to keep both the actual numbers and the percentage in mind. Because it is only by bearing both in mind that we can see the current phenomenon of migration and asylum in a historical context. Historically, these 150 million people mark a significant increase, but they also indicate a larger and longer connection. As has often been noted, people have moved around all through history. The earliest epics, ranging from *Gilgamesh* to the *Odyssey* to the *Mahabharata*, indicate this mobility of people. So does historical and anthropological evidence: as a matter of fact, it is doubtful that any human group is really indigenous to any region. It is always a question of who has been where longer.

But if we move to the second perspective—that of percentage—we are faced with two further complications. First, is three percent really such a high percentage? It could well be that almost a corresponding percentage of the world's total population (which was much less in the past) has lived outside its regions of origin through much of history. Think of medieval Europe with its many mobile people as well as its Jews and Gypsies, Moors and Turks. Think of India. As far as I am aware no reliable quantitative analysis exists to settle this issue, but it might not be too far-fetched to maintain that between one to three per cent of the population of almost any large society in the past might have been born outside that society.

Now, it is not true—as some commentators imply—that 'foreigners' were largely welcomed by their 'hosts' in the past. But it is true that the indicators of identity and foreignness were much more malleable in the past, perhaps because all societies in the past contained largely illiterate and semi-literate persons. Print—and other ways of recording and codifying—had not fixed cognitive borders to the extent to which they have been fixed over the past two centuries or so. Hence, while there was conflict as well as confluence, there was nothing like the sort of overwhelming discourse on abstract 'immigrants' and 'refugees' that exists internationally and nationally today.

This brings us to the second complication. Yes, people have moved around all through history either to further their 'careers' or change their life quality ('immigrants') or because, like Babur, the founder of the Mughal Empire in India, they were booted out of some other place ('refugee'). Migration is nothing new. And yet, one has to maintain the conceptual newness of both the 'immigrant' and the 'refugee': these are terms that came into being, as they are understood today, only with the rise of modern nation states. And in that sense, they are not identical to the term 'migrant'. One can even argue that 'immigrant' and 'refugee'—unlike 'migrant'—are post-imperial terms. They came into being in the present sense only after the British Raj and vestiges of other European empires dissolved under the impact of two World Wars, economic changes and political struggles for independence. Once again, the drawing of national borders across the globe was necessary for the appearance of the 'immigrant' and the political 'refugee': without those borders these 'dislocated people' would have been something else. In fact, the word 'refugee'—with its institutionalized privileging of the political over the economic—is an indicator of this development.

If tomorrow, a high capitalist empire is brought into being by, say, the USA, the terms 'immigrant' and 'refugee' will be transformed into something else. Not necessarily something better, but definitely something else. I do not wish to argue that such an empire is in formation: the US presence in Iraq is still gift-wrapped in the terminology of nation-statism. Anyway, tomorrow is another day, and I am more concerned in this essay with immigration and political asylum as they exist today.

The institutional and international refusal, in practice or theory, to countenance economic asylum has created a situation in which some countries—and the majority of people from these countries—have been transformed into a new global proletariat. If there are sweatshops on one side, there is people-smuggling on the other. Illegal immigrants continue to trickle into West and North Europe. Most of these people cannot claim asylum, for they are fleeing poverty and lack of opportunity (sometimes also allured by the hard sell of the capitalist West), not some tin pot dictator or moronic monarch who refused to kowtow to democratic Western capitalist governments.

This presence of illegal migrants complicates the general and dominant capitalist perception of accredited migrants, who usually contract workers, professionals, political refugees and, in some cases, marriage partners. These migrants are usually seen in terms of 'human capital'—as individuals who rationally weigh and consider their options and then take something like a 'career decision'. But migration is not simply an individual matter: illegal migrants move as families or are heavily funded by the family that stays behind; they are motivated by various factors that go beyond economic calculation; they follow and develop their own networks.

However, whether the labourer enters a relatively privileged socio-political space illegally or legally, she raises—or rather the media raise—some standard issues in that space.

To begin with, there is a general tendency to question the economic wisdom of allowing the immigrant in. It is alleged that immigrants depress the wages of local workers or steal jobs, even though a number of studies exist to show that immigrants, because they are also consumers, actually end up creating jobs in most cases. An eight-nation survey by the Organization for Economic Cooperation and Development (OECD) has shown that, over a decade, unemployment either went down or remained unaffected in the countries with the most immigrants. Similarly, wages seem to remain largely unaffected in most cases. It has also been reliably documented in the US that immigrants—including illegal ones—actually contribute much more to the public coffers than they draw upon. Even though some immigrants might start off by using government funds, particularly to educate their children, in a few years even these are actually paying more in taxes than they are consuming in services. The only group that actually loses—marginally—due to the arrival of new immigrants is the previous group of immigrants.

In Europe and the US, it is often alleged that immigrants sponge off the welfare state. There appears to be some truth in this statement in the US, where new immigrants seem to make slightly more use of welfare than natives. But this perception is faulty, for (new) immigrants are on an average poorer than natives. If one compares immigrants to native families in the same income group, immigrants actually claim welfare less often than natives!

There are many such myths about immigrants (and refugees), most of which can be largely dismantled with reference to hard facts. However, hard facts are not sufficient in all cases. One bit of hard fact that is often used to justify immigration relates to falling birth rates in rich nations. It is argued—and quite logically—that immigration is necessary to sustain the current living standards in such countries. Given a required replacement rate of 2.2 children per woman and an actual birth rate of only 1.4 in the European Union as well as the (in)famous 'greying' of the population—complicated by the fact that older people cost almost double as much to 'maintain' as children do—it has started making economic sense to champion immigration. Consequently, the latest bit of irony: in places like Denmark, it appears to be the chambers of commerce and other assorted capitalist bodies that want more immigrants, while the traditional 'socialist' parties find various reasons to (implicitly or explicitly) barricade the gates!

This hard fact in favour of immigration is attractive, but it is not foolproof. If the calculations of the United Nations Population Division are to be relied upon, the UK will have to import one million labourers every year for the next 50 years to offset falling birth rates and ageing. South Korea will have to take in almost 100 million per year, so that by 2055 its national population will be greater than the current global population! Evidently, such hard facts might get a bit hard to stomach in the longer run.

But there is, to my mind, a greater objection to such justifications of migration. If one justifies immigration —or emigration, which has its own set of problems (mostly accreting around the debate of the supposedly negative 'brain drain' and the supposedly positive 'cash-back')—if one justifies migration by highlighting the benefits it brings to the native population, one has not escaped the central problem. After all, people who oppose migration do so in the name of the native population too. Both the options privilege the native population, turning the migrant into a mere tool. And that, to my mind, is the main problem.

Why is it that both defenders of migration and its opponents finally end up privileging the native population?

To my mind, there is only one satisfactory answer, and it takes us back to my initial remarks about capitalism and nation states. The immigrant and the refugee are living embodiments of what, once upon a time, would have been dubbed a contradiction of capitalism. This contradiction lies in the fact that capitalism, by its own parameters of definition, depends on the 'free flow' of capital, commodities and labour. Of these, however, labour is far less free than capital. The problem of the immigrant—and, often, the refugee (or, increasingly in Europe, the 'Muslim')—arises only when this labour breaches the borders of the nation state to try and match the mobility of international capital. In this moment of penetration, legal or illegal, the nation state—which has mostly served as a regulatory device on the global machinery of capitalism—is made to face its own secondary (but not powerless) status in the global scenario as well as its delicate balance and tension with capitalism. It reacts with prohibitions and permissions. Its populations react in a way that foregrounds their own (partly false) consciousness of an independent national identity and a fecund national machinery. The nation state negotiates and renegotiates its own relationship to capitalism. But, particularly in the rich nations, it and its 'native' populations also refuse to clearly acknowledge the fact that the same capitalism which has obtained for them the comfort and commodities that they cherish is behind the arrival of the immigrant (and even the refugee) on their doorsteps. This failure is a signal failure of our times. It is the material force behind the moral 'failure to empathize' with refugees that Rose George so powerfully documents in *A Life Removed: Hunting for Refuge in the Modern World*.

And hence, again and again, there is an attempt to slam the door on the newcomer, or to slot him as simply necessary to the many comforts of the 'native' inhabitants, to denigrate him as immigrant or unemployable or Muslim or a potential terrorist.

It is in this context that a celebration of the cultural richness brought into a nation by migrant populations—today or in the past—can become a radical political act, and sometimes a necessary one. It is one way of saying—in spite of the various structures that prevent us from making that statement in an economic or political sense—that all of us have made this world and that the world belongs to all of us. It is one way of recognizing that every dusted memento of our supposedly separate 'civilizational' or 'national' identities—whether of science, religion, philosophy, art, literature, architecture, cuisine or complex social practices—bears the fingerprints of people who travelled of necessity or choice.

We need to highlight the richness such mobility has given rise to and the inevitability of human mobility across time. But we also need to recognize a central problem: that we live in a world where many are not free to move from choice and many are forced to move against their will. It is a strange contradiction. It is an immoral contradiction. It is a tragic and, to my mind, unnecessary contradiction. And it is a contradiction that we will have to face and address before we can come to terms with any kind of xenophobia, or even the many fundamentalisms—fascist, nationalist or religious—sweeping across the globe today.

TWENTY-SEVEN

The Politics of Migrancy

This paper sets out to trace not the trajectories of human movement, but the politics of the perception of this movement. In order to do so, I shall play down the distinction between migration and travel. What I am concerned with are not the terms themselves, but how their visibility brings to light some of the structures of the world that we live in: the world of capitalism, casting its faint shadow in the 15th and 16th centuries and with its material body arising from the bog of colonization in the 18th and 19th centuries. Of course, travel is not the same as migrancy, and, in most contexts, the two ought to be distinguished. However, keeping in mind the particular focus of this paper on the politics of the perception of human *movement*, I will use 'travel' in a broad sense—as broad as the sense imposed on the word when Bryan D Palmer describes those overlooked corpuscular moments of sexual and social transgression as 'night travels'.*

When an academic and a writer like me, based in a European university, looks at the visibility of the narration of human mobility from the 16th century to the end of the 20th century, what one sees can be divided into three different phases. It ought to be stressed here that what I am talking about is the *visibility* of the narration, and not the narratives themselves, let alone the actual trajectories of human movement.

If we follow the visible narratives up to the 15th century (using an emblematic cut-off point), human movement appears to have been

---

* First published in *Wasafiri*, UK.

largely a random phenomenon: all communities and cultures could be just as mobile or as static depending on various material and symbolic factors. Even when it comes to written accounts, if there was Marco Polo, there was also the earlier (7th century) Xuanzang (also spelled Hsuan-tsang, Yuan Chwang, etc.), who made a 16 year pilgrimage to the India of King Harsha and left an account of it—an account that illustrates not only the cultural interchange that has taken place between different regions of Asia but also one of the many rich non-European traditions of travel writing. There were 'travel writers' like Ash-Sharif al-Idrisi (1100–1166), the scion of the Hamudid caliphs of Spain and North Africa, born in Morocco, who travelled over most of Western Europe, Africa and Asia Minor as a young man, and Ibn Battutah (1304–1369), arguably the most celebrated of all Arab travel writers. As has often been noted, Ibn-Battutah's travels and accounts far exceed those of Marco Polo, though even this excess has not translated into matching visibility.

However, from the 16th century onwards, even this restricted and retrospective visibility of travel writing from outside European—and later European-settler—sources suffers. I would stress the word visibility, as it cannot be safely argued that non-Europeans travelled less or even that they did not leave behind travel accounts in various shapes, ranging from prose and poetry** to paintings (Liscomb). Extensive areas in Asia and Africa formed a complex network of trade and other routes after the 16th century as well, and these routes were used by Asians and Africans.

** The journey can be almost considered a sub-genre in Chinese Tang Poetry from the 7th and 8th centuries. In India, Kalidasa's 9th century *Meghdootam* is not only a poem but also the description of a journey. Such examples can be multiplied.

Even when it comes to Europe-related movement, there are large areas of blindness in the hegemonic perception of human mobility during these centuries. The transportation of slaves from Africa to the Americas, for example, is one example of human movement that has been largely obscured in favour of the corresponding movement of European settlers to America. Indentured labourers formed another, later, group. So did sailors: Paul Gilroy notes that "at the end of the eighteenth century a quarter of the British navy was composed of Africans." (Gilroy, 13) The etymology of the word 'laskar' reveals the presence of Indian and Asian sailors in the ships of colonization and early capitalism. In his paper, Robert Fraser has focussed on the gypsies, those 'non-European travellers' in Europe whose presence continues to be largely obscured even today. This nexus of occlusion has been continued into the 20th century and sometimes across 'post/colonial' lines: for example, I would argue that the visibility of Australian soldiers in accounts of the First and Second World Wars is far greater than the visibility of Indian soldiers.

Such examples can be multiplied, though even these instances largely leave out the connections that existed outside the presence of Europe. Even much of postcolonial literature, with the exception of work by exceptional writers like Amitav Ghosh, avoids tracing these connections.

In short, even though Asians and Africans continued to 'travel' during and after the 16th century, their movement appears to grow progressively less visible until, in the 19th and early 20th century, all connections come to appear to have been made across the bridge of Europe. It appeared, around the 1930s, for example,[†] that the modern

† Actually, many Europeans and Americans still seem to share vestiges of this view.

world had been made possible only or largely due to the criss-crossing trajectories of European or European-settler adventurers, sailors, migrants, discoverers and travellers. Not only did other travellers disappear, even the complexity of other cultures was seriously reduced in these hegemonic accounts.

To avoid stating the obvious, I will offer only one example of the extent of the latter tendency. The authors of *The Story of English* (a history that is very open to 'new Englishes') write that, "The Raj *created* an essentially bilingual society [in India]" (360). Against this prevalent ahistorical perception, one is forced to point out that the educated classes of India were bilingual even before the Raj and the illiterate classes are (mostly) not bilingual even today. There exist in India not only vast regions of, shall we say, monolingualism but also many *other* kinds of bilingualism than the 'Indian'-English bilingualism being touted in Europe and, often, by members of the Indian/cosmopolitan bourgeoisie.††

It should be noted in this context that the colonial myth of India's lack-of-history isolates India from the cluster of relations that have constituted it (both in its parts and as more-than-its-parts) before European colonization—turning India's history with various other peoples and kingdom-states to an emptiness before the 'arrival' of the colonial presence as the great connecting link. This erasure of pre and para-colonial connections is not merely a consequence of the writing of 'colonial' histories; it also played a significant part in making colonization possible. It appears today that British dominance in the early years of colonization (1780–1820) was not just a consequence of military, informational or even economic advantages. The dominance

†† A recent example of this is Rushdie's *The Moor's Last Sigh*.

itself grew, to a large extent, from the ability of the British to cut the "practical and honorific [and, I would add, symbolic] lines of communication" (Bayly, 58) between the Delhi court and other Indian powers and between Indian powers in general. This was a *conscious* policy—encouraged by Lord Cornwallis and his successors—that broke down the multilateral channels of information between Indian powers. While this policy 'worked' in the political sphere, the colonial myth of India's 'lack of history' sought (and seeks) to extend its effects—that too retrospectively—into the much more complex and resistant fields of culture.

What happened in India can be traced, with regional variations, in other colonized spaces of non-European societies: in all these cases the colonial myth of the 'bridge of Europe' became and, in some ways, continues to be central. We have seen that this myth of the 'bridge of Europe'—largely made possible because of the growing invisibility of other lines of connection in hegemonic discourses of the 19th and 20th centuries—makes English far more central to Indian transculturality[†††] than it has been. Similar trajectories can be traced in other colonial histories and discourses as well. The invisibility of non-European movement (migrancy or travel) in the colonial period is a part of this general problem.

It is true that the 'discovery' of the Americas and Australia added to the self-perception of Europeans as great sailors and discoverers, thus obscuring the achievements of, say, the Arabs and the Chinese. By the 19th century, in Albert Hourani's words, "the growth of large-scale factory production and changes in methods of communication—the

[†††] To employ Rustom Bharucha's term.

coming of steamships, railways and telegraphs—led to an expansion of European trade" (263)—and hence, probably, documented travel. Though even here the word 'probably' should be kept in mind: recent research (Markovits) indicates that Indian merchants continued to operate in a 'global world' in the 18th and 19th centuries as well.

It is also true that various factors, as noted by Giovanni Arrighi among others, ensured that (to quote just one example) Cheng Ho's navy *chose* not to sail around Africa and 'discover' Europe a few decades before the Portuguese rounded the Cape (Arrighi, 33–36). There can, again, be a difference between the *survival* of travel accounts in societies with a high use of printing and those in which printing is new, underdeveloped or unknown. However, even keeping in mind these qualifications, one is faced with the fact that human mobility came to be seen as a thoroughly European prerogative in the 19th and early 20th centuries in spite of the fact that Asians and Africans did leave behind travel accounts in and after the 16th century as well.

I can list, off hand, quite a few such Asian and African travel accounts. Gul-Badan Begum's (1523–1603) autobiographical account contains various travel narratives of her brother Humayun's life. The Bhakti saint and poetess Bahinabai (1628–1700) has given us an interesting account of her journey along River Godavari. Basho's *The Narrow Road to the Deep North* (1689) is undoubtedly one of the masterpieces of world travel writing, where what is often perceived as a 'minor genre' merges with the most concentrated poetry in the Japanese *hoku* tradition and the Zen quest for spiritual enlightenment. Dean Mahomed's account of his days and enterprises in Britain (1759–1851) remains not only the first important text in English by an Indian but also a fascinating travel account. On the other hand, Abu Taleb's *Travels in Europe* (1797–1803) proves that English was not necessary for writing even about Europe: Abu Taleb wrote his account in (Indo) Persian and learnt English only during his stay in Ireland and England. Then we have later accounts like the Shah of Iran, Nasir ad-Din's *Diary of a Journey to Europe* (1873), Emily Said-Ruete's *Memoirs of an Arabian Princess* (1881) and Melek-Hanum's *Six Years in Europe* (1873). There are also somewhat more visible accounts, such as *The Interesting Narrative of Olaudah Equiano*, the only extensive surviving account by a 'slave' on his way out of Africa.

But while the number of 'travel accounts' by Asians and Africans can be multiplied, it does not change the fact that by and until the middle of the 20th century, agential human movement came to be seen as a predominantly European characteristic. This was connected, of course, to the fact that colonial discourses tended to deny rational agency to colonized people. In other words, Europeans and their descendants had a monopoly on both history and agency in most accounts of the recent centuries. No wonder, Europeans and their descendants appeared to have 'travelled', 'discovered', 'settled', etc.—and, thus, made possible the modern world that, it was widely agreed, existed in the first half of the 20th century.

What happened after the Second World War is another story, and this story moves us on to the third phase mentioned at the head of this paper. Even as countries became independent, the myth of the centrality of European agency came to be questioned—not only in the colonies (where some natives had always had doubts about it) or by certain European intellectuals, but by many ordinary, thinking Europeans. It came to be perceived that non-Europeans had also moved, though the extent of their visibility remains restricted and sometimes even entirely obscured in countries like Denmark. But this was, to my mind, a minor aspect of a greater change. What changed was, largely, the character of capitalism: which came to depend, according to Arrighi, less on the space-of-places and more on the space-of-flows. In simpler words, it became far more profitable to use 'free' capital to exploit national markets than to actually colonize and administer regions. (This might well have been an aspect of Marx's famous M-C-M1 equation, but we need not get into that matter here.)

Within the scope of this paper—the exploration of the visibility of different kinds of human mobility—the 1950–1970s not only saw the decolonization of most parts of Asia and Africa, it also marked a gradual change in the perception of the directions in which human beings were seen as moving. Suddenly, the travel, settlement or exploration of Europeans was replaced by the migration of Asians and Africans. The latter perception had a clearly racial logic: white Australians or white Americans, for example, are still seen as posing less of an 'immigration problem' in, say, Denmark than coloured Pakistanis or Algerians or, I am sure, Australian aborigines (if they had a substantial presence). Today, as a glance at the papers read at conferences on contemporary migrancy reveal, non-Europe has suddenly been made visible as moving into the first world nations of Europe or Europeanized, first world spaces (like USA, Canada and Australia).

This academic visibility echoes a greater public rhetoric, even when it sets out to criticise it. Recent instances of this rhetoric in Europe have included the high media visibility of events like refugee movements from, say, Somalia as well as incidents like shiploads of immigrants (economic refugees) abandoned off the French coast, the over-publicized 'organized smuggling of illegal immigrants' from Africa into Spain etc. In themselves, these mark an imperceptible flow into Europe—for example, by far the greatest burden of Somalian refugees has been borne by neighbouring African states—but the

Western media paint such incidents in the colours of a tidal wave set to inundate Europe. Similar tendencies can be noticed in the US.

Once again, the question is not that of scale. It may be true that more Asians and Africans are moving to Europeanized, first world spaces today, though this remains a doubtful conjecture from a relational historical perspective. What concerns me here is the fact that the colonial centuries (to use a convenient emblem) involved a near-complete erasure of Asian and African movements globally, while the post-colonial decades have started to focus inordinately on such movement. I would argue that just as the first erasure was ideologically significant, the second visibility can be ideologically complicit. It remains doubtful that Asians or Africans are more mobile now than they were in the 19th century or than Europeans are today.

It is also significant that the first perception (involving the erasure of non-European movement) coincided with capitalist exploitation based largely on the control of space-of-places.[§] This induced not only the movement of Europeans but, what is more important in our context, compelled the self-perception of Europeans as moving almost solely into other spaces (thus providing a justification for the 'profits' accruing to their 'entrepreneurship').

The second perception (of non-European migrancy in recent decades) has coincided with capitalist exploitation that is increasingly based on the control of space-of-flows and, as we shall see, it provides a similar salve for the capitalist conscience of Euro-Americans.

In some ways, people have never been so tightly penned in by national borders as they are today. What is actually very mobile in

---

§ The difference, of course, is that of degree, for capitalism utilizes both spaces by definition.

our world is capital, and those who own capital or the citizens of countries that 'share' most of the international flow of capital. The body of the African or Asian 'worker' is tightly controlled and seldom allowed to cross national borders, as highlighted (among others) by Amitava Kumar. When this body crosses a national border into the first world, it does so under heightened conditions of the capitalist exploitation of labour.

On the other hand, Europeans, North Americans and Australians enjoy much more mobility not only in the first world but also in Asia, Africa and South America. In short, just as the obscuring of Asian and African accounts of 'travel' served the purpose of hiding the actual realities of colonial empire—and society-building—and hence the capital extracted from the exploitation of Afro-Asian space, agency and labour—the current privileging of Asian/African migrancy often hides the structures of postcolonial high capitalism, as sketched above.

TWENTY-EIGHT

Godly Nations

> "The government of your country! I am the government of your country... You [statesmen] will do what pays us [businessmen]. You will make war when it suits us, and peace when it doesn't. You will find out that trade requires certain measures when we have decided on those measures. When I want anything to keep my dividends up, you will discover that my want is a national need. When other people want something to keep my dividends down, you will call out the police and military."
>
> (Bernard Shaw)

Men made nations in the image of God. Years ago, in a small town in India, when I worked my way to this simple conclusion, I was unaware of Benedict Anderson's *Imagined Communities*. Later, having moved to places that enabled me to read the book, I realized that—unlike many other people writing on nation and nationalism—Anderson had made a connection essential to any understanding of the matter. He had noticed that 'nationalism' belongs "with 'kinship' and 'religion', rather than 'liberalism' and 'fascism'".[1] However, after rejoicing in having my suspicions confirmed by so astute a scholar as Anderson, I read on and realized that my understanding of the matter differed in some ways from Anderson's. And in *many* ways from those currently fashionable, post-Marxist or post-modern scholars who have employed fragments of Anderson's critique outside its socio-economic framework. I was faced with a task that I had hoped, on discovering

---

1 Benedict Anderson, *Imagined Communities*, p 5. While I differ from this book on certain grounds, my paper has been made possible only due to the research of Anderson.

Imagined Communities, would not be required of me: I still had to expand my conclusion into something more than a summary of Anderson (which it is not) or a mere sound bite. Men did make nations in the image of God; but how and why?[2]

Referring to the pre-nation, religion-based conception of such languages as the Bible's Latin, the Quran's Arabic and Examination Chinese,[3] Benedict Anderson rightly notes that these were languages based on the idea of 'the non-arbitrariness of the sign'. The Latin-vernacular debate in Europe or the refusal of Muslim scholars to translate the Quran was based on the idea of the truth-language. Chinese, Latin and Arabic were, as Anderson puts it, "emanations of reality, not randomly fabricated representations of it." Translation was simply not possible, because *all* languages were not seen as alienated and/or equidistant from reality. Having established this point, Anderson notes that as 'truth-languages', Arabic, Latin, Chinese, etc., were "imbued with an impulse largely foreign to nationalism, the impulse towards conversion." (14–15)

But this perception fails to explain all kinds of nationalism, and—what is worse—to distinguish between the two broad 'types' of nationalism. Post-1789 French nationalism was, as EJ Hobsbawn has shown in *Nations and Nationalism since 1780*, largely linguistically defined—though only 50 per cent of all Frenchmen spoke French in 1789 and only about 13 per cent spoke it 'correctly'. However, if one was willing to learn French, one could achieve the status of a French citizen. This contrasted with the other (later) tendency, the

---

[2] First published in Radical Philosophy Review: *Journal of the Radical Philosophy Association*, USA.

[3] And, as an Indian, I would add 'Vedic Sanskrit'.

conservative one, to which the term 'nationalism' was first applied. According to this, one's nationality was a biological and cultural inheritance. This conception of national identity has been dominant in, say, Germany—where nationality depended on belonging to the *volk*. A country like Denmark still exhibits a tension between these two concepts of nationhood—the conservative resistance to 'other peoples' (particularly those from outside North Europe) is countered by Danish social democrats by highlighting an immigrant's ability, willingness, desire, etc., to learn Danish.

As such, the claim that the impulse towards conversion is 'largely foreign to nationalism' is only a partial truth—for 'linguistic' nationalisms do depend on a kind of 'conversion'. More problematically, it identifies the construction of a 'nation' with only conservative discourses of nationalism—of *volk* and not (bourgeois-progressive) 'linguistic' nationalisms.

But there is also a danger in associating 'nation' with linguistic *communities*, and such an association is at times suggested by Benedict Anderson's use of terms like 'nationally-imagined' communities for linguistic minorities. Anderson is aware of the fact that it is erroneous to treat languages as '*emblems* of nation-ness'. But when he notes the capacity of language to generate 'imagined communities', to build 'in effect particular solidarities' (133), he attributes to language an agency that is actually bestowed upon it by the *material interaction and conflict of classes* in bourgeois and capitalist societies.

We have already seen that the relatively progressive linguistic nationalism spawned by the French Revolution itself imposed a language that was not even spoken by 50 per cent of those being defined as French. One can even say that French, as the national language, was spoken by only 13 per cent of all French citizens bourgeois because the 'national language' is always the 'correct' language of universal mass education and not a 'dialect'.

The case was and is similar in many other countries, ranging from Germany and Italy to India. Actually, only 2.5 per cent of the population of Italy used the Italian language in 1860, when Italy was 'united' largely under the banner of the Italian language (Hobsbawm). As such, the attempt to explain nations with the help of linguistic definitions merely replicates the ideology of nationalism. It fails to take into account, as Hobsbawm illustrates, how national languages were themselves codified and created with the rise and spread of 'universal mass education' from the late 18th century onwards.

The question, then, that we should ask is this: Why is it that large patches of largely homogeneous 'one language' peoples did not formulate a nationalism before the age of capitalism or, at least, the rise of the bourgeoisie by way of the burghers? The answer cannot be a "nationally-imagined" people on the basis of language; for one has to explain why such a people needed to be imagined in a language and formed into a nation in a particular phase of history.

Trade, the Bourgeoisie and Language

In order to understand this 'need' one has to refer to the basic fact, stressed by DD Kosambi among others,[4] that trade is crucial to the development of language. For instance, it is in societies based on production *and* trade that one can expect the 'categorization' of language into general terms. This general categorization is achieved and required not only by the increase in human beings' cognitive areas of operation but also by the need of traders, as a separate class, to keep *linear* records.

[4] See DD Kosambi's *An Introduction to the Study of Indian History* and *The Culture and Civilisation of Ancient India*.

Again, extensive and 'vocational' trade and writing complement to each other: some of the earliest instances of writing appear to have served some economic (accounting) and/or administrative purpose. One could claim that large-scale trade would be impossible without general categories in a language; general categories would not be required without regular and widespread trade of different objects.

But trade itself can be divided into, what I will term, internal and external trade. Internal trade is relatively limited in its spatial scope. It is conducted within a region and mostly in one language. External trade, as the term suggests, is conducted *between* linguistic and other spaces: it requires the entrepreneurship (or services) of those who can communicate in two or more languages. Such a sharp division is largely a conceptual aid, but the two 'types' of trade also require different levels of capital, labour exploitation, infrastructural investment, etc. Therefore, the internal or regional capitalist (and bourgeoisie[5]) in a 'universal world'—of the sort created by capitalism (and colonization)—tends to be different from the external or inter-regional capitalist (and bourgeoisie) at least on the so-called 'margins' of the 'metropolis'. The difference is that between what later comes to be seen as a national bourgeoisie and the international bourgeoisie, though there will always be some crossover between the two and their interrelationship would be largely symbiotic in many, especially the early, phases. But the relations between the two alter in significant ways when the regional bourgeoisie grows in wealth, power, numbers and confidence.

---

[5] For the sake of convenience, I have chosen not to differentiate between the capitalist and the bourgeoisie, considering the two to be complicit enough to be mostly considered one in this context.

It is with the rise of a capitalist 'market' that the internal/regional capitalist comes into direct competition with the external/inter-regional capitalist. Earlier pre-capitalist markets permit a more symbiotic relationship by locating profit in the process of 'carrying trade' between two or more relatively independent markets rather than competition in an integrated capitalist market.

Here we have to face the fact—often elided by Western Marxists—that capitalism is a 'market system'. As Ellen Meiksins Wood illustrates in *The Origin of Capitalism*, full-fledged capitalism arose when "England arguably transformed the nature of trade by creating a distinctive national market, in fact the first national market (centred on London), and perhaps the first truly competitive market." (Wood, 57) It is through the creation of a national market—and later a global market—that capitalism could transform 'market opportunities' into 'market imperatives'. Such a 'universal' market was necessary to change the nature of profit-making from that based on 'carrying trade' between different markets to that based on the extraction of surplus capital by wage-based exploitation of labour in the process of competing for consumers in an integrated market. The first national market centred on London was, then, a universal market—with the expansion of capital, it expanded into the colonial market and the current 'global' market. However, while the global—universal—market is the hub of capitalism, it can operate in diverse geographical areas largely (only, until recently) through various integrated national markets. But the national market is not only complicit in the capitalist exploitation of a universal/global market, it can also become the site of a limited bourgeois-competitive 'resistance'. This takes place when, as noted earlier, the regional bourgeoisie grows in wealth, power, numbers and confidence.

Suddenly, the regional bourgeoisie finds its paths increasingly blocked by the greater wealth and power of the inter-regional bourgeoisie. This inter-regional bourgeoisie shares most characteristics of the regional bourgeoisie, except that it usually does not speak (or does not generally speak) those related, mutually-intelligible dialects which are used in the internal market and one of which is perhaps already being codified and universalized by the regional bourgeoisie into a 'language'. (And, ironically, often being codified into a language with the help of an inter-regional bourgeoisie intent on both retaining its differences from the regional bourgeoisie and obtaining greater market penetration for its commodities by way of an organized, locally hegemonic and largely homogenous regional/national bourgeoisie.)

It is evident to all that the regional bourgeoisie's control of the local market depends on its linguistic monopoly. The shopkeeper needs to speak the local dialect, while the large-scale exporter cannot be bothered to speak the languages of the countries or regions to which she exports. It is obvious, then, that the wider the regional bourgeoisie's 'language' spreads, the greater the market available *to the regional bourgeoisie*. Of course, the 'language' itself may not be a particular regional capitalist's inherited language, so long as it is closely related to the dialects (language) of trade and the market. This fact is probably useful in understanding why certain early nationalists did not insist on their particular inherited languages of culture but on the 'language of the people', which was itself usually a newly codified dialect-turned-language imposed on the other dialects of the people. The clash of economic interests between the regional and the inter-regional bourgeoisie is also reflected in the common colonial story of the resistance of *colons* to attempts by 'native' elites to gatecrash 'European schools' and the often special emphasis placed on teaching the native in the 'regional language' (often itself a dialect codified *during* colonization and not a previously codified 'language').

These connections between the 'national language', market capture and the regional bourgeoisie (getting further united on the basis of a class-based relatively uniform education) predicate that the bourgeoisie needs a language not only to maintain its local monopoly but also to expand its markets. The 17th century rise of the book in Europe provides a good early example of this: "Publishers in their search for the largest possible market naturally tended to encourage the growing use of the vernacular for new purposes." (Febvre and Martin, 320) The one may not always lead on to the other, but nationalist aggressions that try to impose the 'national language' on minorities or conquered peoples are partly driven by this logic of the market. Moreover, the control of language is more of an issue in industrial capitalist societies. One has to read manuals in order to operate even simple machines. One has to give more complex instructions than those required in ploughing or digging manually. As Ernest Gellner has noted, agrarian societies are less semantic minded than industrial (capitalist) ones. One need not speak a language very well in order to cultivate a field manually; but extensive trade and mechanical work (including industrialized agriculture) depend on a larger semantic capability and, within regions, greater 'semantic' homogeneity.

There is an administrative corollary to the above factor, and one admirably documented by Anderson. As he notes, in "the late 18th century the imperial administrative unit came to acquire a national meaning in part because it circumscribed the ascent of the Creole functionaries." (ibid.) Here, however, it is interesting to see Creole functionaries as regional bourgeois ideologists: what was happening to them was similar to what was happening to the regional bourgeoisie in general. These functionaries were, for one, confined to the colonial 'margins': an English-speaking, perhaps even England-trained, Indian would seldom be posted to Africa and almost never to Europe or America. On the other hand, English functionaries had the range of the entire imperial 'job market'. Again, as was the case with the regional capitalist, the Creole/regional functionary realized that his essential weapon was the one language of the two or more that the inter-regional/English functionary did not have or did not have to the same extent: the regional 'language'.

It could be that a prospective 'national' language (like *dienstmaleisch*[6]) evolved in a restricted 'functionary' environment and was consolidated by administrative 'pilgrimages'. But for it to become the language of nationalism such a language had to move out (as *dienstmaleisch* did) into the markets and come to be constituted and seen as a major language of the regional market, as part of and distinct from the languages of the inter-regional market. Combined with print-capitalism, such a language is then provided with a putative 'native' ancestor and turned into the nationalist language—*Bhasa Indonesia* in the case of *dienstmaleisch*. Here it is important to note that Anderson's distinction between such functionaries/intelligentsias and the bourgeoisie is not a sound one. Anderson writes that "the key early spokesmen for colonial nationalism were lonely, bilingual intelligentsias unattached to local bourgeoisies." (Anderson, 140) But one cannot imagine such intelligentsias and functionaries as outside bourgeois formations—though within the bourgeoisie, they might well have been marginalized or alienated in the tradition of many bourgeois intellectuals. Even the bilingualism of early colonial nation-

6 To re-deploy an example from Anderson's book.

alists (highlighted by Anderson) is not very relevant in this context. Though they might have been fluent in two or more languages, they were almost always great and obdurate public champions of *the* 'national language'. This even applied to very Westernized nationalists like Jinnah or Nehru, and highly humanist and 'universalizing' ones like Mahatma Gandhi.

Nationalism is not just connected to capitalist trade by way of the spoken and written language. One can even link the numerical logic of nationalism to that language which is central to all trade (capitalist or not)—the language of numbers. The truly original perspective that gave us 'numbers' consisted of the view of all objects as *the same but not identical.* In order to count any heap of diverse objects, one has to state that they exist and that they exist in the same way, none existing differently from others. That, of course, is the statement nationalism makes about the nation and its 'people'. This numerical logic can also be observed in religion—but with a crucial difference. Religion always posits a qualitative difference. In a religion like Brahminical Hinduism, this could lead to theories of pollution or rebirth. In more 'universal', monotheistic religions (like Islam or Christianity), this qualitative difference is reduced in life and projected beyond it—some are saved and some are damned. Nationalists, however, posit a view of the nation as 'the same but not identical'—a numerical view (and, hence, tied to the modern census) that recognizes the discreteness of the units that make a nation, but does not dwell upon their difference. Within the language of nation-ness, all are not identical but all are the same. What is not the same is simply not part of the nation.

(When numbering becomes naming, it perhaps follows that names turn into mere numbers—and hence, to take just one example, the graves of such 'anti-nationals' as Jews, gypsies and communists killed in nazi concentration camps came to bear not names but numbers.)

If one keeps the above relations in mind, it would be problematic to see nationalisms—either linguistic or *volk*-ish nationalisms—*as essentially* emancipatory. The early nationalisms—what Benedict Anderson somewhat misleadingly terms 'popular nationalisms'—were revolutionary only in the sense in which Marx calls the bourgeoisie revolutionary. Early nationalisms were revolutions aimed at unseating the aristocracy, which was not and could not be nationalistic. The monarch had a divine right to rule and was not, until after the rise of nationalism, just a first citizen. Aristocrats, with or without a divine right to rule, saw themselves as *qualitatively* different from the peasantry: vestiges of this perspective survive in, say, the British crown's need to marry only within nobility. Therefore, early nationalisms were basically revolutionary movements led by the lower (educated/professional) middle and new middle classes in the name of the masses. When the traditionally 'superior' classes and their conservative allies responded by positing *given* nationalities (*volk*) they were trying to recuperate the old principle of inherited (divine) right on a per force expanded base. This was basically damage control. The nation had come to stay; now one had to save as many hierarchies as possible. If God could not help protect my privileges, 'nation' would limit the number of potential threats to it. If God denied me the divine right to exploit the peasantry outside my castle, perhaps 'nation' would enable me to exploit those outside the nation with no twinge of conscience.

Incidentally, the connection between such conservative (even feudal) 'damage control' and ethnic (*volk*) nationalisms is not confined to Europe. Zulu nationalism (arguably the only example of 'ethnic nationalism' in South Africa) was itself a product of "a revival in the fortunes and influence of the Zulu royal family" and was "sponsored by *amakholwa* intellectuals hoping to anchor their own political position through this alliance." (Ross, 138)

It is to this conservative reaction that the term 'nationalism' was finally given. But even early nationalism was not a revolutionary movement in the sense of being a "popular" one or a proletarian-type revolution—not even when it took advantage of or sought to remedy some popular grievances. In some ways, one can argue that even this early, bourgeoisie-induced nationalism was a class-specific consolidation and usurpation of popular revolutionary tendencies. In both forms, the 'nation' was constructed to protect and, at times, extend the privileges of a minority. It is in that sense that men (and initially not women) *made* nations in the image of God.

The fact that nations inspire love and often "profoundly self-sacrificing love" (Anderson, 141) should not blind us to the fact that nations, as we know them, are largely bourgeois hegemonies. Love, after all, is not just commanded by what is 'one's own'. More often than not, we love what we have been conditioned to love—just as we hate what we have been conditioned to hate. The story of Laila and Majnu (or Romeo and Juliet) becomes significant and ends in a tragedy simply because the lovers break a rule and love what they were socially conditioned not to love. But, even there, a prior biological and cultural conditioning is required—they are physically desirable and satisfy each other's criteria of beauty. It may be that Othello, being black, is seen as physically unattractive by white Europeans like Iago; but his deeds and demeanour make him attractive to many, like Desdemona, who have also been conditioned to love bravery and heroism. The poor retarded hunchback of Notredame, on the other hand, loves his beautiful gypsy girl, but does the gypsy girl ever really reciprocate that great love?

It is relevant to remember that much 'profoundly self-sacrificing love' has been bestowed by workers on the two 'things' central to the exploitation of the proletariat: capital and commodity.[7] Actually, the purpose of nationalism is not just to empower the (no doubt sincere) values of a particular bourgeoisie but also to promote such 'love' and 'self-sacrifice' in those less-privileged classes whose labour keeps the nation—and the bourgeoisie—going. One could trace this effect even in the early stages of the rise of nationalism (and capitalism). The Prussians freed their serfs after the disastrous battle at Jena not because they were suddenly moved by some abstract ideal of liberty but because of the practical observation that free peasants appeared to fight better and more loyally than serfs. Already, the vertical imposition of power was changing into a more 'horizontal' hegemony. The divine right to rule was being replaced by the leadership of the 'first citizens' of the nation—citizens who 'just happened to be' members of the national bourgeoisie or aristocrats trying to save the day by clinging on to triumphant bourgeois coat-tails and ideals.

It won't be too rash to claim that just as God was necessary to keep the rich man in his castle and the poor man at his gate (or, rather, in his fields) in the past, the nation is necessary to keep the capitalist in his office and the worker in the 'factory' today.

It could be that the French Revolution of 1789 contained truly revolutionary aims—in the sense of equality, fraternity and liberty as a *political* demand for *all* human beings. As aims, anyway, such notions have been in the air for centuries. But the post-1789 'nation' has functioned more as a symbolic *and* material instrument with which

---

[7] For non-Marxists, a word of clarification: 'commodity' is not the same as 'product', and 'capital' need not be the same as 'money'.

to maintain a hegemonic status quo and to indoctrinate and exploit the working majority. Within the nation, this exploitation is imposed on the working classes in the name of 'the national spirit' or the 'national cause'—even by rich countries in times of war or economic failure. The working classes are also incorporated into the ideology of the bourgeoisie classes that use the nation to maintain a certain monopoly on the market. Outside the nation, other proletariats are exploited for so many 'national interest reasons' that they can hardly be enumerated. It is these new 'needs' that explain why nationalism arose when it did.

The apparently 'horizontal' organization of society needed by capitalism in order to produce more (and, hence, make more profit), its need to match increasing productivity with an increasing market, its miracle of turning a daily exploited and dehumanised labour force into willing consumers—all these needed the hegemony, the 'love and self-sacrifice', the numerical sameness of discrete units that nationalism imposes. This is the reason why while the problem of nationalism could arise in the Agrarian Age in the shape of "the question of political power to culture" (Gellner, 16), a theory of nationalism only arose with the rise of industrial capitalism.

The role of trade and a rising bourgeoisie in fomenting nationalism is crucial to understanding the odd exceptions to Gellner's otherwise-sound rule linking nationalism to what I would call industrial capitalism and what he terms 'modernity' and 'industrialization'. The first outbreak of nationalism, claims Gellner, took place among the Greek minority in what is now Romania and was then not half as industrialized a place as England (Gellner, 41). But here it is interesting to note that the Greeks were "privileged and powerful intermediaries between the populace and the Muslim overlords." (Gellner, ibid.)

In trade and educational terms, they were an evolving bourgeoisie. Again, later examples of nationalist movements in agricultural areas of a largely industrializing world should be seen in terms of the complexity and global reach of capitalist ideologies and/or attempts by 'proto-bourgeoisies' to 'develop' their 'nation' and in the process constitute themselves as full fledged bourgeoisies.

Finally, as indicated earlier, the bourgeois 'hand' in nationalism is reflected, among other things, in the nation's desire for a *particular type* of order and 'democratic hierarchy'. As Gellner has noted, the most emotive element in the nationalist attitude is that it not only defines the limits of the nation, but it assumes that the nation has an institutional leadership ('the state') controlled and manned by 'genuine nationals' (Gellner, 6). This bid to exclude 'foreigners' from power in the nation is always a bid by the regional bourgeoisie to empower itself and its adherents. The otherwise complete Wallerstein encapsulates only one half of the issue when he notes that "capitalism was from the beginning an affair of the world economy and not of nation states." (Wallerstein, *The Capitalist World Economy*, 19)

While it is true that, always in theory and often in practice, capital does not allow national boundaries to limit its aspirations, capitalism is also central to the creation and perpetuation of nation-states and the nationalism associated with and required by them. At its simplest, this is so because capital is owned by capitalists (mostly) who, unlike capital, itself have a face and a location. But, of course, the matter is much more complex (as indicated in this essay) and this is one of those contradictions of capitalism that make it such a volatile concoction. In short, the logic of nation-statism is just as inherent in capitalism as the logic of 'globalization.' These are not mutually exclusive terms but dialectical ones. They follow the logic of capital itself, which as

Marx and the 20th century have illustrated, is both faceless and mono-polistic. One can simplify the above statement to the remark that capital 'tends' to accrete in certain hands and be more closely associated with certain faces (such as those of Ted Turner, prospective American presidents and Bill Gates) even as it remains faceless and renders its own origin, labour, faceless.

This nexus between capitalism and the nation-state has been noted by others. Giddens, for instance, notes in passing that the two have been 'intertwined' in their 'mutual development'. It is this realization which enables Giddens to note that capitalism is 'international in its scope' and that "a capitalist society is a 'society' only because it is a nation-state." (Giddens, 57) However, Giddens, like most others, lets the matter rest there—and merely ends up suggesting a casual collaborative link between nation-statism and capitalism without exploring the dynamics of the matter. Moreover, in Giddens' account both the concepts misleadingly retain their independence as concepts: they seem to have been twins who simply shared the same womb and hospital. My account of their relationship is evidently different.

All this is not to suggest that 'nationalism' is a theory consciously manufactured and promoted by a wicked bourgeoisie for nefarious ends. Rather, it arises from the relations and forces that capitalism brings about—being, so to say, one of the symbolic sides of the material changes of capitalism.[8] To understand this aspect of 'nationalism', we have to remember (as Marx pointed out) that the bourgeoisie, as a class,[9] does *not* act out of some abstract 'evilness' but because it is

[8] Both the symbolic and material fields effect and constitute each other.

[9] Though, of course, individuals (bourgeois or not) may be perfectly capable of 'evil'—or, at least, selfish—acts.

convinced that the conditions of its own emancipation are the (only) conditions under which all (other classes) can be emancipated.

As is obvious, 'nationalism' has its advantages—and most of these accrete to the national bourgeoisie. Nationalism creates the half-true myth of a horizontal (and not vertical) division of society which obscures the fact that some continue to live at the cost of many. It constitutes the 'serfs' into 'free peasantry' which can defend the status quo better and can be 'freed' even further into the condition of workers forced to sell their labour: that is, it not only gets workers to *work*, but also gets them to *consume* on bourgeois terms.[10] Finally, it constitutes a state that while keeping 'order' in the nation also protects the national bourgeoisie from external threats (not least economic ones) to the best of its ability. The argument that first world capitalist states do not indulge in much 'economic protectionism' is blind to the fact that their bourgeoisies are in such positions of strength that they stand to gain *more* by competing on 'equal terms' with other bourgeoisies. This is a fact not lost on other bourgeoisies—witness the hamstrung attempts by a rightist party like the Bharatiya Janata Party to keep international *capitalists* out of India while trying to invite international *capital* into the country! On the other hand, wherever and whenever first world nations risk competition on unfavourable terms (such as in the fields of agriculture and textile) their governments obligingly 'call out the police and the military'—that is, implement protectionist policies.

The above observation does not mean that the state is a creation of nationalism. Anyone with even a rudimentary acquaintance with history knows that, in their various forms, states preceded nationalism

[10] A 'revolutionary nation', in this sense, is an oxymoron—attempts to create such nations often mark (as in Stalinist and post-Stalinist USSR) the hegemony of another elite group standing in for the bourgeoisie.

by at least a couple of millennia. But while the state is not a creation of nationalism, the current 'universality' of states *is* a creation of nationalism. Pre-capitalist societies could be organized in forms other than that of a state. Moreover, pre-capitalist states could contain diverse peoples, sometimes even called 'nationalities'. Even as late as the nineteenth century, one comes across the following statement in Article 19 of the imperial constitution of the multicultural Austro-Hungarian empire: "All the peoples in the state are equal before the law and each has an inalienable right to cultivate its nationality and language."[11]

However, the theory of nationalism *insists* not only on a state but also posits *one state for one nationality*. This is what I mean by 'nation-statism'. In cases where there is a reasonable chance of success—either due to numerical strength, economic growth, geographical factors or international support—this assumption leads to demands for independence. As in the case of India/Pakistan from the Raj, Bangladesh from Pakistan or, more recently, a number of 'new countries' in East Europe. But if success and support are seriously in doubt, the word used is 'autonomy'—as in Kashmir until recently, and Kosovo today. Thus, heartless as this may sound, the tragedies of Jews in Nazi Germany, of Kurds in Turkey and of Kosovars in Yugoslavia have been *doubly coded* into the very theory of nationalism.

But is nationalism, per se, a bourgeois fief, or can some of it be retrieved and employed for revolutionary purposes? To answer that final question, we shall have to return to rumours of a now-obscured revolutionary face of nationalism. Such rumours need to be read with some scepticism, but we need not dismiss them outright. After

---

[11] Cited in Yves Plasseraud, "Choose your own Country", *Le Monde Diplomatique* (*The Guardian Weekly*), London, May 2000, p 8.

all, nationalism was 'revolutionary' in the struggle of the bourgeoisie against the aristocracy.

Perhaps, one may have a kind of 'revolutionary nationalism' even today. Perhaps, one might even *need* a kind of revolutionary nationalism in developing countries—but only if such nationalism considered itself a necessary and evanescent category of a revolutionary international socialism. To confine ourselves to the terminology of nation-states and nationalism is to negate the revolutionary option of going beyond capitalism. Here, it is necessary to see the rise of nationalism as an aspect of capitalism and not just as an 'interlinked' development. Hence, suggestions that 19th or 18th century models of statehood[12] (such as the one from the constitution of the Austro-Hungarian empire quoted above) might offer ways out of the current nationalist double-bind seem to miss the point. What one needs to do is to go through and beyond the processes of nationalism (and capitalism) rather than go back—for, given the flow of time and events and the nature of the relations and means of production, there never is any going back in the material world.

In a letter dated 21 May 1894, Engels confesses being "driven to despair by these English workers with their sense of imaginary national superiority," while in a letter dated 18 January 1893 he ticks off the Fabians for aiming at a municipal socialism rather than a national socialism (Marx and Engels, *On Colonies, Industrial Monopoly and Working Class Movement*, 56–57). These two contradictory responses

---

[12] Even Plasseraud comes up with such implicit or explicit suggestions in an otherwise excellent article. See, Yves Plasseraud, "Choose your own Country", *Le Monde Diplomatique* (*The Guardian Weekly*), London, May 2000.

to the 'nation' by even such a 'Marxist' scholar as Engels highlight the limitations of 'revolutionary nationalism': nationalism tends to maintain the hegemony of the bourgeoisie classes and, in that sense, it seeks to create the condition of Engels' English workers. One can only use 'nationalism', if forced, as an evanescent stage in the endeavour towards a revolutionary international socialism.[13] Without that, the nation simply fills a gap left by God, and those who define and control nationalisms are the new priests of our society. Like God and religion, the nation reduces human beings to fungible commodities and human existence to a mere means. But the *revolutionary* idea[14] of God—as an index of the limits and the potentials of human beings—has itself always undergone a capture similar to the one imposed by 'nation' on the revolutionary politics of universal community. The God of religion is mostly a god of rules and sects: but a God of rules and sects is a limited god of specific men and women, not that *emblem* of the limits and potentials of embodied human *life* which we need to constantly recognise and address. Just as, at a more limited level, we need to constantly recognise, address and contest the limits of elitist, bourgeois and capitalist nationalisms in order to posit a revolutionary future.

In the post-colonial context, such a redefinition of 'nationalism' not only bestows agency on post-colonial nationalisms (which cease to be 'copies'), it also helps us trace the close connections between the

---

13 But won't it, like Banquo's ghost, refuse to leave the banquet room when we so desire? Especially if we, like Macbeth, have been instrumental in bringing it about?

14 'Revolutionary' merely in the symbolic realms if not supported by a materialist theory of the world: the basic limitation of religion that made Marx dismiss discussions of religion (and atheism) as finally beside the point.

nationalist celebrations of the late colonial period and the celebration of cultural and linguistic 'ethnicities' today. The seed of the latter was always present in the former, and for largely the same socio-economic reasons. Both, again, are expressions of the logic of capitalism, even as they offer some internal opposition to it. Contrary to the beliefs of some nationalists or most post-colonialists, both these internal 'oppositions' are also necessary for the growth and preservation of capitalism.

TWENTY-NINE

Lifting the Veil on Islam: The Ghost Busters

Two types of error plague the '*udlænding debat*' (foreigner debate) and the debate on Islam in Denmark. The first type contains errors of fact. These can be simple, such as the claim that (most) second-generation Muslim Danes marry their 'cousins from outside Denmark' or that Muslim employees waste their working time praying or that there had been no gang rapes in Denmark before a recent gang rape by youths from an immigrant background. A simple look at the actual facts would dispel such notions. But there are also more complex errors of fact. This can be best illustrated with reference to the claim by a major Danish politician that 'foreigners' (implicitly, visible—coloured—foreigners) have a crime rate that is higher than the Danish national average. Ostensibly, a convincing 'fact' but it appears so only because it has been taken out of context. The crime rate of many marginal groups (including *pære dansk* ones) would be higher than the national average, for crime rates have a lot to do with unemployment, low-prestige jobs, lack of education, living conditions and a general sense of worth. With regard to all these factors, coloured foreigners mostly belong in the bottom quarter of Danish society. It is as useless to talk of the crime rate of any group outside its actual socio-economic context as it would be to say that the crime rate among professors is significantly lower than that among taxi drivers.

---

1 Published in *Kritik*, Denmark.

These errors of fact proliferate in Denmark even though the country has a high literacy rate and readily accessible sources of information. That is the reason why I am not concerned with such errors of fact. If people persist in making them, it shows a desire to think on those particular lines—and one can not do much about people who have made up their mind to be wrong. What I am concerned with in this essay is the other type of error: errors of conceptualization. It might be best to discuss this type of error with a concrete example.

It seemed just a few months back that a spectre was haunting Denmark—the spectre of the veil. It has not been exorcised even today, but in those days it appeared to be particularly rampant. Women had veils ripped off their heads by total strangers (this happened again for a short while after the September 11 tragedy), a supermarket tried to ban its employees from wearing the veil, and similar bans were imposed by other Danish companies. The media filled with discussions on the role of the veil. Even when well-meaning, these discussions were often run along essentialist and ahistorical lines associating Islam with the 'ideology' of 'shame and honour' (a crass simplification based on colonial binarisms of the 19th century but kept alive in our times by various books, including some by privileged immigrants). And still the gem of genuine concern about women's rights sometimes lay under even some of these crass discussions.

The Spectre of the Veil

The fact that refugees and immigrants to Denmark have included women is, of course, central to any understanding of the veil. Some of these women came already possessed by the spectre of the veil. What made matters worse was the fact, discovered later, that the naturally bracing air of Denmark did not automatically drive such spectres from the minds of ignorant refugees and such-like. Many of them continued to wear veils. And, horror of horrors, even some children of unveiled immigrant mothers put on the veil—as a bid to preserve and stress their 'identity', they claimed.

Around this time, 'average Danes'—convinced of their own free and unpossessed nature—were hurrying back with two or more overloaded bags from the supermarket, intent on catching a particular show on TV. They saw veiled 'second-generation' spectres haunting Denmark. They stopped in shock. They were faced with a dilemma. And 'average Danes'—being, as is always the case, not really 'average' and 'identical'—solved the dilemma in different ways depending on their political sympathies. Some wanted to give the spectres a few generations, convinced that with time they would mature into Danishness. Others wanted more active steps: education, indoctrination, legislation. Some would just have these spectres out of Denmark—or at least ensure that more of the sort did not come in.

I do not agree with any of these ghost-busters. The veil remains a problem, but it is not *really* a spectre brought in from far-away misty lands by strange foreigners. The veil that some refugee women wear is a piece of cloth that *should* soon get worn out in a society like Denmark. No doubt, women who grew up in cultures where both decency and respectability are associated with wearing the veil cannot be expected to give it up just because a political upheaval or a marital relationship has transported them to Denmark. But women like these represent only a short generation. Growing up in Denmark, their daughters can be reasonably expected to discard the veil. The spectre of the veil, thus, rises on the grounds of Denmark when these daughters *refuse* to discard the veil. And when other daughters put on the veil that their mothers and grandmothers had discarded.[2]

As such, the spectre of the veil is a problem that has to be addressed on the material grounds of today's Denmark. It has to be addressed in its material reality—which relates to the position of the concerned immigrants in modes and relations of production characterizing Denmark (and 'developed' capitalist Europe) today. But it also has to be addressed in its symbolic constituents and repercussions—for example, both as a sign of male hegemony *and* as a relevant gesture of protest (or sign of identity). To ban it or accept it completely in relativist terms is to ignore at least one side of this complex issue.

Moreover, the reactionary bid to ban the veil and persecute those who wear it shares much with what appears to be its diametrical opposite—the relativist attempt to accept it unquestioningly. This relativism appears radical and progressive but is not so. In fact, it shares the main premise of the reactionary response to the veil.

The main premise of the reactionary response to the veil can be described as a nexus of essentialisms. It is based on essentialist definitions of both Danishness and 'foreignness'. These essentialisms may be worded in terms of Europe-and-the-rest, Science vs Religion, Christianity vs Islam, Danes vs non-Danes, 'freedom' vs 'shame', 'individual' vs 'society', etc. But they are based on essentialising assumptions on both sides of the binary opposition posited. Danes are seen as having

---

[2] I am momentarily skipping the argument—made and backed by various scholars—that the 'veil' (like *sati* in the case of Hinduism) has been constructed as a generalized symbol of the otherness of Islam, largely by simplifying facts, reading cultures ahistorically and avoiding issues of cultural contradictions and complexities. Such Western construction of 'otherness', as I have indicated in this book, always suits Islamic fundamentalists too, for their worldview is just as binary and oppositional.

certain *basic characteristics* which are, often, *essentially lacking* in certain non-Danes. One evidence of this kind of essentialist thinking is the failure, noted above, to see the rise of the veil in its immediate Danish/European context and the associated tendency of simply relating it to the *past* of immigrant groups in other countries. Another evidence is the call to deport immigrants or arbitrarily ban veils.

Now, when the 'multicultural' relativist accepts the veil unquestioningly, he is indulging in similar essentialism—but on the other side. Just as the reactionaries essentialise Danishness or Europeanness, some well-meaning relativists end up accepting essentialisms about, say, Islam or the East. It is true that the recourse to the veil by second-generation Danes is partly a gesture of cultural protest and a bid to enact one's own identity. The *gesture* is valid and should be supported. But the *symbols* chosen for the gesture *cannot* be taken for granted. In other words, just as we cannot take for granted the claim that one needs to wear trousers in order to be Danish, one cannot uncritically accept the claim that one needs to wear a veil in order to be, say, an Indian Muslim or an Egyptian. The veil is only one in a range of symbols associated with the identity under consideration. Many Muslim women do not wear veils, and never have in the past.

Whenever a material practice like the veil is fetishized as a central and unavoidable symbol of identity, one ought to listen for the noise of clashing interests and obscured 'cultural contradictions'.[3] For example, essentialising claims about Danishness always represent attempts by some spokesperson to advance certain agendas by excluding certain

[3] As Aijaz Ahmad points out in his book, *In Theory*, no culture is self-identical with itself to the extent that it can be considered a site of resistance in its totality: all cultures contain within themselves various 'cultural contradictions'.

peoples or to gain power through ideological homogenization. When a spokesperson claims that you can be a Dane only if you have 'x', she is actually excluding all those who do not have 'x' or forcing them to acquire 'x'—and in both cases the spokesperson, as the champion of 'x', stands to gain. The contest over the veil is similar: it is an attempt by certain forces to define 'Muslim' or 'Pakistani' or 'Arab' in ways that suit their agenda. One cannot take for granted that the 'veil' is a symbol of Muslim, Pakistani or Arab identity—because, of course, Muslim, Pakistani and Arab identities are much more varied and internally critical, contain many other elements and continue to change with time and place.

Why, then, do so many second-generation Danes seem to be returning to the veil? Firstly, this question is itself incorrect: many second-generation Danes do *not* wear the veil. However, *some* do—and a few of these are, surprisingly, daughters of women who never wore the veil.

To say that the reason is the relative success of Islamic propaganda is to utter an oxymoron. One wonders, why such propaganda succeeds in a country like Denmark where it can hardly make itself heard? But 'Islamic propaganda' is not the answer, and 'male-dominated family structures' is only partly and indirectly an answer. Both these answers, moreover, posit veiled second-generation women as empty vessels incapable of thinking on their own. This not only reduces these women to much less than what they are, it is even opposed by its own logic. If these women were so impressionable, why didn't they adopt so-called 'Danish values' with which they are bombarded (via media, job and education) more often than with 'foreign/Islamic values'? Neither does male dominance explain it all, for a number of these women are independent working women and most of them are capable of turning the argument upside down. One such woman recently claimed in an interview that the veil was a defiance of the male gaze and, as such, an emancipating *feminist* practice. Of course, this claim is faulty—defiance that imposes limits on *yourself* is more compulsion than resistance. But such an articulate claim highlights the fact that one cannot dismiss these women as brain-dead automatons.

As said earlier, one has to examine the material siting as well as the symbolic stances of the women who have gone back to the veil or refused to discard it in spite of a lifetime in Denmark. We have seen that these are often immigrant women who see the veil as either a mark of identity or a gesture of cultural protest. We have also explained how such a *gesture* is justified, but the *veil* is not. The veil marks a hegemonic discourse from persons and forces that actually wish to appropriate long, living and complex cultural traditions by reducing them to a few tractable and fixed elements. They mark the impoverishment of these rich and fertile traditions. These persons and forces are actually *helped* by dominant Western (and Danish) discourses about, say, Islam or the East. As Asian and African peoples are already presented as greatly impoverished in European discourse—not impoverished materially (which is often a fact) but impoverished culturally and historically—children of 'third world' immigrants growing up in the 'West' have very few symbols to relate to. A second-generation Muslim Dane grows up with the image of 'the Muslim world' as, say, 'veiled women' or the reactionary Taliban—and not as the many *positive* historical and contemporary examples. In such a situation, reacting to mainstream Danish assumptions and faced with her own 'impoverishment', a second-generation Muslim Dane often has no option but to clutch at straws. The veil is the one obvious straw that—thanks to Western discourses *and* Islamic fundamentalism—is always within reach.

Of course, the matter is much more complex: such impoverishment has roots that go into the arid soil of colonization and neo-colonization as well as the muddy, shifting waters of capitalism. But in its basic shape it enables us to understand how the spectre of the veil is no airy apparition. One can leave it at this, but for the fact that one has not explicitly answered those fundamentalists who project 'veils' as a mark of identity. They are, as the discerning reader would have guessed, indulging in another round of essentialising. The 'veil' has a certain social and material existence: it came about in certain classes in cultures, times and places where it served certain material and symbolic purposes. We have already seen that a woman who has grown up wearing a veil in, say, middle class, small-town Egypt cannot be expected to discard it on emigrating to Denmark. That would be the equivalent of stripping her naked in public. The veil, of course, no longer serves any material purpose in Denmark, but it still serves such a vital symbolic need for that particular woman that we cannot strip her of it.

But when the daughter of a woman who never wore a veil puts it on in Denmark, she has fallen prey to the reification and fetishization of identities. Though one can and should support her *gesture*, one can and should also point out that the *symbol* she has chosen is limiting and impoverishing. And that she is essentialising her identity in a way that is similar to those Danes who do *not* want *her* in Denmark because she does not fit *their* essentialist notion of Denmark. Cultural symbols cannot be fixed in time; they are always in the process of being actively constituted. One has to point out that the veil no longer fulfils a material need in Denmark and that a second-generation Dane can choose many other symbols from her living cultural heritage that fulfil her symbolic needs just as much without limiting her as a person or a woman. But one can point that out only if other cultural symbols are as *visible* in Denmark as the veil is, only if other cultures are not so grossly appropriated and impoverished in European discourse as they have been until now.

Other Terms of Definition

There is, of course, the 'Islamic' aspect to the veil. Islamic fundamentalists claim that the veil is central to Islam. But is it? While I do not feel that reference to the past —even to 'holy books'—is enough to justify something in the present, I will for once refer to the past and to holy books. Fatima Mernissi has illustrated the historical character of the veil in her book, *Women and Islam: An Historical and Theological Enquiry*. She has also noted that, even theologically, the veil can be seen as imposing a limit on male vision and as dividing private and public spaces rather than imposing restrictions on women.

According to the concerned Hadith (traditions associated with Prophet Mohammad) as well as major commentaries on it by al-Bukhari and al-Tabari, the veil was "a division of the space into two areas, isolating each of two men present, the Prophet on the one hand and Anas, the witness [to the Hadith] who describes the event, on the other." According to the Hadith concerned, the veil (*hijaab*) was pulled down by Mohammad to separate the private space of his married life from the public space occupied by other men: it fell between two men. It was only later—and through a historical and social process—that the veil became primarily an instrument of male dominance in many Muslim societies and was imposed on women. In this context, it also marked the continuation of pre-Islamic traditions. However, it is always pertinent to recall in this context that the veil (in different forms) was also an instrument of male dominance in many Christian societies until recently.

Is it, then, possible to talk of these differences in other terms than the ones currently employed in the Danish debate and also by Islamists?

For the rest of this essay, I will not talk of what Muslims are or are not, in the Danish context or outside it. Neither will I quote the Quran to highlight the multiplicity and past/potential progressiveness of Islam. I will not dwell on, for example, the fact that the rise of Islamic fundamentalism has much to do with the systematic persecution of Marxists and radical Socialists in Muslim countries, very often with the direct support of the 'West'. I will not focus on the contradiction that while Muslim history teems with tens of thousands of differing exegeses of the Quran, the leaders of Islamic 'fundamentalism'—people who claim authority on the basis of that holy book—have hardly written any such work of exegesis. There are only two such exegeses by Islamists in the 20th century, as against approximately 3,000 until the 19th century: by al-Maududi (d. 1979) and Sayyid Qutb (d. 1966).

I will not even try to strain myself defending the 'spirit of Islam' against the frequent charge of misogyny by placing the relevant Hadiths and Quranic verses in historical context, a task performed admirably by Fatima Mernissi in *Women and Islam: An Historical and Theological Enquiry*. Neither will I examine the ahistorical idea of a clash of civilizations as used in the media—at best a case of the boy who cried wolf—or examine the extent of the so-called Islamic threat. The latter examination has been performed with much intellectual honesty by John L Esposito in *The Islamic Threat*.

What I am interested in is a contemporary formulation that might enable us to understand the 'problem of the veil' in a broader context, a context that does not get pegged down by hegemonic or essentialist definitions of Islam, Christianity, Hinduism, European, Arab, civilization or culture, etc. Once again, the 'problem of the veil' is used simply as a concrete example—a touchstone for conceptualization—instead of beating about the vague and varied bush of Islam. Let us begin, then, by reformulating the 'problem' within the context of the one sweeping reality of our world: capitalism.

A Body of Abstract Capital

Capital is abstract. It does not exist simply as money, cowries, cash, coin or cheques. Capital comes into being as a social relation. One can, of course, trace this abstracting nature of capital throughout the past few centuries until one reaches the high capitalism of our times when world trade is valued at a mere US$ 2 billion while international capital movements are estimated at US$ 50 billion! In the poorer countries, including much of East Europe now, this abstract nature of capital is best symbolized by their outstanding debts, which grew from US$ 900 billion in 1982 to US$ 1,500 trillion in the 1990s, of which half was expended on *interest.*

This abstract nature of capital imposes an abstract structure of power. The structure of power in capitalist societies is based on capital: it depends on the control of abstract capital and not directly on the control of the human body. The human body is, of course, controlled in the final run, for all power over human beings needs to be inscribed on the body finally. But this control is exercised abstractly: for example, through wages. Or through the concept of 'nationality', which enables the capitalists of rich nations (like Denmark) to exploit the labour of poor nations while maintaining the unequal mobility ratio between (global) capital and (world) labour.

Having said that, let us return and look again at the countries most Muslim immigrants to Denmark come from. The capitalist mode of production is un(der)developed in these countries. These countries (with the partial exception of a country like Malaysia, which has been held up as such a good 'Muslim' example during the Afghanistan war) also have a very small bourgeoisie in general.

This lack of developed capitalist modes of production has 'local', 'national' and 'global' reasons, of which the most important might well be the nature of capitalism itself. As Samir Amin notes in *Capitalism in the Age of Globalisation*, favourable conditions, like the massive accumulation of capital permitted by colonization as well as Europe's ability to get rid of its surplus population in a crucial period, have not been available to the rest of the world. In the present too, as Amin notes, "most of [the immense amounts of floating capital in the world] seeks investment by roaming from one financial metropolis to another, only rarely paying a visit to third world financial systems."

The lack of capitalist modes of production in Muslim countries is not just a consequence of the failure of the local elite: it has much to do with the position of Asia, Africa and South America in the evolution of capitalism. These countries—with the exception of some colonial powers, like Japan—have not had the opportunities to accumulate wealth and export surplus population enjoyed by capitalist European powers and settler countries during the colonial period. It is doubtful that European capitalism would have thrived without at least these two advantages. However, lack of success has deprived Asian and African bourgeoisie of both size and the wealth, to impose the sort of hegemony on other classes in the nation that one sees in developed capitalist nations.

Hence, we have in these Muslim countries a ruling elite that seeks and often obtains all the benefits of global capitalism. On the other hand, the modes of capitalist production remain un- or under-developed within the nation. What actually exists in these countries has many similarities with various pre-capitalist modes of production—though it is not simply pre-capitalist, for capitalism does effect ground realities in various ways. As such, the tendency—in Denmark, for example—to see Islamic fundamentalism or even the Taliban in terms of the past is incorrect. These movements are very much of the present, though they derive their legitimacy partly from a peculiar version of the past.

This version of the past is created in the present as a consequence of the position of these societies in the capitalist world. Let us repeat the two conditions obtaining in these nation-states: (i) the vast majority form a reserve of labour and live under un(der) developed modes of capitalist production and (ii) the (small) bourgeoisie or elite enjoys many of the privileges of capitalism but does not have the success to either impose its hegemony on other national classes or to compete with the international bourgeoisie.

This lack of success not only leaves the bourgeoisie unable to oppose or divert conservative/reactionary forces, it is actually forced to reformulate the conservative/reactionary appeal to the 'past' as its final justification. Not being successful in capitalist terms forces these national bourgeoisie to function economically only in collaboration with the international bourgeoisie—thus, abandoning its other role of a limited competition with other national (and international) bourgeoisie. This further weakens its legitimacy and the bourgeoisie is forced to seek in the symbolic realm what it cannot reasonably claim in the material sphere: its 'national' legitimacy. Here we have to note that the national bourgeoisie (by definition under capitalist conditions) needs to exist simultaneously with the nation-state. It is in the name of the nation-state, that the bourgeoisie—successfully in the first world and unsuccessfully in the third world—has been able to exercise hegemony over the other classes.

It is in this context that the national bourgeoisie in Muslim countries takes up a particular version of 'Islam.'[4] This evocation of 'Islam' enables the elite or the bourgeoisie to profit from its complicity in global capitalism while keeping the people alienated from the partly-democratic tendencies of capitalism (fetishized into the 'West') and singularly unable to comprehend the real structures of their oppression.

Here, however, I should warn against the vulgar Marxist tendency of blaming exploitation simply on the 'exploitative nature' of an evil elite. The bourgeoisie or the elite in Muslim (and third world) countries is forced by the very logic of global capitalism—including capitalism's imbrication with the nation state—to seek to establish its hegemony over the other classes by means of the only thing it can press into service: the evocation of a past ('Islam') that, in its pre-capitalist tendencies, might serve as an (ineffective) critique of capitalism (or, more exactly, the capitalist 'West'). Had the Muslim or third world bourgeoisie been successful in capitalist terms (something precluded by the very mechanism of historical capitalism), this would not have been necessary to the same extent. And had revolutionary critiques—such as radical socialism or Marxism—been allowed to flourish in these countries, there might have been other alternatives to this recourse to an Islam defined by and 'refined' into its most body-impacted, pre-capitalist elements.

---

[4] This also happens in other nations that have not shared in capitalist success, such as, to a lesser extent, the Hindu bourgeoisie in relatively more successful India, the Buddhist elite/bourgeoisie in Sri Lanka and the Christian bourgeoisie in parts of Latin America and Africa.

The point to note, however, is that the 'past' that comes into being due to the nexus of these interests and forces has been created very much in the present. This is underlined by the technical and vocational education of many supporters of Islamic (and Hindu) fundamentalism, the highly political character of much of Islamic (and Hindu) fundamentalism as well as the fact that Islamists are not really interested in writing exegeses of the Quran.

It is in this context that Islam is constructed in these countries—sometimes even changed in the name of being 'restored'—on largely pre-capitalist symbolic lines. This effects the symbolic logic of power in such societies—for if power cannot be exercised abstractly through capital, it has to be exercised directly on the body of the agent. Earlier on, I had noted that power operates through abstract capital under capitalism. But, if one does not have capital—as in pre-capitalist societies —power would need to be more directly inscribed on the human body. Power will not be enacted abstractly (say, in the shape of wages, fashions etc.); it will be enacted directly on the body (say, in the shape of patronage, serfdom, prohibitions, etc).

It is revealing that in their evocation of Islam, conservative forces as well as the national bourgeoisie in many societies choose particularly those 'traditions' which most visibly inscribe power directly on the human body: the veil being just one of them. I am not saying that this happens because these societies are pre-capitalist. While they have un(der)developed modes of capitalist production, they are touched and even at times penetrated by the global structures of capitalism. This happens because the structures of power 'selected' in these countries have to be at least *outwardly in opposition* to the structures of power that operate under capitalism. Hence, the fact that even pre-capitalist societies did have *other* limited enactments of power—particularly so in high mercantile Muslim regions—is conveniently obscured. The 'traditions' chosen are often not those that are similar to capitalist ('Western') tradition; they are those that appear most visibly opposed. Whipping or stoning is visibly opposed to a three months sentence; hanging is graphically opposed to a life sentence.

Islamic fundamentalist parties are a spin off from this game, a game that (it must be stressed) *mostly* suits dominant business and political interests in the 'West' most of the time. Even when they end up challenging the legitimacy of the government of a Muslim country, fundamentalist parties do not really upset the capitalist apple cart. Reacting to the abstract structures of power under capitalism, the leaders of these fundamentalist parties try to restore what they consider Islamic: obviously, stressing the structures of power that impact directly on the body under pre- or quasi-capitalist conditions. The problem with this opposition remains the same: it is unable to fight the real structures of power under global capitalism. It can only indulge in pointless violence, like the bombing of the WTO building in New York.

But the story is not one-sided. It does not simply involve an ideological failure on the part of Muslim elites. While the fully capitalist 'West' and many members of the bourgeoisie elsewhere (including Muslims, at times) often perceive the bodily structures of power which are made to dominate traditional Islam with great repugnance, they also fail to address their own abstract structures of power.

It is here that we can return to the veil finally and examine the entire problem in a different and more complex light.

I continue to be surprised by the vehemence of the Danish opposition to the veil and even the *dupatta* when contrasted to the increasing lack of opposition in Denmark to consumerist definitions of female (and, increasingly, male) identity, the common display of women as sex objects on TV, etc. As such, it is sad but not surprising that women who wear the veil turn a blind eye to the enactment of male power coded into the act of donning that piece of dress while pointing out, quite correctly, the enactment of male fantasy and power in various advertisements of half/naked women in Denmark. In both cases, it must be added, dress—or lack of it—is not the issue; the issue is the complex of discourses inducing one to opt for a particular option and only that option. And in that regard, more than one veil has to be raised.

THIRTY

Why Muslims Cannot be Modern

> "...what is masked here, by modernists and anti-modernists alike, is the fact that these spiritual and cultural movements, for all their eruptive power, have been bubbles on the surface of a social and economic cauldron that has been teeming and boiling for more than a hundred years. It is modern capitalism, not modern art and culture, that has set and kept the pot boiling—reluctant as capitalism may be to face the heat."[1]

Writing about the crusades, the Arab historian Amin Malouf notes that the Frankish incursions marked a closing down of the Arabo-Muslim world.[2] "Henceforth," he states, "progress was the embodiment of 'the other'. Modernism became alien. Should cultural and religious identity be affirmed by rejecting this modernism, which the West symbolized [now]? Or...should the road of modernization be embarked upon with resolution, thus risking loss of identity?... Even today we can observe a lurching alternation between phases of forced Westernization and phases of extremist, strongly xenophobic traditionalism." (Amin Malouf, p 264–5)

Writing about very different times (the late 18th, 19th and early 20th centuries) and from a different space, Hindi writer Nirmal Verma notes that "European colonization cast a shadow, right at the center

---

1 Marshall Berman, *All That Is Solid Melts Into Air: The Experience of Modernity*, p 123.

2 First published in *Third Text*, UK. Slightly revised.

of Indian consciousness.[3] Tradition, which was a way of life, was externalized as something belonging to the past; Europe, which was an external factor, was internalized as the iron in the soul." (Nirmal Verma, p 42)

Both Malouf and Verma are actually writing about the same equation, though their perspectives differ slightly. But before we go on to examine the problem—and that is what this essay sets out to do—it is best to start from a third, a more personal, vantage point.

***

In the on-going process of editing an anthology of travel writing and while teaching a course on 'Orientalism', I had the occasion to read or re-read a number of 20th century accounts by European travellers writing about Asia, Africa and (in one case) South America. These ranged from travel classics like those by Wilfred Thesiger and Robert Byron to contemporary publications in English and Danish. What struck me was the common focus that all the writers (with the partial exception of Thesiger) put on the discrepancies that they observed in Asia, Africa and South America. These were not always termed 'discrepancies'—and were sometimes celebrated in the light of an implicit Eurocentricity or, what is more common today, of 'multiculturalism' and hybridity. However, the world these authors described was a 'discrepant' one: a world of fragments. This perceived fragmentation of the non-European world *increased* progressively as the traveller moved from rural areas to urban ones. Remarks and descriptions, ironic or

---

[3] Nirmal Verma passed away in the years between the first publication of this essay and its inclusion in this book. His lack will be felt not only in the realm of Hindi literature but also that of world literatures.

appreciative, about the abrupt juxtaposition of the 'modern' and the 'traditional', the 'European/American' and the 'native' grew in volume with the proximity of the narrative to an urban center. It started to appear, at times, that the non-European world was in some ways *more fragmentary* than the European one. The fragments of modern existence, to twist T S Eliot's line from "What the Thunder Said" (*The Wasteland*), appeared to have been shored up more in the 'traditional' or 'backward' non-West than the 'modern' and 'progressive' West. This essay attempts to put together the fragments of this perception into a larger mosaic that, inevitably, bears upon the twinned issues of modernism and modernity in the contemporary world of nation-states and 'globalism'.

Modernity and modernism, we have often been told, are two different things. However, in at least one sense, modernism and modernity refer to the same thing: pan-Europe and the Eurocentric world whose current navel is USA. This is a connection that is not lost even on those people from Asia, Africa and South America who have little to do with any intellectual 'ism' and prefer a greasy fat cheque to a clean political manifesto. Both modernism and modernity meet in what the non-West is most often encouraged to achieve by the West: modernisation. It is also what the non-West is always on the verge of achieving: modernisation is the Holy Grail of the third world.

It is this connection that explains why, in the middle of an argument, a senior member of my family—one of those usually quiet professionals who 'return' to religion in their middle age—dismissed the entire 'project of modernity'. In the process, he also dismissed most of science and, in spite of being an engineer himself, much of technology and planning. He was not a widely read person. He had merely repeated sentiments which run through many contemporary fields of the humanities—not least post-modernism and post-colonialism—and are so well integrated into general discourse that they can be imbibed through newspapers, radio broadcasts and TV shows. These sentiments are also replicated—implicitly or explicitly—in much of contemporary fiction and poetry, though the best writers (Amitav Ghosh in *The Calcutta Chromosome*, Albert Wendt in *I Will be our Saviour from the Bad Smell*, Angela Carter in *Nights at the Circus*, etc.) manage to seriously complicate the dualities on which they are based.

But, in spite of a few blows struck in favour of a more complex understanding of the world, a generalized dismissal of the 'project of modernity' is more typical of current discourses in fashionable and thinking circles. My relative's dismissal reminded me of a person, from a North Indian Muslim background like him, who lived at a time when modernity had not been so rigidly defined as to be dismissed en masse.

In 1797, Mirza Abu Taleb, a minor aristocrat,[4] embarked on a journey to England, travelling (on the way there and back) over much of continental Europe, Turkey, Persia and parts of Africa. When he set off, he spoke Persian, other Indian languages and Arabic; he learnt English on the outward voyage. When he came back, he wrote down an account of his travels. There are various remarkable things about Abu Taleb's travel account—things that, as I have pointed out in a paper due to appear in *Wasafiri*, complicate some of the readings of literary studies, colonial historiography and postcolonialism. But

---

[4] Though he was popularly billed, as he remarks with a tinge of humour, 'the Persian Prince' in London and evidently returned with 'Londoni' (One who has been to London) tagged on to his name.

here we are interested in only Abu Taleb's attitude to the new and the modern. Nowhere in the book does Abu Taleb associate modernity solely or essentially with Europe. While he is highly appreciative of European technical progress, even when it comes to European scientific observations, he measures them against his own scientific knowledge and traditions. He recognizes the greatness of European cities, but seldom loses the critical perspective of someone who feels that he has the equipment to understand even what is new and different. Finally, his account is not written as a Europe-facing defence of his people and culture in India. His main reason for writing the book is of great interest to us. Abu Taleb writes that he "was of the opinion that many of the customs, inventions, sciences, and ordinances of Europe, *the good effects of which are apparent in those countries*, might with great advantage be imitated [in the East]." (Abu Taleb Khan, p xv).

Not having attributed all of modernity, science, etc., to Europe, Abu Taleb can ask for a selective adoption on the twin assumption that this adoption is not 'ontologically foreign' to cultures in the East and that such adoption can be justified on the basis of *concrete evidences of success*. This is very different from a dismissal of 'the project' of modernity or science. In spite of the 19th century essentialisms that often afflict his discourse, there is no absolute tension between modernity and tradition, science and religion, rationality and belief in the account of Abu Taleb. He mostly does not even situate them on the East-West axis—they are both part of his own heritage and background, though he remains acutely aware of European developments and differences. This is not surprising, for rationality and belief, science and religion remain emblematic descriptions of tendencies to be found in many non-European traditions, as Sudhir Kakar notes with reference to the traditional healing practices of India.

On the other hand, an unavoidable tension runs through the narrative of Marshall Berman's book, *All That Is Solid Melts Into Air: The Experience of Modernity*. This tension has little to do with Berman's erudite and thoughtful readings in the book and much to do with the very term that enables the narrative: modernism. The problems of employing this term are fore-grounded in a sheer quantitative way when, on page 16, Berman states that people have been going through the experience of modernity for 'close to five hundred years' and, on page 35, he goes on to claim that our modern roots 'go back two hundred years'. Why this difference of 300 years between two accounts of being modern in the same chapter by the same author?

In order to understand this difference, one has to realize that Berman—in spite of providing a sympathetic reading of Karl Marx—is operating from a perspective that is not a fully dialectical materialist one. This perspective should not be blamed on Berman: it is coded into the very discourse of modernism and modernity.

Modernism *and* modernity? Haven't we been told again and again, and on good grounds, that modernity is not the same as modernism? And yet in a crucial way, as noted earlier, modernity and modernism refer to the same thing in most accounts: pan-Europe and the Euro-centric world whose current navel is USA. As Geeta Kapur puts it in her excellent collection of essays, "Imposed on the colonized world via selective modernization, modernism transmits a specifically bourgeois ideology." (Kapur, p 276) The word to be stressed here is not just 'bourgeois' but also 'specifically': not any bourgeoisie, but a *specific* bourgeoisie. Given this, to my mind, greater complication, I am not concerned with pedantically extricating the strands of modernity from those of modernism.

My point of departure in this essay is to question whether one can talk of something called 'modernism'[5] or 'modernity' at all in the discursive terms currently employed. It is my contention that one needs to address capitalism first—especially in its industrial forms—before moving on to whatever modernism and modernity may or may not be. Berman is, of course, very conscious of capitalism. At times, as in the extract quoted at the head of this essay, Berman's awareness of capitalism as one of the defining forces enables him to avoid some of the pitfalls of purely idealist definitions of modernism or modernity. However, much of the time, Berman subsumes capitalism and industrialisation to modernism—thus, so to say, inverting the sequence of events and rendering his erudite reading of modernity problematic.

The problems are evident in the very first line of the introduction: "There is a mode of vital experience—experience of space and time, of the self and others, of life's possibilities and perils—that is shared by men and women all over the world today. I will call this body of experience modernity." (Berman, p 15) Shared by men and women all over the world today? To what extent do the aborigines living in Chhotanagpur share the experiences of a Wall Street businessman? Or, for that matter, to what extent did servants in my grandparents' house at Gaya share the experiences of my parents in the same town—not to mention my own experiences in Gaya, Patna, Delhi and Copenhagen? Sharing an experience, in the above sense, is *very*

---

[5] I have avoided a discussion of 'modernism' as an art movement, simply because I am neither an artist nor an art theorist. But for a discussion of the art of modernism which substantiates my general reading here, the reader may refer to the artist and theorist Rasheed Araeen's "A New Beginning", *Third Text*, 50, London, Spring 2000.

different from being profitably or exploitatively *effected* by the global structures of capitalism.

Sharing, of course, is a revealing word, just as revealing as words positing essential dichotomies and dualities. Both these groups of words derive their logic from an idealist/symbolic perception of the world. In the material world, however, sharing is always accompanied by conflict. There is no 'clash of civilizations', but there is no simple sharing either: there are clashes (and convergence) of interest, inequalities of wealth, conflicts of gender, 'race', 'nationality' and class. Experiences are shared in an unequal world only to the extent to which they are contested. For example, while both the capitalist and the proletariat might 'share' the experience of industrial capitalism, they do not share it in the same way. It is this realization that is ignored if we allot priority to a symbolic/idealist 'modernism' over a materialist 'capitalism' in our bid to address and understand our world.

Moreover, even at the symbolic level, experiences are subjective things: one can occupy the same space and time without really sharing the same experiences. What one can share are the material conditions that enable certain experiences and make certain other experiences impossible or unlikely. This again returns us to the primacy of dialectical materialist explanations, such as those based on the role and nature of capitalism.

Berman is aware of the sheer physicality of much of what we call modernity. As he writes:

> "The maelstrom of modern life has been fed from many sources: great discoveries in the physical sciences, changing our images of the universe and our place in it; the industrialization of production, which transforms scientific knowledge into technology, creates new human environments and destroys old ones, speeds up the whole tempo of life, generates new forms of corporate power and class struggle, immense demographic upheavals...; rapid and often cataclysmic urbam growth; systems of mass communication...; mass social movements of people, and peoples, challenging their political

> and economic rulers, striving to gain some control over their lives; finally, bearing and driving all these people and institutions along, an ever-expanding, drastically fluctuating capitalist world market." (p 16)

The problem is not his lack of awareness of capitalism, but his relative lack of awareness of *current definitions* of 'modernity' as a by-product of capitalism and *dominant versions* of 'modernism' as a capitalist-bourgeois 'sales gimmick'. By taking 'modernity' and 'modernism' as his starting point, Berman fails to explore how and why the 'modern' got to be constituted as it has been. The problem is similar to the one Marx associated with religion: that an 'explanation' purely at the symbolic level cannot help us get to grips with the material realities of our world. Modernism is often constructed in purely symbolic terms: it is almost a state of mind, at best a collocation of texts, styles and ideas. It can be only understood if we address the material changes that made the symbolic superstructure of 'modernism' not only possible but almost inevitable in certain parts of the world—and how this particular modernism has colonized our notions of the modern. My concern is not that much the proscription of participation[6] but

6 Paul Gilroy, for example, has exposed the whitewashing of Black and coloured stories in the writing of the history of 'Atlantic modernity' in *The Black Atlantic: Modernity and Double Consciousness*. Noting factors like the neglect of Black slaves and their descendants in the radical history and working class politics of the North Atlantic, Gilroy states that "modernity might itself be thought to begin in the constitutive relationships with outsiders that both found and temper a self-conscious sense of Western civilization." (p 17) However, Gilroy is still concerned with modernity in the North Atlantic, while my scope is the world of capital, based as it is on a history of colonization, in general. However, the occlusion of radical Coloured agency in dominant accounts of modernity—as read by Gilroy or by Winston James in *Holding Aloft the Banner of Ethiopia: Caribbean Radicalism in Early Twentieth-Century America*—provides the other side of the coin being examined here.

more the prescription of definitions implicit in most constructions of modernity and modernism.

The constitution of the world into an *integrated* market, a process that started sometime in the 16th or 17th century but was significantly achieved only in the 18th, is central to an understanding of not only capitalism (as Ellen Meiksins Wood has argued in *The Origin of Capitalism*) but also to an understanding of modernism and modernity. Modernism/modernity—as it came to be constituted in the late 19th and 20th centuries—was partly or wholly a monopolistic consolidation of the material changes brought about by (European) capitalism and industrialization. It ensured that all non-European attempts to harness the forces of production unleashed by capitalism and industrialization had to be *necessarily* mediated through European channels. Abu Taleb's touchstone of 'good effects' was replaced by an implicit or explicit myth of 'good (European) forms'—the 'referent' was already being dumped in favour of the 'sign'. As Malouf puts it, 'modernism became alien' (cited earlier). The very ease with which Malouf's discourse slips in the course of two lines from 'modernism' to 'Westernization' illustrates the crux of the problem and the depth of the equation.

Verma makes a similar point when he states that "tradition, which was a way of life, was externalized as something belonging to the past; Europe, which was an external factor, was internalized as the iron in the soul." (p 42) Here, Verma is on to an important and often obscured fact, but such is the power of Eurocentric discourses that he falls into the very trap that he has set out to spring. For the opposition is not really between 'tradition' and 'Europe'. It is between 'tradition' and 'modernity', in the sense that modernity was removed from the cultural and historical space of countries like India in the course of colonization. Europe could move naturally from 'tradition' to 'modernity' within its own intellectual heritage, but India, Egypt, China could only be 'modernized' on European models. This introduced a synchronic and diachronic rift between 'tradition' and 'modernity' that 'post-colonial' countries have yet to bridge. This rift explains the 'lurching' from Eurocentric modernization to reactionary traditionalism that Malouf notes in the Arab countries and that we can notice in all ex-colonized states. The problem is reflected also in the arts, where third world or post-colonial artists are likely to achieve international visibility largely in terms of 'tradition'. The problem, noted by Rasheed Araeen, of the occlusion of modernist art from post-colonial countries in favour of 'traditional' art (aboriginal, folk, etc.) arises because of this nexus. As does the fact that contemporary art from post-colonial countries is seen in terms of tradition rather than modernity, though even many new 'aboriginal' styles and genres are modern recoveries and elaborations. To simplify: Picasso can adopt aboriginal elements and create *modernist art*, but an aboriginal artist incorporating, say, European techniques, themes or material in his work would nevertheless continue to create 'authentic', 'traditional' or 'aboriginal' art.

The flip side of the coin is best illustrated by quoting Araeen on an exhibition of African culture in the West: "The word 'authentic' was emphasized, on the basis that the modernism of the third world artists was *derivative*, which raised many disturbing questions. Not because one wants to deny the influence of the European art movements on the work of so-called third world artists, but the assumption that this influence had only produced derivative works was based on the assumption that the third world *could have not produced* original modernist works of art." (Araeen, p 13) Once again, the patented fragments of modernity not only prevent the non-West from becoming anything other than 'traditional', they dismiss the elements of modernity from the non-West as merely derivative. This is exactly the situation etched in political and historical terms in the quotation by Malouf at the beginning of this essay.

*****

As is obvious, whatever the original revolutionary possibilities of the 'modernization' ushered in by the dissolution of feudal and tribal hierarchies in Europe and elsewhere and the release of new productive forces, the term 'modernism' and the term 'modernity' became indexes of European hegemony. This association of the modern with 'Europe' started well in the 19th century though it was fetishized in the term 'modernism' only with the turn of the century. It is this movement that explains why, as Immanuel Wallerstein puts it, "...the extra-European world represented 'tradition': the pan-European world represented modernity..." (Wallerstein, p 14). It is a dichotomy that has been maintained in our times, and sometimes even by writers, such as Salman Rushdie and VS Naipaul, who partly hail from the 'extra-European' world.

Wallerstein points out another contemporary example: "No one who has read the press in Western Europe can have missed the degree to which the coverage of the post-communist world has focused on the absence [in the post-communist world] of the higher level of modernity found in the pan-European world." (p 11) The media implication is that these post-communist countries should learn the high modernity of rich Europe—a pedagogic process that, no doubt, would include not only the transfer of ideas but also of second-hand expertise and exploitative industry. In short, this is good business for the capitalists and bourgeoisie of the rich countries of North

Atlantic[7]—but it is only good business if one has a monopoly on the goods to be offered. The 'fragments' on offer have to be patented. It is this monopoly that is packed into the very definitions of 'modernity' and 'modernism'. The case has not been different historically either. To quote Immanuel Wallerstein again, in the past:

> "Analysis of the extra-European world was consigned to separate disciplines: anthropology for the barbaric 'peoples without history' and Oriental studies for the non-Western 'high civilizations' that were, however, *incapable of proceeding to modernity without European intrusion and reorganization of their social dynamics.*" (Wallerstein, p 14) (My stress)

Arguments similar to the one succinctly paraphrased by Wallerstein above continue to hold European and American thought in thrall—not to mention the thoughts of many 'thinkers' and politicians in the third world. The extent of this discourse becomes visible when one reads an ostensible Marxist like Bill Warren coming up with a defence of imperialism as a beneficial force and a force of development and progress in the non-European world.[8] Warren is forced into this defence because he, like most Europeans and many non-Europeans, can only imagine the 'modern' in European shapes.[9] The power of the

---

[7] To employ Richard Rorty's convenient term for Europe (North and West, in my account) and North America.

[8] Bill Warren, *Imperialism: Pioneer of Capitalism*, New Left Books, London, 1980. For a rebuttal of Warren's arguments, see Aijaz Ahmad's essay 'Imperialism and Progress' in Ahmad's *Lineages of the Present: Political Essays*, Tulika, Delhi, 1996.

[9] What I am stating here is not the common post-colonial argument against any kind of modernity. The fact that modernity does not necessarily have European forms does not imply that there is no difference between a modern perspective or structure and its reactionary or traditional 'alternative'. Moreover, the 'modern' can have—but need not have—non-European forms. Similarly, all that is 'non-European' need not be celebrated against its 'modern' European alternatives simply because it is 'native' or 'natural' or something else. What is most necessary is to consider the relations that constitute something as modern—relations promoting greater human agency in general—rather than perpetuate the common attempt to construct European or non-European fetishes or to dismiss the "entire project of modernity."

discourse—and its obvious symbolic and material advantages—also becomes evident when one thinks of the bid of Jawaharlal Nehru, a liberal-socialist, to build a modern Indian city. It was a bid that could come to fruition for Nehru only through the mediation of the French modernist, Le Corbusier. The result, Chandigarh, is only one example of the Eurocentric hegemony that modernism has exercised on the possibilities of various non-European peoples to become truly modern. All Asian and African towns and cities are full of such examples. As are the palaces and flats of Asian and African politicians whose assemblage of 'Made-in-Europe/USA' artifacts—cars, furniture, paintings, clothes, etc.—occlude their role in repressing the freedom of thought and action that was and is the revolutionary idea behind the fetish of European modernism and modernity. As, for that matter, was the first consciously 'modernist' city built on the margins of the West—Petersburg, whose construction "was planned, designed and organised entirely by foreign architects and engineers, imported from England, France, Holland and Italy." (Berman, p 177)

When it comes to architectural matters, perhaps the most revealing continuity of the fetishized prestige of 'modernity' and 'modernism' can be traced back from the Capitolio in Havana (Cuba). Built during the government of Gerardo Machado (1925–1933), the first (American-supported) Cuban dictator, the Havana Capitolio was modelled on the Capitol in Washington. But the idea of the American Capitol itself came from Europe—assuming prestige from an invocation of ancient Rome while at the same time standing for the 'modernity' of America and Europe. This movement of the 'blueprint' of the Capitol—from Europe to the USA in the centuries of European hegemony of 'modernity' and from USA to the 'third world' in the century of the American take over is revealing and significant. It is just as significant that Fidel Castro, in spite of his opposition to the USA and the capitalist regime under which the Havana Capitolio was built, is not above basking in the prestige of 'modernity' and 'progress' bestowed by that copycat building.

As indicated above, 'modernism' and 'modernity' remain the selling edge of the capitalist hegemony of dominant nations and cultures. It is not surprising then that in *Still the Old World*, Philip Fisher comes up with a thesis that associates 'modernity' with the dominant capitalist culture of the age. Fisher claims that American culture is identical with the culture of modernity (Fisher, *Still the New World*). Fisher's argument is not as atrocious as it may sound to non-Americans. He is correct, though largely for all the wrong reasons. Modernism or modernity is and (under capitalism) will always be, by definition, identical with the hegemonic capitalist culture. But it is not modernism or modernity that creates the hegemonic capitalist culture in its own image; it is the capitalist culture that determines what we see and recognize as modernism and modernity.

This, however, is not to make a regressive claim. I do *not* mean to suggest that modern life is inherently indistinguishable from what went before it or that certain freedoms have not been won, at least for some people, during the course of the capitalist and bourgeois ascendancy that has left us with the current myths of modernity or the current forms of modernism. It also does not mean that the 'signs' of current capitalist modernity and modernism: (i) should be either dismissed as having nothing at all to do with the idea of the modern or (ii) should be used to dismiss the fact that we may have certain referents which are sought to be addressed, even at the risk of being appropriated, by these signs.

Neither do I lean over to the latter side of a 'dualism' that Berman rightly criticizes:

> "Our vision of modern life tends to split into material and spiritual planes: some people devote themselves to 'modernism', which they see as a species of pure spirit, evolving in accord with its autonomous artistic and intellectual imperatives; other people work within the orbit of 'modernization', a complex of material structures and processes—political economic, social—which, supposedly, once it has got under way, runs on its own momentum with little or no input from human minds or souls." (Berman, p 131–132)

The point is exactly that 'modernism'—and most definitions of 'modernity'—actually imply a system that "once it has got under way, runs on its own momentum with little or no input from human minds or souls." It is this assumption that explains the endless scramble to catch up with the West—a rigged race that the non-West can *never* win—as well as the copycat monstrosities of 'modernization' that dot much of Asia, Africa and South America. While the material costs of such a definition of 'modernity' are evident enough—and are daily footed by both non-Western governments and individuals—the symbolic costs are perhaps even more frightening. For these costs include not only the predicated inability to evolve locally and culturally sustainable *modernities* but also the inability, noted by Malouf, to become modern without ceasing to be different from the West. In other words, symbolic 'modernism' predicates that the non-West cannot continue to be itself (and the non-West) and still be(come) modern. This is a choice that has not been faced by the West to the same extent, for in the West 'modernity' is a questioning and reworking of traditions, even when it seems to be a case of complete erasure or replacement.[10]

[10] One can see how this situation can lead to claims of 'restoration' and divergence in the non-West.

If, however, one sees modernity as arising out of material and symbolic changes associated with, first, capitalism and then industrialization, one is left with far more scope for different modernities and modernisms. For capitalism and industrialization indicate material *and* symbolic changes—changes in the means and relations of production. These material changes—arising out of the constitution of an integrating market that is necessary for the extraction of 'capital' from (waged) labour—can be seen as taking place in areas with different cultural histories as well as material backgrounds and opportunities.

In other words, the 'modernism and modernity' brought about by capitalism in different parts of the world *need not* have the same shape and colour as the modernisms of Europe or the USA: these non-Western modernisms will be affected and shaped by what is *already* on the ground in these non-European spaces. But neither do they *necessarily* have to be different. It is here that the act of dismissing something simply as 'European' or 'foreign' is revealed (yet again) as deeply illogical as well as problematic and potentially reactionary. The matter can be put in context by quoting Memmi on difference: "Differences can exist or not exist. Differences are not in themselves good or bad."[11] In simpler terms, all peoples should have the right of not only differing (internally and as a group) but also of abandoning those differences which are 'not good' for their agency and their continuity as human beings in a complex social and environmental context. Here, as is obvious, 'good' is not moral, essential or universal (in the idealist sense); it is contextual, as Abu Taleb would have understood in the 18th century. *What was good in one space and time might cease to be good in another. But not necessarily.*

---

[11] Albert Memmi, Racism, Trans. by Steve Martinot, University of Minnesota Press, Minneapolis/London, 2000, p 52.

In short, only a materialist view of modernism and modernity would help us focus on the relations behind the changes rather than their outward forms. What we ought to be worried about are not the signs of differences but their effects. In other words, we may finally have the theoretical equipment to focus less on the model of cars being driven on a third world street and more on the intellectual and physical space available on those streets. Berman is aware of these issues. But his determination to focus on 'modernism' and 'modernity' as the primary terms makes it impossible for him to come up with answers.

*****

Describing the situation in post-Soviet Uzbekistan, Chris Aslan comments that "the Silk Road has become a bizarre blend of traditional, Soviet and Western sexual norms." (Chris Aslan, 'Silk Road Witnesses as Marriage of Moralities', p 21) What he has in mind is the purported increase in the number of polygamies in Uzbekistan, fuelled by the post-Soviet prosperity of a few and running against Soviet policies favouring nuclear families. But the article makes it clear that Aslan associates polygamy, 'bride-stealing', male promiscuousness, etc., with 'tradition' in Uzbekistan. Here he is only echoing a widespread attitude to the persistence of elements from the past in societies of the present, especially when these societies are not Western ones. What actually exists is, however, much more complex.

Here is what a young Uzbek has to say (in Aslan's article) about his 'need' to skip the conjugal bed for an occasional night with prostitutes: "Now I watch *Playboy* and I see what happens in the West. I want to do these things, but I can't do these sinful acts with my wife, so I find a bad girl or a prostitute." Evidently, to this young Uzbek the act of having sex with more than one woman is not a leftover of 'traditional' patriarchal values; it is an intensely modern experience. More than that, it is a modern experience that derives its modern surcharge by being associated with the West. It would, perhaps, not have been experienced as modern if it had not been associated with 'Playboy' and the West.

In other words, not only does Aslan commit the mistake of segregating the Uzbek man's experience of modern life into 'traditional' and 'modern' components (with the latter associated implicitly with the West[12]), the Uzbek himself feels a need to assert his *modernity* by replicating the 'playboy-West'. This is the typical double bind in which the symbolic discourses of 'modernism' and 'modernity'—with their inherent surcharge of Eurocentricity—place the non-Western woman and man.

*****

The role that a similar colonization of the possibilities of being 'modern' has always played in subsequent colonization and neo-imperialism has seldom been examined. But contemporary accounts are full of relevant details. Here, for example, is an account from the late 1960s when the USSR, after decades of extraordinary industrial growth, started lagging significantly behind the fully capitalist world. Revealingly, this lag was based on an attempt to catch up on terms which were 'modern' in those decades, terms condensed into the image and prestige of the 'car' in the extract below.

---

12 Revealingly, Aslan uses 'Soviet' as a buffer term.

> "In the fiftieth year of Bolshevik power the Soviet Union stands on the edge of the automobile age that the United States entered in the 1920s...But this will not be soon enough to cut off the wave of popular grumbling. 'When I see that an ordinary worker in Italy or France has a car,' says a [Soviet] writer just back from one of his frequent trips to Western Europe, 'I wonder what we have been doing in the last 50 years...'"[13]

I do not want to enter the complex and, no doubt, fruitful matter of the automobile and its role in 20th century urban life though an interesting essay on the topic was written by Sweezy (*Monthly Review*, 51) around the same time as the essay from which the above extract has been quoted. What is significant is the association that car has for the Soviet writer quoted above. Now, the automobile has its uses, but it is by no means the best mode of transport: one would imagine that very good public transport facilities and convenient city planning (not to mention other professional and social factors) would be better indications of 'progress' and 'modernity'. One could also give Reagan's Satan its due and concede that, for all its shortcomings, Bolshevik communism did give rise to a state and society with cheap and largely well-organized public transport facilities.

But not so for the Soviet writer, who, significantly, is a frequent visitor to Western Europe. Here the car is a good example of the symbolic colonization of the modern by discourses of capitalist (US-centred) modernism and modernity. What the 'car' replaces is the 'content' of modernity—space and mobility in both the symbolic and material senses—with one particular form (car) in which it has been achieved to some extent in a *few* environments given *certain* conditions.

---

13 Harrison Salibury, "A Balance Sheet of Fifty Years of Soviet Rule", *New York Times*, 2 October 1967, cited in Paul M Sweezy, *Post-Revolutionary Society*, Monthly Review Press, New York and London, 1980, p 24.

In this context, even scholars of the stature of Giddens are completely off the mark when they claim that 'modernity is inherently globalizing'. (Giddens, p 63) Here they have set up a symbolic term, with ill-defined characteristics, and imposed it on the world at the expense of more carefully definable materialist terms, such as capitalism. For it is capitalism that is inherently globalizing (though not in a simplistic way). To call modernity globalizing is to risk the replication of certain forms of modernity. For, the 'car' may be an aspect of 'modernity' that has become global. But the force driving the car is the capitalism of industries, consumerism, ecological alienation and divided urban spaces. In both its good and bad aspects, current 'modernity' is an expression of capitalism—and, as such, can assume similar or different shapes in different contexts.

*****

One can consider the act of being 'modern' as denoting a capacity and achieved ability to live substantially in the present in a way that does not depend for ultimate justification on the past or the future but is highly cognizant of both the past and the future. It is in this sense that 'tradition' (and even current forms of religious fundamentalism) is a modern phenomenon.[14] Whenever modernity is reduced to European

---

[14] Tradition, as Anthony Giddens points out in *The Consequences of Modernity* and as the essays in Eric Hobsbawm and Terence Ranger's *The Invention of Tradition* illustrate, is a purely chirographic and largely modern development. One can argue, against dominant assumptions in postcolonialist circles, that a purely oral society (arbitrarily assuming the existence of one today or in the recent past) would have fewer 'traditions' than New York. This perception reveals the attempt by certain spokespersons of marginalized communities to restore 'traditions' as equivalents of similar hegemonic endeavours elsewhere.

fetishes, not only are alternatives lost but the very act becomes deeply counter-modern. For copying from the (European) past reduces one's capacity to live fully in the present. It is this realization that comes up every time people like my relative implicitly or explicitly dismiss the 'project of modernity'. To this extent the dismissal is understandable. *What makes it problematic and reactionary is the fact that it allows the entire space of what is or can be 'modern' to be colonized by Eurocentric discourses of modernity and modernism.* Moreover, the dismissal is itself based on essentialist and/or symbolic terms: a thing need not be rejected because it is 'European' if it provides the best available tool by which agency can be extended and people enabled to live fully in the present. An oppositionary mind that accepts the European-modern connection has no choice but to reject all that is European—even if this process may leave one with little alternative but to accept what is local *and* reactionary/regressive.[15] Such an attitude usually leads to a complete disregard of the tendencies towards the 'modern' which existed and exist in non-European cultures (as well as the willing and unwilling parts played by non-Europeans in constructing the 'modernity' of Europe and USA).

The above statements, however, require a few words of clarification about the material 'nature' of the modern. I do not mean to recuperate that superfluous debate: are modern institutions capitalist, or are they industrial? While there can be a theoretical agrarian capitalism—and I actually consider it essential for the development of capitalism—and there can obviously be agricultural societies outside capitalism (at

---

[15] Moreover, it is a mind so trapped in essentialist and symbolic paradigms that it fails to consider the material fact of interaction between Europe and non-Europe—and the change of relations that this implies.

least historically), it seems to be mere sophistry (and it is extremely unproductive) to oppose capitalism to 'industrialism'. Capitalism is a system of social relations based on commodity production—and, as such, would be significantly underdeveloped without industrialization and industrialized agriculture.

Industrialism, on the other hand, is supposed to be "the use of inanimate material power in the production of goods, coupled to the central role of machinery in the production process." (Giddens, 56) When put like that, it ought to be possible to envisage industrialization without capitalism—that, actually, has been the effort of many socialist and communist projects. But such a non-capitalist industrialization would be very different from what we understand by industrialism today—because industrialism is not just the use of 'machinery' but of "inanimate material power in the production of goods." What renders this 'material power' inanimate is not the fact that it is outside the human body. Much of what is associated with agriculture is and has always been outside the human body: seeds, hoes, ploughs, soil etc. Moreover, it is not rendered inanimate simply because human beings are not used to operate it—for human beings continue to operate machines and computerized units and will do so in the foreseeable future, though their numbers may decline. What renders material power inanimate in industrialism is the prior presence of capital. Actually, Gidden's anti-Marxist bias determines his very definition of industrialism, which posits a natural 'machinery' and fails to see machinery in terms of accumulated capital. Once capital is revealed as the informing reality of 'industrialism' we can understand why material power is rendered 'inanimate'—because productivity is divorced from human needs, because the act of production is alienated from the process of living, because the machine can come into being as 'inanimate' due to the prior (and occluded) presence of alienated, inanimate capital.

It is in this sense that we have to agree with Marx when he claims that capitalism preceded industrialism and created the conditions for it. It is difficult to imagine industrialism without competitive universal markets and 'freed' workers *forced* to sell their labour—both created by and under capitalism. It is the inevitable restlessness, the constant need of capitalism to expand that sets the agenda for industrialism. It is the capitalist alienation of the worker from her 'species life'[16] that gives machines (also as capital)—and not workers—the central role in industrialism.

Above all, it is capitalism that explains why the money invested in industrialism is not 'money' but capital. Money is primarily a communicative medium and a disembedding device that provides more space for human activities by disembedding the human being from restricted time-space positions. Capital, on the other hand, is a social relation. In other words, money becomes capital when constituted within capitalist conditions of the private ownership of property and the subsistence of the worker on the basis of the imperative sale of her wage labour. It is in these conditions that money—as capital—becomes more 'real' than the worker and the worker gets to be progressively unreal.

Hence, there is little profit in pitting capitalism against industrialism. *But there is good sense in putting the two before modernity*, as we have seen earlier in this essay. It is remarkable that Giddens, for one, fails to do so: attributing both capitalism and industrialism to

---

[16] A complex term. My use of it defined and discussed in my book, *Babu Fictions: Alienation in Contemporary Indian English Novels*.

modernity. What such a definition does is create exactly that fetish of modernity and modernism which ensures that the dominant capitalist and industrial cultures will always be up ahead in the long walk to the never-beginning future, with the rest limping behind perpetually. Instead of addressing the material structures of industrial capitalism, such a vision of the world entangles us in an acceptance or bland rejection of symbolic or culture-specific forms of modernity/modernism. This has three major consequences:

1. It preserves the material status quo, by changing the focus to symbolic elements which are unlikely to effect the real structures of inequality.
2. It makes even this version of modernity/modernism impossible to attain. For it can be attained only in a dialectical relationship with material changes, which are largely obscured or evaded. All the non-West, for example, can do is limp after the mirages of modernity, erecting a superfluous stadium here and a boastful bridge there.
3. It enables a fetishized opposition to 'modernity', 'science', the 'West' etc. This opposition is just as hamstrung as the imitative attempt described above, and for exactly the same reasons.

The claim that modernity has "swept us away from *all* traditional types of social order" (Giddens, p 4) is a partial truth based on a symbolic myth. Its roots in myth become evident when one looks around oneself for the 'modern' and the 'traditional' in Western and non-Western societies—the divide is absolute in the non-West (thus resulting in the 'fragmentation' and 'discrepancies' noted by Western travel writers) while the modern in the West is seen more in terms of organic opposition to (at times even synthesis with) the 'traditional West'. Hence, to take the most obvious examples, the maintenance of state religions, religious taxes, aristocracies and monarchies over much of Western and North Europe—the very things that go and/or are expected to go whenever the non-West attempts any 'modernization' that is credible to the West. Hence, also the restoration of the 'past'—both as customs[17] and as artifacts and monuments—in the West. It is revealing that this project of 'restoration'—which has ranged from folk-fairy tales to 'medieval' castles—has coincided with late enlightenment and 'modernism'. That is, it stretched across the early phases of colonization to the latest period of capitalism.

Thus, Giddens' comment that "inherent in the idea of modernity is a contrast with tradition" (Giddens, p 36) seems to be a bit short of the reflexivity that he associates with modernity. There are contrasts and there are contrasts. In the 'West', modernity is seen as a *response* to tradition. In some liberal-conservative versions, it may even be an alteration or development of tradition. In any case, whatever its level of 'contrast', Western modernity is seen as a response to *Western* tradition. But in the non-West, modernity is seen as disjunct from tradition. Modernity is something that is traced to another space and time—either Europe or the effects of European colonization. The 'fragments' of the 'non-European' present come from the two separate/d spaces of 'tradition' (read: the recent 'native past') and 'modernity' (read: the recent Euro-American past)—and, hence, one or the other space has to be vacated in any conception of a holistic future.

This myth and problem is embedded in the very definitions of modernity and modernism. The very usage of these terms as primarily symbolic ones (and primary to materialist explanations, such as capitalism and industrialization) predicates the problem discussed above. The experience of being modern is captured by the symbolic terms, 'modernity' and 'modernism', whose hegemonic forms themselves grew out of certain *specific* material changes. However, once the

---

[17] See, Eric Hobsbawm and Terence Ranger (Ed.), *The Invention of Tradition*.

symbolic takes precedence, the matter is displaced in a way so as to aid the capture of the potential and the referent by a specific Eurocentric form and sign. Modernity assumes a specifically European face, while the body of material factors around it disappears from view—leaving us with the simplistic discourse of 'accepting' or 'rejecting' Western words and practices.

In the above conditions, the 'modern' grows out of the 'traditional' in the West, where the basis for evaluating the modern is rooted in the traditional—as opposition, divergence, alteration or development. Not so in non-Europe, where the two stand discursively and spatially separate. The extreme—and extremely ineffectual—politics of identity (with its simple oppositions) stems from this situation. And it is this situation that explains the similarity in the 'equations' highlighted, in different ways, by Malouf and Verma at the beginning of this essay.

So, whenever I come across a Western commentator claiming that Muslims are incapable of modernity—and I hear such explicit or implicit claims at least once every month—I feel like shaking his hands and congratulating him on the extent of his unconscious self-awareness. And I would do so too, if only there were any such thing as unconscious self-awareness!

THIRTY-ONE

A Muslim Consciousness: The Space of Definitions

Islam came to me in two ways. The first one was the Islam I was born into. It fell on my shoulders as lightly as a silken shawl embroidered by hand. I was hardly conscious of it, though the month of Ramadan was special, even when I did not keep a fast (which was often, though my parents fasted regularly), and there were festivals to look forward to. This Islam was filled with the smoke of incense sticks during Shab-é-Baraat; it wore white *churidaar kurta*—the sleeves carefully crinkled with the help of a special kind of stone—for both Hindu and Muslim festivals. There was no purdah in this Islam; my mother and my father's sisters were mostly university graduates and one of them had an independent academic career. Both my grandmothers—even my mother's mother, who spent her days praying and reading the Quran—would never wear a purdah. This Islam did contain relatives who wore the purdah—but once they took it off indoors, they spoke and thought like everyone else in the family. Moreover, many of these purdah-wearing distant relatives were working women—more so than my aunts, who were relatively affluent. I was hardly conscious of all this being Islam (or 'not-Islam').

But it is the other kind of Islam that concerns me here. For this is the Islam of which the world, for better and for worse, made me conscious. When did this Islam penetrate into my consciousness? My

---

[1] Unpublished. Written in 2002, revised in 2004.

parents and my aunts narrate a story about a time when I was four years old. They had caught me arguing with an older boy, the son of one of the maidservants. According to them I had been asking him in Urdu: "Don't Hindus have one nose and two eyes like you and me? How can you say that they are different?"

This is Episode one in my story of the Islam that the world made me conscious of. We will return to it later. Let me put on record the other episodes first.

Episode two: I am older, probably 11 or 12. I am in the playground of our Roman Catholic missionary school in Gaya, sitting on the railings of the sliding board. I am too old to use the sliding board, but evidently not old enough to dissociate myself from it. Two of my class friends, boys who have studied with me for at least six years, come to me. They are arguing. One of them says, ask him, ask Tabish yourself. The other turns to me and puts the matter to test. He asks, "You are not Muslim, are you?"

Episode three: I am in my late teens, and travelling alone by train for some reason or the other. A distant cousin has been requested to book a railway berth for me. When I get my ticket—or is it when I see the passenger list pasted at the station?—I realize that I have been listed as 'T. Kher'. The cousin explains to me that it would be safer to travel under a 'Hindu' name, as there is communal tension in many parts of North India and riots might break out between Muslims and Hindus. I remember feeling proud, ashamed, excited: proud of my ability to pass for a Hindu, ashamed of the need to do so, excited to be playing a kind of teen agent.

Episode Four: I am in my 20s. I am still living in my small home town but have started writing for the *Times of India*. The Delhi edition carries a long piece by me criticizing Rushdie's lack of understanding of Muslim sentiments and beliefs but defending his rights as an artist and a human being, a piece written without reading The *Satanic Verses* (a novel I could lay my hands on only much later). Emboldened by the success of the piece, which provokes healthy debate in my circles, I collaborate with my best friend, Gyanendra Nath (who was to die later in a road accident), to write a critique of the Mahabharata TV serial. This evokes more extreme reactions. A couple of our acquaintances—supporters of what was a small Hindu-rightist party in those days, the BJP—get very angry with Gyanendra. To me, they only say: Gyanendra is at least a Hindu; why don't you write about your own Mullah religion?

Episode Five: I am stung by the challenge to write about my own 'Mullah religion'. I decide to take it up and write an article on Islam in India. It is published by the *Times of India*. The article is simple to my mind: highlighting the tradition of ijtihad, I ask why Indian Muslims—or rather Islamic scholars in India—do not reform aspects of religious practice in keeping with the spirit of Islam and changing times? I mention things I would like to see reformed—for example, it might be a good idea, I argue, to consider replacing the ritual sacrifice of animals during Eid with charity in the shape of cash. Nothing happens for a week. Then (I am told) the article is taken up for discussion on radio and all hell breaks loose in my town. Only in my town though. The local mullahs start preaching against me, I get anonymous phone calls by people who threaten me with death and worse, my defence of Rushdie is suddenly recalled in the vivid colours of apostasy, a mob surrounds my father's clinic demanding that I should be turned over to it to be 'disciplined'. My father, a religious man and a respected doctor, does not want to call the police because he is afraid the matter would turn into a Hindu-Muslim riot if (Hindu) policemen are involved in it. He goes out to speak to the leaders of the mob: He is alone, except for one of my uncles, the Urdu writer Kalam Haidri. The mob is on the verge of turning violent, but there is still some respect for my father. My father, who knows his Quran and Hadiths inside out and can speak the language of the crowd, argues with them for three or four hours. By the end, he has convinced them that I have not done anything 'unislamic'. They go away, some of them still muttering.

Episode Seven: I have just moved to Denmark. My first novel has been published in India. A (Danish) journalist requests me for an interview. During the interview, I tell him about the mob. But I narrate the incident to highlight the local character of the threats (the result of small town conservatism and intrigues rather than global Islamism), its transitory nature (after a few months I could enter even Muslim mohallas without feeling threatened) and, above all, the complexities brought forth by the fact of the mob's discussion with my father. I insist on these points. Imagine my surprise when the article appears bearing the heading, "Indisk forfatter-talent betalte dyrt for at støtte Salman Rushdie (Budding Indian writer pays dearly for supporting Rushdie)."

Episode Eight: I am in my early 30s and doing a PhD at Copenhagen University. At a highly cultured dinner, I am seated next to a highly cultured and literate Danish woman and an African Muslim scholar based in UK. The wine is poured. But do you drink wine, the woman asks the Muslim professor. When he replies in the affirmative, she bursts out: You are the first normal Muslim I have met.

*****

What if the hands are powerless, these eyes
Still see: O let the wine stand where it lies!

Thus said the great 19th century Urdu poet and Indo-Persian writer, Asadullah Khan Ghalib. One can quote so much by and about writers, thinkers, travellers, mystics, scholars from Muslim societies of the past (and the present) that contradicts all definitions of Muslim normality, whether formulated by Islamists or non-Muslims, whether formulated in criticism or admiration.[2] And yet the definitions keep on being pushed into my flesh, pinning me to this worldview or that. It is these easy and obdurate definitions, these piercing definitions that worry me most of all.

When I look back at my first episode narrated above, I am surprised by its lack of definitions. My parents were practising Muslims; they would not touch any kind of alcohol. They were also urban people, with a very middle class 'Islamic' suspicion of sages and sants, faqirs and mysticism. So their openness to Hindus was not a direct gift of Sufism. They were, moreover, not the kind of people who would think or talk too much of secularism or other such abstract ideas. And yet

---

[2] Just as interestingly, both 'cider' and 'alcohol' in English come from Arabic words.

not only did I say what I said to the older boy, all the elders around me heartily appreciated a child's refusal to allow abstract definitions to divide living bodies. Having one nose and two ears was what counted. When I look back on that first memory and through the following years, what I sense most of all is a stiffening of definitions, the concrete enactment of abstract boundaries. It changed so soon to a choice being forced on to me in a playground: Are you Hindu or Muslim? And that forced choice itself excluded me from a large part of my cultural heritage: write about your own 'mullah religion' not about Hinduism, as the two BJP supporters put it. It ended with the Muslim mob surrounding my father's clinic and the cultured woman in Copenhagen excluding practising Muslims (like my parents) from the bounds of 'normality'.

The hardening of definitions. The constricting of the space of definitions. It reminds me of another *sher* by Ghalib, a *sher* that would sound like blasphemy to many Islamic fundamentalists. Here it is, in a somewhat free translation:

> For God's sake leave the Kaaba's veil alone;
> There too may lie hidden a god of stone.

But I do not wish to lament the end of multiplicity, like the Moor in Salman Rushdie's novel. Laments and tears are what we might sometimes owe the past, but I live in the present. I have an 11-month-old son who, I hope, will grow up into the future. I seek not lamentation but understanding. But, above all, I seek understanding that avoids the old definitions, the definitions that, once adopted, pin you to the board of the same answers as always.

As such, for the rest of this essay, I will not talk of what Muslims are or are not. Neither will I quote the Quran to highlight the multiplicity and past/potential progressiveness of Islam. I will not dwell on, for example, the fact that the rise of Islamic fundamentalism has much to do with the systematic persecution of Marxists and communists in Muslim countries, very often with the direct support of the 'West'. I will not highlight the links of Bin Laden with CIA or point out how Israel, considered a democracy in the 'West', remains a living illustration of the success of rampant power and authoritarianism to most Muslims. I will not focus on the contradiction that while Muslim history teems with tens of thousands of differing exegeses of the Quran, the leaders of Islamic 'fundamentalism'—people who claim authority on the basis of the Holy Book—have hardly written any such work of exegesis. As Abdel Salam Sidahmed and Anoushiravan Ehteshami point out in *Islamic Fundamentalism* "apart from al-Maududi (d. 1979) and Sayyid Qutb (d. 1966), there is hardly any significant work by Islamists in this regard."

I will not even try to defend the 'spirit of Islam' against the frequent charge of misogyny by placing the relevant Hadiths and Quranic verses in historical context, a task performed admirably by Fatima Mernissi in *Woman and Islam: An Historical and Theological Enquiry* (Blackwell, 1991). Neither will I examine the ahistorical idea of a clash of civilizations as used in the media—at best a case of the boy who cried wolf—or examine the extent of the so-called Islamic threat. The latter examination has been performed with much intellectual honesty by John L Esposito in *The Islamic Threat.*

What I am interested in is a contemporary formulation that might enable us to understand the problems—and explore the possibilities—in a broader context, a context that does not get pegged down by hegemonic definitions of Islam, Christianity, Hinduism, European, Arab, civilization, culture etc. For the problem of stiffening definitions is the consequence of attempts at hegemony by various elites in the 'West' and in Muslim countries.

Again and again this attempt forces the mask of the past on the Islam I grew up with. Islamists evoke the 'glorious past' and urge a return to what they think were the Islamic values of yore. Critics in the 'West' see aspects of Muslim societies—including fundamentalism—as throwbacks to the past or, if they are kind, its remnant. A recent editorial in one of Denmark's leading paper, the left-of-center *Politiken*, for example, urged European Muslims to eschew tendencies from the 'Middle Ages'. After the fall of the Taliban, TV hosts and commentators celebrated the deliverance of Afghanistan from the 'Stone Age'. Even Muslim progressives or reformers, fighting Islamic fundamentalism with their backs against the barbed wall of Western hubris, spend much of their time proving that the *past* of Islam was progressive and revolutionary.

This constant reference to the past as the decisive element in world serves to further ossify the terms and definitions in question, for they are mostly retrieved as fossils which, at the best, are supposed to help us understand the almost predetermined character of contemporary Islam. No doubt, the past has a role to play, but this role is not greater in Muslim societies than in non-Muslim ones *per se*. When Muslim societies, in spite of their obvious variety in the past and the present, start appearing to be suffering more from the nightmare of the past, then we have cause to examine the present of these societies. And that is what I intend to do in a very limited way—by focussing on capitalism—for the rest of this essay.

*****

The structure of power in capitalist societies is based on capital: it depends on the control of *abstract* capital and not directly on the control of the human body. The human body is, of course, controlled in the final run, for all power over human beings needs to be inscribed on the body finally. But this control is exercised abstractly: for example, through wages. Or through the concept of 'nationality', which enables the capitalists of rich nations to exploit the labour of poor nations while maintaining the unequal mobility ratio between capital and labour, now internationally.

The growth of capital marks a significant break with the structure and logic of power in pre-capitalist societies. As Maurice Bloch pointed out in *Marxism and Anthropology*, one ought to resist the tendency of turning pre-capitalist societies into paradises of equality. The absence of capitalism does not mean the absence of structures of power in pre-capitalist societies. It simply means that if power cannot be exercised abstractly through capital, it has to be exercised directly on the body of the agent.[3] One could illustrate this point with reference to the family, religion, legislative codes and social structures of pre-capitalist peoples, but for lack of space and the redundancy of such illustration.

We can see a distorted recognition of this direct enactment of power on the body of the agent in pre-capitalist societies in the way in which dominant agents in capitalist societies look at their own marginalized members—'women' and 'peasants' in Europe in the 19th and even the 20th century. European women have been depicted in

---

[3] It is relevant to remember that pre-capitalist societies, especially under mercantile conditions, do have structures of power that do not impact directly on the body, though these are usually very limited. Similarly, areas of capitalist society which are not directly effected by capital—such as the family—might retain elements similar to pre-capitalist structures of power.

much of 19th and some of 20th century European literature as creatures of the body: not only is their sexuality a threat, their speech is often relegated to the level of screams and similar bodily noises. It is only under capitalism that we mark a reverse movement, when some 'cultured women' start getting more and more refined and ethereal. Peasants too have not only been seen as earthy, their acts of agency have been portrayed as involving excessive physical violence. Even though one might argue that peasants were no more prone to violent agency than other sections of European society, it is remarkable that the dominant discourse in a capitalist society tends to segregate the marginalized on the basis of their *bodily* characteristics and tendencies. Is this merely the fear of the social other, or does it also contain a warped recognition of the fact that the structures of power under capitalism are very different? They are, actually, based on replacing labour with capital, replacing the human body with abstract 'value'. As such, the body has to be brought under these abstract structures of power in capitalist societies; previous structures of power have to be systematically undermined and opposed. This abstract logic of power, which capitalism does not really acknowledge, makes the capitalist bourgeoisie acutely conscious of the preceding logic of power—and, with it, also of the *othered* body.

It is in this context that we have to return to Islam today, remembering well that the capitalist mode of production is un(der)developed in most Muslim countries. These countries (with the partial exception of a country like Malaysia, which has been held up as such a good 'Muslim' example during the Afghanistan war) also have a very small bourgeoisie in general: the Muslim bourgeoisie in India might well exceed that of all Arab countries combined.

This lack of developed capitalist modes of production has 'local', 'national' and 'global' reasons, of which the most important might well be the nature of capitalism itself. As Samir Amin notes in *Capitalism in the Age of Globalisation*, favourable conditions, like the massive accumulation of capital permitted by conquest/colonization as well as Europe's ability to get rid of its surplus population in a crucial period, have not been available to the rest of the world. In the present too, as Amin notes, "most of [the immense amounts of floating capital in the world] seeks investment by roaming from one financial metropolis to another, only rarely paying a visit to third world financial systems." The Arab countries, in spite of the oil wealth that is largely controlled by a few in collaboration with multinational corporations, are particularly lacking when it comes to developing capitalist modes of production. This lack is exceeded only by parts of Africa.

But it is not my thesis in this essay that the 'reactionary' tendencies in many Muslim societies today are the reflection of their pre-capitalist or quasi-capitalist status. Such a thesis would return us to the past as providing a simple and direct explanation of the present. And that is something I wish to avoid. Moreover, such an explanation would also obscure the 'globalizing' nature of capitalism today. Capitalism touches almost everyone in the world today, though of course it does not touch everyone in the same way or to the same extent.

What I wish to highlight is the fact that Muslim countries—along with other 'third world' and 'fourth world' countries—have undeveloped or underdeveloped modes of capitalist production. This—combined with the lack of historically favourable conditions for the development of Europe-style capitalism—leaves these countries with a small and insecure bourgeoisie, which does not have the success/wealth to incorporate or force the other classes to accept its hegemony. In these countries, as Samir Amin puts it, "the local bourgeoisie has failed to achieve the building of a modern self-reliant economy." This local/national bourgeoisie lacks the courage and the wealth to really compete with the international bourgeoisie in economic terms, and is thus confined to only one half of its role as a *national* bourgeoisie: collaboration with the *international* bourgeoisie. However, in keeping with the nation-state-based political structure of post-war international community and its own self-definition, this local bourgeoisie can only exist as a national bourgeoisie if the nation-state continues to exist—and to exist simultaneously with it. For that the national bourgeoisie needs both the resources that it can obtain from the international bourgeoisie—by trading, trafficking or begging—and, above all, it needs to keep on differentiating itself *symbolically* from the international bourgeoisie. This differentiation can only be made in the symbolic sphere because its inability to compete with the international bourgeoisie deprives the national bourgeoisie of both hegemony in the nation-state and a plausible appearance of material/economic differentiation.

It is here that 'Islam' steps into the picture in many Muslim countries.[4] This, however, is not just a 'Muslim' characteristic. 'Hinduism' is being used in similar ways in India, a usage altered slightly by the fact that India has a relatively large bourgeoisie.

The game that has been played in most Muslim countries is a two-edged one. On the one hand, the bourgeoisie and the traditional elite

4 Its appeal to the 'immigrant' population from these countries is consolidated by the fact that religious identity, unlike national identity, exceeds national borders—hence, religion becomes doubly attractive to many immigrants in the West, who are caught outside or between national borders.

seek and often obtain many of the benefits of capitalism. On the other hand, the people live under conditions of un(der)developed modes of capitalism. This quasi-capitalist state of economic activity to which most of the population is confined due to the failures of the national bourgeoisie and the structure of (global) capitalism, necessitates a corresponding 'quasi-capitalist' symbolic world, which is largely achieved with the help of a reductive reading of Islam. For reasons of prestige (borrowed from the 'past') and availability, this 'quasi-capitalist' symbolic world has to rely heavily on certain 'pre-capitalist' tendencies which appear most opposed to the capitalist symbolic world.

Apart from the logic of its evocation, this also enables the elite to profit from its complicity in global capitalism while keeping the people not only alienated from the partly-democratic tendencies of capitalism (fetishized into the 'West') but also singularly unable to comprehend the real structures of their oppression. Instead of partly competing and partly collaborating with the global capitalist (as it would have if it had been a full and vigorous national bourgeoisie), the Muslim national elite simply collaborates with the global capitalist in material terms while appearing to provide an alternative to the people in symbolic terms. This suits all the elites and bourgeoisie concerned most of the time, for the fully abstract nature of capital today makes it more sensible for the global capitalist to keep away from territorial entanglement (which, by the way, also helps us understand the kind of wars being waged by the US in recent years and perhaps predict the future in Afghanistan).

Islamic fundamentalist parties are a spin off from this game, a game that (it must be stressed) suits dominant business and political interests in the 'West'. Even when they end up challenging the legitimacy of the government of a Muslim country, fundamentalist parties do not really upset the capitalist apple cart. Reacting to the abstract structures of power under capitalism, the leaders of these fundamentalist parties try to 'restore' what they consider Islamic, inevitably stressing the structures of power that impact directly on the body under pre- or quasi-capitalist conditions. (The Taliban was but the expression of this oppositional logic taken to its limit; Saudi Arabia continues to present its institutionalized face.) The valid attempt to resist the abstract structures of power under capitalism leads to not a (revolutionary) re-evocation of the body under changed conditions but a defensive/ conservative/reactionary attempt to preserve the body under old pre-capitalism-like structures of power. From a radical perspective, the main problem with this oppositional formulation is its inability to fight the real structures of power under global capitalism. It can only indulge in pointless violence, like the bombing of the WTO building in New York; violence that, if anything, enables capitalist leaders to consolidate their hold on power.

Here I should spell out the hitherto implicit fact that I am not indulging in the vulgar Marxist tendency of blaming exploitation simply on the 'exploitative nature' of an evil elite. The bourgeoisie or the elite in Muslim (and third world) countries is forced by the very logic of global capitalism—including capitalism's imbrication and tensions with the nation state—to seek to establish its hegemony over the other classes by means of the only thing it can press into service: the evocation of a past that, in its pre-capitalist tendencies, might serve as an (ineffective) critique of capitalism (or, more exactly, the cpitalist 'West'). Had the Muslim or third world bourgeoisie been successful in capitalist terms (something precluded by the very mechanism of historical capitalism), this would not have been necessary to the same extent. And had revolutionary critiques—such as radical socialism or

Marxism—been allowed to flourish in these countries, there might have been other alternatives to this recourse to an Islam defined by and 'refined' into its most body-impacted, pre-capitalist elements.

The point to note, however, is that the 'past' that comes into being due to the nexus of these interests and forces has been created very much in the present. This is underlined by the technical and vocational education of many supporters of Islamic (and Hindu) fundamentalism, the highly political character of much of Islamic (and Hindu) fundamentalism as well as the fact that Islamists are not really interested in writing exegeses of the Quran and Hindu fundamentalists tend to turn the Ramayana into a pulp serial rather than study it in Sanskrit.

Islamists and their critics in the 'West' use terms of definition that play out this contrast between capitalist and pre-capitalist structures of power, which is often translated into: (a) the resistance of the body to abstract capital, if you are anti-capitalist or anti-West and (b) the freedom of the body from the tyranny of society/religion, which is the dominant view in the capitalist 'West'. Here it must be added that the intense 'Muslim' suspicion of the 'West' is not just due to the lack of self-criticism in the Muslim world that Salman Rushdie has castigated. Actually, from at least the day in 1099 when Abu Sa'ad al-Harawi burst into the *diwan* of al-Mustazhir Billah decrying Muslim decadence and weakness in the face of the advancing crusaders, Muslim communities have indulged in as much (reactionary or revolutionary) self-criticism as any other community. The Muslim suspicion of the 'West' is due to a garbled realization by the average Muslim of the structures of power under capitalism, structures that touch him very differently from how they touch Rushdie or an Arab Sheikh or even a humble white clerk in London. The 'Muslim failure' is not a consequence of that suspicion; it is due to his limited ability to see through the false choice being imposed upon him: the choice that fixes him permanently and wriggling to the board of someone's idea of the past.

And the failure is not just his; it is mutual. While the capitalist 'West' and many members of the bourgeoisie elsewhere often perceive the bodily structures of power which are made to dominate 'traditional Islam' with great repulsion, they also fail to address their own abstract structures of power. A minor proof of the latter is the fact that the debt of the 'peripheral economies' grew from US$ 900 billion in 1982 to US$ 1,500 trillion in the late 1990s, of which half was expended on interest. The failure, then, has not been simply that of Muslim societies or individuals. It is a mutual failure and a deeply ideological one. Most immediately, it is not due to the so-called 'failure of socialism' but due to the failure of socialist parties in the 'West' to retain or revive the internationalist character of socialism in the wake of their pacts with national capitalism.

Almost everywhere the problem of the present is being resolved with recourse to the past, simply because there is no real attempt at resolving the contradictions of capitalism that lie at the heart of the problem. Almost everywhere the terms of definition are turning dead and rigid, for they are mostly fossils from the past.

To address the problem one would need to shift the terms of discussion from the symbolic realm preferred by the various elites (even when in opposition to one another, as Bin Laden is/was to the ruling family of Saudi Arabia or the US Government) and locate these terms in the dialectical realm of the actual activities of living *bodes*. One would need to read the past in the present and not vice versa. In short, one will need to examine capitalism more seriously than one is allowed to today, both in the 'West' and in Muslim countries.

That lack, finally, is what I can read in the episodes that I lined up at the head of this essay to press my case against Islam as it has been imposed upon me by Muslims and non-Muslims. Starting with a realization of the shared body, the material basis of our existence, all the episodes narrated lead us further and further into the symbolic: though there remains the possibility of communication, as when my father spoke to the angry mob. The boy who saw no difference between the Hindu body and the Muslim body travels through the increasingly constricting definitions of abstract naming until finally, in Copenhagen, his 'normality' is hung on the symbolic hook of his personal decision to drink wine. That boy still feels many things about being 'Muslim' in India and in Denmark: but if you were to ask him he would tell you what he feels in terms that could be shared by many from his background, Hindu, Muslim, Sikh or Christian. Surely we need to create more space for that boy to speak the language that would make sense to so many like him—not only in 'Muslim' countries, but even more so in the globally dominant 'West' which is just as closed ideologically.

In the lack of that space, that boy–like all of us–will be faced with one danger. And here I have to narrate one more episode from the story of that boy's growing and changing awareness of his Muslim name. It is an episode I have had to force myself to narrate. Chronologically, it would be Episode number 6.

Episode Six: I am working as a news reporter in Delhi. I have not left for Denmark yet, though I am considering a switch to academia. The Ram Janam Bhoomi/Ayodhya movement is simmering on. There have been Hindu-Muslim riots in Delhi. I have started resenting the coverage of the paper I am working for, because I feel that it sometimes plays into the hands of communal elements in the BJP. I particularly resent the fact that Muslim reporters are sent to cover stories of police violence against Muslims. I feel it places them under the obligation of proving their secularism—thus inducing them to be soft on the police at times—while creating the impression of objective reporting. When my chief reporter asks me to cover one such report, I refuse rather shortly. The chief reporter has never given me any ground to suspect him of any communal feeling, but suddenly I see him as a Hindu trying to exploit my Muslim name. I have become fully conscious of this Muslim name. I have started seeing invisible differences. My definitions are hardening, and so are my prejudices.

I am shaken by my own reaction. I spend months thinking through all my values again, examining my past in the present. I spend years studying. I return to texts that I had been made to believe were 'dated'—not least the actual writings of Karl Marx. The conclusions I reach are those I have stated, to the best of my ability, in this essay. I have put them down for the sake of that boy who saw no difference between Hindus and Muslims. I wish him other terms of definition. I wish him the space to define himself..

Part III

THIRTY-TWO

Prospect for the Future: Only Sporty Muslims Need Apply!

Should I have started compiling this book by announcing theatrically that I condemn terrorism? Or should I have started by saying that I condemn, in particular, the Muslims who might (or might not) have sparked the latest terror alert in England (in the year 2006)? Or should I say that I condemn Bin Laden, pet monster? Or should I add that I condemn the treatment of women in Saudi Arabia? Or should I go further and condemn Muslim liberals for being 'too understanding' when it comes to the dilemmas confronting Muslims in the West today? Or perhaps even that won't do, and I will be required to condemn Islam and particular lines from the Quran?*

When the editor of a magazine like *Prospect* (Foreword, September 2006) takes Muslim liberals to task for 'not condemning enough and for understanding too much', it is time to sit up. David Goodhart's accusation deserves a thought or two. It is true that many Muslims feel they are being pushed against the wall by Islamic fundamentalists as well as media and political interests in the West. They see Islamist militancy as something not that different from neo-nazism in Europe or Ku Klux Klan-type racism in USA. They see it as minority extremism, and want to make others see that too. After all, Goodhart does not write a condemnatory essay every time there is a racist attack on a Black American or an immigrant in Europe.

---

* Written in Aarhus, 12 September 2006.

But that does make Muslim liberals seem suspect in the eyes of many people, who would want them to condemn first and analyse later. Still, these Muslim liberals are more interested in analysis: because their concern is to remove the causes that enable a kind of minority extremism from becoming attractive to large numbers of ordinary Muslims. One way to understand this is to realize that extremist views, like those of Nazis, will always be espoused by small fringe groups, but when these groups start crawling out of the woodwork—as they did under Hitler, for instance—then one cannot simply condemn. One needs to understand why an extremist stance starts becoming attractive to ordinary men and women.

But if you are a Muslim and do so, you are likely to make yourself conspicuous. It is a bit like an experience narrated in Albert Memmi's *Racism*. A well-meaning, non-racist White European sees a group of coloured teenagers making a lot of noise on a bus or on the metro. They shouldn't do this, the man tells Memmi, alluding to the fact that by calling attention to themselves the coloured teenagers add to existent prejudices against immigrants. But, as Memmi asks, is this not the behaviour of any gang of street kids?

So, perhaps it's true that some Muslim liberals are quite defensive in the face of redefinitions of Islam from both sides, and sweeping criticism of Muslims in the West. But then are they so unusual? British historians and intellectuals are still writing entire books defending and justifying the British empire!

Why is it that Goodhart wants a certain kind of discourse from Muslim liberals, all of whom have already condemned terrorism quite clearly? (I have too, and also the recent rise of anti-Semitism in Islamist circles). Why is it that this feeling is so strong in him that it leads to a glaring error when he claims that a change in British foreign policy is basically being demanded only by 'three percent of the British population' that is Muslim? I am afraid Goodhart has allowed himself to slip into the position of the well-meaning, non-racist gentleman on Memmi's bus. His way of looking blinds him to the fact that many non-Muslim British citizens are also unhappy with the current British foreign policy. (And actually, some of these three percent British Muslims might even be happy with aspects of the policy!)

Finally, it is pathetic that Goodhart can only come up with a tired old symbol of 'successful integration'—England's new fast-bowling star, Sajid Mahmood. One has heard this in so many places. Tell it to any politically-aware and history-conscious Black American and she would fall over laughing. After all, the dominance of American sports and athletics by Black Americans has not removed (or even, I would argue, significantly reduced) the differences between Black Americans and White Americans as peoples, differences that are based partly on the dominant 'white' tendency to talk down to all others. Surely, Mr Goodhart, you can set those presumably faint-hearted Muslim liberals an example by doing better than that!

What is interesting, as Tariq Ramadan pointed out in a BBC programme on 11 September 2006, is that Muslims of all sorts (except a minority of fanatics) have condemned terrorism from the very moment that the import of 11 September 2001 sank in. And yet a veritable chorus in the West accuses Muslims of not condemning enough. I fear that what this chorus wants is not condemnation of terrorism, which any sensible Muslim is willing to offer, but a silencing of the political criticism of draconian immigration-related internal politics in the West and short-sighted or Machiavellian international politics orchestrated by the Liberal Right from places like USA. This no sensible Muslim—or human being—should be willing to offer.

So I am sure that a certain type of critic will take me to task for not 'condemning enough' in this book, glibly skipping the unqualified condemnation of terrorist violence that exists in these pages. Because while I condemn terrorism, I am not willing to be browbeaten into saying only what people like Mr Goodhart want to hear. Let alone what people like Mr Blair or Mr Bush wish to hear.

The essays and articles collected in this book are, perforce, the responses to recent events and discourses by an Indian born in a Muslim family and currently located in Denmark. It is true that they are not an engagement with Islam or even with Islamic fundamentalism, though they do say quite a few things about the latter. As a thinking person, I feel that I need to engage in greater detail with my own religious, cultural and philosophical traditions, of which Islam definitely forms a part. But that engagement awaits another book and another time—a time when what people like me have to say about Islam won't be turned into sticks with which to beat and browbeat ordinary Muslims, a tendency that is very much in evidence in the West today.

In the meanwhile, I hope that this book will enable some people like me (and a few unlike me) to examine their views about various things—religion, Islam, immigration, modernity, capitalism etc.—that effect all of us, and perhaps in the process learn to see Muslims as a disparate people engaged in different ways in making sense of their own lives and of the world. I hope that this book will help create a world in which we won't just mourn the innocent victims of the tragic terrorist strike in New York on 11 September 2001 but also mourn the innocent victims of various other acts of needless violence in Asia, Africa and South America, some of them perpetuated by or through the support of Western powers. Let not our mourning, whether in the USA, Denmark, Iraq or Lebanon, refuse to include those who are not like us, for in that refusal the humanity of feeling turns into the inhumanity of not-feeling. A person who can only mourn his own 'kind' is always a potential terrorist: this applies to nationalist Americans as much as to fundamentalist Arabs.

I also hope finally that sometime in the future when the next generation, the generation of my children, engages with similar issues, this book will be among those enabling the formation of identities that are neither singular and reductive nor vague and indeterminate. For while every human being needs to be someone, we are also always and at the same time more than just one.

THIRTY-THREE

The Arrest of Dr Haneef and the Questions of Fundamentalism

Much has happened in the year that lapsed between compiling this anthology and its date of publication. Most of it you might not have heard of. For instance, it is unlikely that you know that the entire population of Denmark died out twice in this one year. Oh well, the equivalent: for over 10 million infants died of malnutrition and similar avoidable causes, in a world that produces enough food to feed almost double the number of people alive today. If Denmark had been wiped out twice in this one year, you would have heard of it. But these 10 million children lived in parts of Asia, Africa and South America, mostly. As such, they did not make it to the news.

Some other things did make it to the news, but just barely: like the train to Pakistan that was bombed in India, or the eight Indian workers who were chased through the streets of an East German town and beaten up by a gang of 50 neo-Nazis. However, one bit of news that we all heard was related to the Indian doctor, Muhammad Haneef, 27, who was arrested in Australia, on the charge of complicity in terrorist activities in the UK. "He has been charged with providing support to a terrorist organization," police had said in a statement at the moment of his arrest. The maximum penalty for such 'support' is 15 years of imprisonment.

Later on, the doctor was released, as his 'support' appears to have comprised of lending his mobile phone's SIM card to a cousin, who had passed it on to someone who might or might not be involved in terrorist activities. For those of us who, Muslim or not, come from

Asia or Africa, this appears to be an innocuous act. We are accustomed to operating in immigrant networks. Immigrant networks are not confined to Asians and Africans, though some cultural traits might be. The Irish, the Italians, all of them have had their networks in the USA or Australia. When you move from one country to another, as Dr Haneef did, you give away whatever can be used to your relatives and friends. It is a part of being an immigrant.

Anti-terror policemen, who cannot or will not recognize the vitality or existence of these networks, are either ignorant, or wilfully prejudiced. One thing for which the current anti-terror laws are being used, is to break up and hound certain kinds of networks. These networks are sceptical of the *status quo*: immigrant, anti-racist, eco-friendly (as in the UK in August 2007, when anti-terror laws were imposed to cow down an environmentalist's demonstration) and alternatively political in general (various instances, ranging from the USA to Denmark over this year alone).

One of the major problems with Islamic fundamentalism is that it has diverted its attention from such protests. We are living in a grossly unfair world. It is not unfair because people do not offer the *namaaz* or do not respect the Prophet as much as Muslims think He should be respected. It is unfair because two Denmarks can die out every year, without making it into the news because they happen to be in Asia, Africa and South America. Islamic fundamentalism, by reducing protest to religious/cultural matters and confining itself to one religion (and actually to a very small percentage of members of that religion who are 'Islamic' enough), has done the world the signal disservice of providing reactionary and rightist forces with the cudgel of 'anti-terror', increasingly being wielded on any kind of protest whatsoever. The arrest of Dr Haneef was an indication of this development; his release a sign that there still are people—Muslim or non-Muslim, black or white—who care for justice and decency.

It is time to pause and think again. On all sides.

Ziauddin Sardar is one of the very few writers who have managed to say something perceptive and balanced in the wake of Islamic 'jihad' and the Western 'war against Terror', as I indicated in my review of a book co-authored by him earlier in this anthology of essays. As such, when even Sardar succumbs to the reductive analysis that jihadis are empty-headed, brain-washed morons ('The Terror of Self-satisfaction', *New Statesman*, 23 April), I find it more disturbing than all the bombs dropped on Iraq or suicide-attacks by Islamic terrorists.

From our perspective (and I speak firmly from the West, which is where I am located geographically and discursively), it is easy to spot the rot coming from Islamic fundamentalists: their inane analysis of modernity, as offered in texts attributed to Bin Laden and others, or their copycat anti-Semitism are just two obvious instances. Again, not having bought the hard-sell of Bush and Blair, we can also spot the obvious rubbish coming from various born-again imperious crusaders of the West. But can we spot the rubbish that we ourselves—educated, left-leaning, open-minded that we are—have been pushed to spout more and more, often under the new circumstances inflicted on us by Bin, Bush, Blair and Sons, Unlimited?

Let me tell you a story. When I last returned to my hometown in Bihar, I was visited—as is the case in such places—by anyone who knew me, or had known my father, or my grandfather. And sometimes even by people who knew my mother, or grandmother. As I had a reputation—vain-gloriously exaggerated by family and friends in a small and backward place—as an 'internationally-published writer', a number of these visitors turned out to be people with literary ambitions.

One of them offered me a book, privately printed, on the 'Middle East'. I shuddered to flip through it, but there was no polite way by which I could refuse to do so. I had already been told that the book discussed Israel, and I hardened myself for the usual invective. More so, I knew that the person offering it to me, and the author (let us call him X), would be considered Muslim fundamentalists by most liberals in the West. It turned out, however, that I was mistaken. The book did not fulminate against Jews. In fact, it argued that Jews and Muslims share (and had shared) much. Then, it argued—somewhat more predictably—that Jews have been turned into scapegoats by powers (and religious Christians) in the West in order to control the Middle East.

I suggested to my benefactor that perhaps X's second thesis revealed a degree of paranoia and had to do with his overly religious (Islamic) view of the world. He was surprised. He drew me a verbal map of Asia-Africa-Europe. He then traced on the map how 'Europeanized Christianity' had been encroaching upon the Muslim world for '300 years', and how every century the Muslim world had been shrinking and was now hardly left with a country without Western military presence.

Not tending to think in terms of 'Muslim' or 'Christian' worlds, I was taken aback by this view of history. I did not agree with the version provided by X or the man who had given me X's book, as I prefer seeing matters in term of capitalism, modernity, etc., but I could not dismiss him as a moron. By no means. True, he is not the kind of fundamentalist who would toss bombs, or not yet anyway. He might share the kind of anger and frustration that I have also heard in the voices of Muslim youth who are capable of violent reaction. Could I simply dismiss his version of history? Could I tell him that he was a brain-washed person, whose humanity was being 'flushed out' by Islamic fundamentalism (as Sardar puts it in *New Statesman*)?

I know—and I agree with Sardar—that a jihadi suicide bomber is another matter. Any person who can take the life of innocent bystanders, must have lost some essential part of his humanity. And yet, when did this loss take place? How did it take place? And why? It is these questions that we sweep under the carpet when we focus on the jihadi suicide bomber, rather than on the Islamic fundamentalist. The jihadi suicide bomber is too much the Other: he, and it is mostly a he, is beyond our comprehension. But he is not beyond the comprehension of most Islamic fundamentalists. Ask them about it, and you will find out that they, even when they disagree, do not view the jihadi suicide bomber as an Other, someone who can only be understood in terms of absolute negativity (Bush's 'evil') or absolute emptiness (Sardar's 'flushed humanity').

No, most Islamic fundamentalists can comprehend the jihadi suicide bomber. And most of us can comprehend the Islamic fundamentalist, if we do not reduce him or her to the absolute otherness of the 'suicide bomber'.

Flying back to Denmark and later in England, I discussed the attraction of Islamic fundamentalism with a number of young people. All of them were from Muslim backgrounds, though many were non-religious. Their reaction to both the 'war against Terror' and the discourses of 'Islamic jihad' was sceptical—and this scepticism did not always depend on how religious the student was. But then I found a vague pattern of difference between religious Muslim students and students from Muslim backgrounds who did not practise their faith. It appeared that the religious students had a greater sense of a world community, often but not always a 'Muslim community'.

I looked around and noticed that despite academic discussions of globalization, the actual socio-political and legal reality in places like Denmark or England was strongly defined along national lines. And even more so, if you came from Africa and Asia—for the relative mobility available to European Union citizens would be seldom extended to you. The political discourse was often—more in Denmark and Austria, less in England or France—in terms of national identities, sometimes conflated with 'European-ness'. However, the lived experience of these students was predominantly that of 'globalization'. In this context, suddenly, I realized that at least some of them related to religious Islam as a 'progressive' category. It provided for them a clear acknowledgement of aspects of their varied identities that exceeded national boundaries. (Dr Haneef's story is part of this larger story, whether or not he has religious sympathies).

Perhaps if socialism had not been dismissed in Europe or mostly reduced to nationalist protectionism, these young men and women might have had another discourse about being citizens of the world, and not just citizens of Denmark or England, or immigrants. Lacking that alternative, Islam appeared to, at least the religious students, more in tune with their present—and the future—than the discourses implicit in the rhetoric of politicians who worried about 'Islamic fundamentalism'. These students were not fundamentalists, but perhaps some of them would not need to be 'brain-washed' in order to be recruited to some version of Islamic fundamentalism in the future?

It is time for us in the West to realize that Islamic fundamentalism—in very different ways in Afghanistan, Iraq, Denmark and the USA—is providing many people with answers, however flawed and distorted, to questions that we do not even bother to ask at times, especially in the privileged West. Sometimes these answers come from the past—as is the case of the Madrasa students who, mostly reared on a staple diet of dysfunctional Islamist propaganda served as education, seldom have a choice but to turn to narrow, fundamentalist versions of Islam. But sometimes the answers are attempts to cope with the present, grope towards a better future. Above all, these are answers to questions that worry many men and women. Even if we disagree with the answers, as I do, we have to face the questions. We cannot ignore these questions simply because, given our affluence, passports, careers or location, they do not concern us overly.

All of us have to answer these questions, just as all of us have to take a stand against injustice. And if you are a Muslim, you have to take a stand not just against the injustice faced by Muslims, but also against those faced by non-Muslims, including non-Muslims in Muslim countries.

For centuries, Muslims have been brought up with the belief that the primary duty of a Muslim is to fight against injustice, for the God of Islam is a just God. But justice is not something one can have at someone else's expense. Either there is justice for everyone, or injustice. A fair world is a world in which all are entitled to fair treatment. It is this that Muslims have to remember, for Islamic fundamentalism, even of the non-militant variety, isolates Muslims in this global fight for rights, equality, justice. It is a fight that will be easy to win, but only if all of us fight for the rights of others. More and more Muslims need to ask themselves if that is what they have been doing. And the so-called West needs to put the same question to itself, for there are unanswered questions on all sides.

Selective Bibliography

1. Adams, Hazard, Ed. *Critical Theory Since Plato*. Revised Edition. Fort Worth and London: Harcourt Brace Jovanovich College Publishers, 1992.
2. Ahmad, Aijaz *Lineages of the Present: Political Essays*, Tulika, Delhi, 1996.
3. "The Politics of Literary Postcoloniality", in Mongia, P, Ed. *Contemporary Postcolonial Theory: A Reader*. London and New York: St Martin's Press, 1996, p. 276-293.
4. *Iraq, Afghanistan & The Imperialism of Our Time*. New Delhi: Leftword, 2004.
5. Ali, Monica. *Brick Lane*. London: Black Swan, 2004.
6. Amin, Samir. *Capitalism in the Age of Globalisation*. London: Zed Books, 1997.
7. Anderson, Benedict. *Imagined Communities: Reflections on the Origin and Spread of Nationalism [1983]*. London: Verso, 1991.
8. Arrighi, Giovanni. *The Long Twentieth Century: Money, Power and the Origins of Our Times* (1994). London and New York: Verso, 2000.
9. Araeen, Rasheed. "A New Beginning: Beyond Postcolonial Cultural Theory and Identity Politics", *Third Text*, 50, London, Spring 2000.
10. Aslan, Chris. "Silk Road Witnesses as Marriage of Moralities", *The Guardian Weekly*, London, May 24, 2000.
11. Atwan, Abdel Bari. *The Secret History of Al-Qaida*. London: Saqi Books, 2006.
12. Austin, Allan D. *African Muslims in Antebellum America*. New York: Routledge, 1997.
13. Barnes, Julian. "This war was not worth a child's finger", *The Guardian*, London, April 11, 2003.
14. Barthes, Roland. "The Death of the Author", 1968. *Modern Literary Theory: A Reader*. Ed. Philip Rice and Patricia Waugh. London: Edward Arnold, 1989.
15. Berman, Marshall. *All That Is Solid Melts Into Air: The Experience of Modernity* [1982], Penguin, New York, 1988.
16. Bauman, Zygmunt. *Liquid Modernity*. Cambridge: Polity, 2000.

17. Bayly, C. A. *Empire and Information: Intelligence Gathering and Social Communication in India 1780–1870*. Cambridge: Cambridge University Press, 1996.
18. *The Birth of the Modern World 1780–1914*. Oxford: Blackwell, 2004.
19. Bhabha, Homi K. *The Location of Culture* [1994]. London and New York: Routledge, 1995.
20. Bharucha, Rustom. *The Politics of Cultural Practice: Thinking through Theatre in an Age of Globalization*. New Delhi: Oxford University Press, 2001.
21. Bloch, Maurice. *Marxism and Anthropology*. Oxford: Clarendon Press, 1983.
22. Brodber, Erna. *Myal*. London and Port of Spain: New Beacon Books, 1988.
23. Brontë, Charlotte. *Jane Eyre* (1847). Ed. Beth Newman. Boston and New York: Bedford/St. Martin's, 1996.
24. Brontë, Emily. *Wuthering Heights* (1847). Ed. Linda H. Peterson. Boston and New York: Bedford/St. Martin's, 2003.
25. Césaire, Aime. *Discourse on Colonialism* [1972]. Trans. By Joan Pinkham. New York: Monthly Review Press, 2000.
26. Chomsky, Noam. *Doctrines and Visions*. London: Penguin Books, 2003.
27. Conrad, Joseph. *Heart of Darkness* (1899). Ed. Robert Kimbrough. New York and London: W. W. Norton and Company, 1988.
28. Curtis, Mark. *The Great Deception: Anglo-American Power and the World Order*. London: Pluto Press, 1998.
29. Dummett, Michael. *On Immigration and Refugees*. London and New York: Routledge, 2001.
30. Eagleton, Terry. *Holy Terror*. Oxford: Oxford UP, 2005.
31. *Marx and Freedom*. London: Phoenix, 1998.
32. Esposito, John L. *The Islamic Threat*. Oxford: Oxford University Press, 1992.
33. Evangelisti, Valerio. 'The truth is in here', *Le Monde Diplomatique*, August 2000, p. 15.
34. Febvre, Lucien and Martin, Henri-Jean. *The Coming of the Book*. 1976. Trans. David Gerard. London: Verso, 1998.
35. Fraser, Robert. "Mapping the Mind: Borders, Interrogation and Myth." Keynote Address. Writing Europe 2001: Migrant Cartographies Conference. University of Leiden/University of Amsterdam. March 2001.
36. Fisher, Philip. *Still the New World: American Literature in a Culture of Creative Destruction*, Harvard University Press, Harvard, 1999.
37. Forster, E. M. *A Passage to India*. 1924. London: Edward Arnold, 1978.
38. Gellner, Ernest. *Nationalism*. London: Phoenix, 1998.
39. George, Rose. *Hunting for Refuge in the Modern World*. London: Penguin Books, 2004.

40. Giddens, Anthony. *The Consequences of Modernity* [1990], Polity Press, Cambridge, 1997.
41. Gilroy, Paul. *The Black Atlantic: Modernity and Double Consciousness* [1993]. London and New York: Verso, 1999.
42. Girard, René. *Violence and the Sacred.* London: Continuum, 2005.
43. Ghosh, Amitav. *In an Antique Land* (1992). London: Granta Books, 1994.
44. *Countdown*. Delhi: Ravi Dayal, 1999.
45. Heaney, Seamus. *New Selected Poems* 1966–1987. London: Faber and faber, 1990.
46. Hensher, Phillip. *The Mulberry Empire.* London: Flamingo, 2002.
47. Hobsbawm, Eric and Ranger, Terence, Ed. *The Invention of Tradition* [1983], Cambridge University Press, Cambridge, 1997.
48. Hobsbawm, Eric. *Nations and Nationalism since* 1780. Cambridge: Cambridge UP, 1992.
49. Hosain, Attia. *Phoenix Fled.* [1953]. London: Virago, 1988.
50. Hossaini, Khaled. *The Kite Runner.* London: Bloomsbury, 2003.
51. Hourani, Albert. *A History of the Arab Peoples* (1991). London: Faber and Faber, 1992.
52. Jameson, Frederic. 'Taking on Globalization', *New Left Review*, 4, London, July/August 2000.
53. James, Winston. *Holding Aloft the Banner of Ethiopia: Caribbean Radicalism in Early Twentieth-Century America*, Verso, London, 1998.
54. Jung, C.G. *Modern Man in Search of a Soul.* London: Routledge & Kegan Paul, 1945.
55. Kakar, Sudhir. *Shaman, Mystics and Doctors: A Psychological Inquiry into India and its Healing Traditions* [1982], Oxford University Press, Delhi, 1998.
56. Kapur, Geeta. *When Was Modernism.*, Tulika, Delhi, 2000, p. 276
57. King, Bruce. *New National and Post-Colonial Literatures.* Oxford: Clarendon Press, 1998.
58. Kipling, Rudyard. *Kim.* 1901. London: Penguin Classics, 1994.
59. Khan, Abu Taleb (Trans. by Charles Stewart in 1814), *The Travels of Mirza Abu Taleb in Asia, Africa and Europe* (Appeared in Persian in 1803), Sona Publications, New Delhi, 1972.
60. Khair, Tabish. *Babu Fictions: Alienation in Contemporary Indian English Novels.* Delhi: Oxford University Press, 2001.
61. Kumar, Amitava. *Passport Photos.* Berkeley and London: University of California Press, 2000.
62. Lewis, Mathew. *The Monk* (1794). London: Penguin Books, 1998.

63. Lindqvist, Sven. *A History of Bombing*. Trans. by L. H. Rugg. London: Granta Books, 2002.
64. Liscomb, Kathlyn Maureen. *Learning from Mount Hua: A Chinese Physician's Illustrated Travel Record and Painting Theory*. Cambridge: Cambridge University Press, 1993
65. Malouf, Amin. *The Crusades Through Arab Eyes*. Trans. from the French by Jon Rothschild, Schocken Books, New York, 1984.
66. Martel, Yann. *Life of Pi*. Edinburgh: Canongate, 2002.
67. Marx, Karl. *Economic and Philosophic Manuscripts of* 1844. Trans. by Martin Milligan. Moscow: Foreign Languages Publishing House, 1961.
68. Marx, Karl and Engels, Frederich. *On Colonies, Industrial Monopoly and Working Class Movement: Extracts from article and letters* 1847–1894. Copenhagen: Publishing House Futura, 1972.
69. Matar, Nabil. *Turks, Moors and Englishmen: In the Age of Discovery*. New York: Columbia University Press. 1999.
70. Markovits, Claude. *The Global World of Indian Merchants 1750–1947: Traders of Sind from Bukhara to Panama*. Cambridge: Cambridge University Press, 2000.
71. McCrum, Robert; MacNeil, Robert; Cran, William. *The Story of English*. London and Boston: Faber and Faber/BBC Books, 1992.
72. Memmi, Albert. *Racism*, Trans. by Steve Martinot, University of Minnesota Press, Minneapolis/London, 2000.
73. Mernissi, Fatima. *Woman and Islam: An Historical and Theological Enquiry*. Oxford: Blackwell, 1991.
74. Meyer, Susan. "'Your Father Was Emperor of China, and Your Mother an Indian Queen': Reverse Imperialism in *Wuthering Heights*", in Brontë, Emily. *Wuthering Heights*. Ed. Linda H. Peterson. Boston and New York: Bedford/St. Martin's, 2003, p. 480–502.
75. Midgley, Mary. *Wickedness*. London: Routledge, 2001.
76. Mitter, Partha. *Much Maligned Monsters: A History of European Reactions to Indian Art*. Chicago and London: The University of Chicago Press, 1992 (1977).
77. Mongia, Padmini, Ed. *Contemporary Postcolonial Theory: A Reader*. London and New York: St Martin's Press, 1996.
78. Oxford University Press. *The Concise Dictionary of English Etymology*. 1986. Oxford: OUP, 1996.
79. Palmer, Bryan D. *Cultures of Darkness: Night Travels in the Histories of Transgression*. New York: Monthly Review Press, 2001.

80. Rhys, Jean. *Wide Sargasso Sea* (1966). New York and London: W. W. Norton and Company, 1992.
81. Richardson, John E. *(Mis)Representing Islam: The racism and rhetoric of British broadsheet newspapers.* Amsterdam: John Benjamins Publishing Company, 2004.
82. Ross, Robert. *A Concise History of South Africa.* Cambridge: Cambridge UP, 1999.
83. Roy, Arundhati. *The Algebra of Infinite Justice* [2001]. Delhi and London: Penguin, 2002.
84. *An Ordinary Person's Guide to Empire.* London and Delhi: Penguin Books, 2005.
85. Rushdie, Salman. *The Moor's Last Sigh.* London: Jonathan Cape, 1995.
86. *Midnight's Children.* 1981. London: Picador, 1982.
87. Sardar, Ziauddin and Davies, Merryl Wyn. *The No-Nonsense Guide to Islam.* London: Verso, 2004.
88. *Why Do People Hate America*? London: Icon Books, 2004.
89. Said, Omar ibn. "An Autobiography of Omar ibn Said, Slave in North Carolina, 1831", *American Historical Review*, XXX, No. 4, July 1925, p. 787 – 795.
90. Said, Nicholas "A Native of Bornoo", *The Atlantic Monthly*, October 1867, p. 485–495, accessed from Cornell University Library's online "Making of America" section.
91. Salibury, Harrison. 'A Balance Sheet of Fifty Years of Soviet Rule', New York Times, October 2, 1967, cited in Paul M. Sweezy, *Post-Revolutionary Society*, Monthly Review Press, New York and London, 1980, p. 24.
92. Seabrook, Jeremy. *The No-Nonsense Guide to World Poverty.* London: Verso, 2003.
93. Sertima, Ivan Van. *The African Presence in Ancient America: They Came Before Columbus.* New York: Random House, 1976.
94. Sidamed, AS and Ehteshami, A, Ed. *Islamic Fundamentalism.* Oxford: Westview Press, 1996.
95. Smith, Zadie. *White Teeth.* London: Hamish Hamilton, 2000.
96. Spivak, Gayatri. *Outside in the Teaching Machine.* London: Routledge, 1993.
97. Stalker, Peter. *The No-Nonsense Guide to International Migration.* London: Verso, 2001.
98. Stallabrass, Julian. *Gargantua, manufactured mass culture.* London and New York: Verso: 1996.

99. Stevenson, Robert Louis. *The Strange Case of Dr Jekyll and Mr Hyde* (1886). Ed. Katherine Linehan. New York and London: W. W. Norton and Company, 2002.
100. Stoker, Bram. *Dracula* (1897). Ed. Nina Auerbach and David J. Skal. New York and London: W. W. Norton and Company, 1997.
101. Sweezy, Paul M. "Cars and Cities"[1972], *Monthly Review*, 51, 11, New York, April 2000.
102. *Post-Revolutionary Society*, Monthly Review Press, New York and London, 1980.
103. Tilly, Charles. *Big Structures, Large Processes, Huge Comparisons.* New York: Russel Sage, 1984.
104. The United Nations Human Development Report (2000), as cited in Victoria Brittain and Larry Elliott, "Rich live longer, poor die younger", *The Guardian Weekly*, July 6-12, 2000, p. 3.
105. Verma, Nirmal. *India and Europe: Selected essays.* Ed. by Alok Bhalla. Centre for the Study of Indian Civilization and Indian Institute of Advanced Study, Shimla, 2000, p. 42.
106. Viswanathan, Gauri. *Masks of Conquest: Literary Study and the British Rule in India.* New York: Columbia University Press, 1989.
107. West, Cornell. "Marxist Theory and the Specificity of Afro-American Oppression", Cary Nelson and Lawrence Grossberg (Ed.), *Marxism and the Interpretation of Culture*, Urbana and Chicago: University of Illinois Press, 1988.
108. Wallerstein, Immanuel. "The Albatross of Racism", *London Review of Books*, Volume 22, Number 10, 18 May 2000, p. 14.
109. *The Capitalist World Economy*. Cambridge: Cambridge UP, 1979.
110. Warren, Bill. *Imperialism: Pioneer of Capitalism*, New Left Books, London, 1980.
111. West, Cornell. "Marxist Theory and the Specificity of Afro-American Oppression", Cary Nelson and Lawrence Grossberg (Ed.), *Marxism and the Interpretation of Culture*, Urbana and Chicago: University of Illinois Press, 1988.
112. Williams, Raymond. *Marxism and Literature*. Oxford: Oxford UP, 1977.
113. Wood, Ellen Meiksins. *The Origin of Capitalism*. New York: Monthly Review Press, 1999.